PERFORMING HAMLET

Jonathan Croall is a distinguished biographer and theatre historian. He is the author of over 20 books, notably the acclaimed biographies *John Gielgud: Matinee Idol to Movie Star* (Methuen Drama) and *Sybil Thorndike: A Star of Life*. His other titles include *The Coming of Godot: A Short History of a Masterpiece* (short-listed for the 2005 Theatre Book Prize); *The Wit and Wisdom (& Gaffes) of John Gielgud* and *In Search of Gielgud: A Biographer's Tale*; two collections of theatre journalism, *Buzz Buzz! Playwrights, Actors and Directors at the National Theatre* and *Closely Observed Theatre: From the National to the Old Vic*; and three books in the series The National Theatre at Work – *Peter Hall's 'Bacchai'*, *Inside the Molly House* and *Hamlet Observed*.

His most recent book is *Performing King Lear: Gielgud to Russell Beale*, published by Bloomsbury Arden Shakespeare in 2015.

Other *Hamlet* productions to accompany this book are available at: https://www.bloomsbury.com/performing-hamlet-9781350030756/. Please type the URL into your web browser and follow the instructions to access the Companion Website. If you experience any problems, please contact Bloomsbury at: contact@bloomsbury.com

RELATED TITLES FROM THE ARDEN SHAKESPEARE

Emotional Excess on the Shakespearean Stage
by Bridget Escolme
ISBN 978-1-4081-7967-3

English Renaissance Tragedy
by Peter Holbrook
ISBN 978-1-4725-7280-6

Performing King Lear: Gielgud to Russell Beale
by Jonathan Croall
ISBN 978-1-4742-2385-0

A Year of Shakespeare: Re-living the World Shakespeare Festival
edited by Paul Edmondson
ISBN 978-1-4081-8814-9

*Shakespeare on the Global Stage: Performance and
Festivity in the Olympic Year*
edited by Paul Prescott and Erin Sullivan
ISBN 978-1-4725-2032-6

Performing Hamlet

Actors in the Modern Age

Jonathan Croall

THE ARDEN SHAKESPEARE
LONDON · NEW YORK · OXFORD · NEW DELHI · SYDNEY

THE ARDEN SHAKESPEARE
Bloomsbury Publishing Plc
50 Bedford Square, London, WC1B 3DP, UK

BLOOMSBURY, THE ARDEN SHAKESPEARE and the Arden Shakespeare logo
are trademarks of Bloomsbury Publishing Plc

First published in Great Britain 2018

Cover design by Irene Martinez Costa
Cover image: Jude Law as Hamlet, Wyndhams Theatre, 2009 © Johan Persson

A catalogue record for this book is available from the British Library.

A catalog record for this book is available from the Library of Congress.

ISBN: HB: 978-1-350-03076-3
          PB: 978-1-350-03075-6
          ePDF: 978-1-350-03073-2
          eBook: 978-1-350-03074-9

Typeset by Integra Software Services Pvt. Ltd.
Printed and bound in India

To find out more about our authors and books visit www.bloomsbury.com
and sign up for our newsletters.

CONTENTS

Descriptions of 22 other productions are available online. See the end of the introduction for details.

LIST OF ILLUSTRATIONS

ACKNOWLEDGEMENTS

I owe an incalculable debt to the five leading actors who found time in their busy lives to talk to me in absorbing detail about playing Hamlet. So many thanks to Simon Russell Beale, Jude Law, Adrian Lester, Maxine Peake and David Tennant. I am equally grateful to the six directors who gave me such excellent insights into their productions: John Caird, Greg Doran, Sarah Frankcom, Simon Godwin, Michael Grandage and Nicholas Hytner.

I must also thank my two editors at Bloomsbury: Margaret Bartley, for accepting the book for the Arden Shakespeare, and Mark Dudgeon, for giving me his usual valuable support during its production.

REFLECTIONS

Simon Russell Beale Hamlet is a very hospitable role: it will take anything you throw at it.

John Caird Simon's fascination for the development of the character, his appetite for experiment, and his daring as an actor are constantly astonishing.

Adrian Lester The more we left convention behind, the happier Peter was.

Peter Brook Adrian has many special qualities. Above all he is somebody of tomorrow, and the audience immediately recognises that.

David Tennant You're being asked to stand in a line of Hamlets, which is flattering and seductive and absolutely terrifying in equal measure.

Greg Doran David was the funniest Hamlet I have ever seen.

Jude Law You get to speak possibly the most beautiful lines about humankind ever given to an actor, and ask the biggest philosophical questions.

Michael Grandage I wanted to use Jude's extraordinary ability to communicate with a young audience.

Rory Kinnear The soliloquies are supposed to be one-person events, but they can be the most collaborative moments in the play.

Nicholas Hytner I realised I'd found in Rory an actor whose intellect measured up to Hamlet's.

Maxine Peake I wanted to play a strong, physical part, but there aren't many female warrior roles.

Sarah Frankcom Maxine is a mercurial actress, who transforms herself for every role she takes on.

Paapa Essiedu If I'm the first black Hamlet, that tells its own story.

Simon Godwin I was drawn to the clarity of Paapa's verse-speaking and his charisma, but also his personal narrative.

Introduction

Hamlet is one of the glories of world literature. It is arguably the most famous play on the planet, the greatest of all Shakespeare's works. It's the one which most profoundly examines the nature of mankind; T.S. Eliot called it 'a Mona Lisa of literature'. It probably remains the most frequently performed of his plays, staged throughout the world in countless venues and spaces. It is certainly the one most written about and, at 4,000 lines, the longest. Its rich and complex story has provoked enormous debate and myriad interpretations, with productions set in every period and setting imaginable.

Just as King Lear is the role leading actors aspire to at the zenith or culmination of their career, so Hamlet, as Max Beerbohm observed, is 'a hoop through which every very eminent actor must, sooner or later, jump'. Those who do so face a daunting challenge in attempting to convey the formidable and unmatched mixture of qualities in Hamlet, a character whose intelligence is arguably unmatched in classical drama. His is a potent brew of wit, melancholy, verbal dexterity, cynicism, charm, cruelty, sweetness, rashness, theatricality, energy and finally stoicism. It's a role that is uniquely exposing in requiring an actor to bare his soul. It's become a truism to say no actor can totally fail in the part. As the scholar John Dover Wilson wrote: 'There are as many Hamlets as the actors who play him.'

Performing Hamlet provides a panoramic view of how *la crème de la crème* of the English theatre sought to conquer this supremely challenging work. The actors (and actresses) varied in how they prepared to tackle this uniquely demanding part, at more than 1,500 lines the longest in Shakespeare. While Simon Russell Beale learned his lines well in advance, David Tennant went to the opposite extreme. Rory Kinnear learned the soliloquies by himself, the rest only when he started working with the other actors. Several Hamlets had valuable one-to-one sessions with their director before the company rehearsals began.

There were contrasting opinions about the value of research. Jude Law, with a year to prepare, read around the play, studied the period and scholarly opinion, as well as works which Shakespeare had probably read, such as Montaigne's *Essays*. Maxine Peake, on the other hand, decided initially not to examine past productions, but eventually succumbed and watched various Hamlets' performances on DVD.

Several Hamlets said that in creating the part they had to dig deep within themselves, and that in exploring and trying to understand his psyche and inner self they had better understood their own. In some cases (Jonathan Pryce, Daniel Day-Lewis, Simon Russell Beale) this was connected to the death of a parent. Some claimed that such an exploration will make you not only a better actor (Adrian Lester), but a better person (Michael Pennington); others that it will in some way change your life (Paul Rhys, Simon Russell Beale, Jude Law). It was also common to feel a deep ambivalence about the role, to experience a mixture of rampant fear and profound satisfaction, leading in certain cases (David Tennant, Maxine Peake) to a sudden and strong desire to flee the theatre.

Directing *Hamlet* is also a supreme challenge. Played uncut the play is well over four hours long. Although a few directors such as Peter Hall have risked staging this version (dubbed 'Hamlet in its Eternity'), for most the question is how much and which lines to cut to make the story as coherent as possible and keep the audience's attention. Directors also have to decide whether to move certain speeches, the classic example being whether to shift 'To be or not to be' to earlier in the action as, controversially, Lyndsey Turner chose to do.

Rehearsal methods varied substantially, generally beginning with a read-through on the first day, sometimes preceded by a talk from the director (Peter Hall, Trevor Nunn) about the meaning of the play and their intended staging. Some directors, including Nicholas Hytner, liked to get the actors on their feet as soon as possible, and start blocking the scenes. By contrast John Caird spent several days simultaneously discussing and cutting the text in conjunction with his company. Greg Doran adopted an equally democratic approach: avoiding a read-through, he and his actors explored the play together scene by scene. Simon Godwin chose a similar method, but also asked each actor to write a biography of their character.

In recent years the question of colour-blind casting has come to the fore. Now broadly accepted, it's a measure of how slow the process has been that it was 2016 before the Royal Shakespeare Company cast its first black Hamlet, Paapa Essiedu. In 2000 Adrian Lester took on the role, but that was for Peter Brook, who invariably used an international cast. But a mixed cast can sometimes create problems for the audience: for instance, will a black Laertes and a white Ophelia prompt distracting thoughts about their family history?

Though less widely accepted, cross-gender casting has become increasingly popular. With her admired performance as the Prince in 2014, Maxine Peake was following in a tradition of female Hamlets that goes back to the eighteenth century. More unusual was her director Sarah Frankcom's decision to give five of the male characters to actresses, most notably turning Polonius into Polonia, and making the Gravediggers a female double-act.

The play's many inconsistencies, omissions and ambiguities have faced directors with key decisions. Should the Ghost be a supernatural ancient warrior, or a more recognisable human being? Did Hamlet truly love Ophelia? Does he know Polonius is eavesdropping on their conversation? Does Gertrude see the Ghost during the closet scene? Why did she simply observe Ophelia's drowning rather than try to save her? How accurate or trustworthy are Hamlet's descriptions of Claudius and Polonius, or his benign one of his father?

A broader question for the director is how far their production should reflect the spirit of the age. Those staged by Nicholas Hytner and Robert Icke focused strongly on our increasingly surveillance-dominated society. But there is a growing trend, especially for productions in smaller theatres, to focus on the family story, and leave out Fortinbras and the Danish/Norwegian politics. A compelling example of this was Peter Brook's version, which he cut down to two-and-a-half hours and pointedly re-named *The Tragedy of Hamlet*.

Performing Hamlet deals with a wide range of productions staged in England since 1950. It initially covers the second half of the twentieth century, and consists of portraits of a handful of major performances from each decade. It goes on to use a similar formula for the present century, but includes my interviews with five star actors and six leading directors. These are followed by 'Hamlet Observed', my fly-on-the-wall account of Simon Russell Beale's hugely acclaimed Hamlet in John Caird's 2000 production at the National Theatre, which toured the UK and visited Elsinore. The book was previously only available through the National Theatre bookshop; for this reissue both actor and director have added later thoughts about the play and the production. Finally comes a chapter on Hamlets at Elsinore.

My descriptions of a further 22 productions can be found online at https://www.bloomsbury.com/performing-hamlet-9781350030756/

The actors who played Hamlet in them were:

1950s John Neville, Peter O'Toole, Ian Richardson
1960s Ian Bannen, Richard Pasco, Tom Courtenay, Richard Chamberlain
1970s Hugh Thomas, Alan Bates, Peter Eyre
1980s Frank Grimes, Philip Franks
1990s Timothy Walker, Alan Rickman, Russell Boulter, Damian Lewis, Richard McCabe
2000s Toby Stephens, Ed Stoppard
2010s John Simm, Joshua McGuire, Ladi Emeruwa, Naeem Hayat

1

Stage History

When he wrote *Hamlet*, Shakespeare was at the mid-point of his career and at the height of his powers. The histories and comedies were behind him; ahead lay the mature tragedies. In 1599 he had written *Julius Caesar*, *As You Like It* and *Twelfth Night*. He wrote *Hamlet* during 1599 and 1600; it was first published in July 1602. It's claimed that it was initially written for a tour of the English universities; from records of payments made to the actors the first performance could have been at Oxford. An entry in 1602 in the Stationers' Register showed that it had been 'latelie Acted by the Lord Chamberleyne his servantes' at the Globe theatre.

The figure of Hamlet had been around for five hundred years. He appeared first in an Icelandic poem of the eleventh century. Hamlet's feigned madness had been a powerful theme in Viking and Celtic folklore, and his name was a synonym for a wild man or imbecile. A brutal version of the story, with 'Amleth' emerging as king, was included by the Danish scholar Saxo Grammaticus in his twelfth-century Latin history of Denmark and its heroes, *Historica Danica*. Around four hundred years later it was re-told by the French chronicler Belleforest for inclusion in his *Histoires Tragiques*, published in 1576. There is evidence that an English version existed before Shakespeare's, and was popular in the 1590s. Now lost, this was probably a revenge tragedy written by Thomas Kyd, the author of *The Spanish Tragedy*; but it was conceivably by Shakespeare himself, based on Belleforest, and already in his company's repertory.

Hamlet is unique among Shakespeare's works for having three significant texts: the first Quarto, the second Quarto and the first Folio. The first Quarto appeared in 1603, indicating the play had at 'diverse times' been acted in the City of London, Cambridge and Oxford universities, and 'elsewhere'. Known as the 'Bad Quarto', this was a pirated edition of around 2,200 lines. A short and garbled text full of grammatical and printing errors, it may have been taken down in shorthand during a performance at the Globe, then dictated to the printer. Another suggestion is that it is Shakespeare's own first draft. The soliloquies included variants such as 'To be or not to be, Aye, there's the point' and 'Why what a dunghill idiote slave am I?'

The second Quarto, a much longer text of 3,800 lines, followed in 1604 or 1605. This version was inscribed as 'newly imprinted and enlarged to almost as much againe as it was, according to the true and perfect Coppie'. It is believed to be based on the first draft Shakespeare submitted to the Lord Chamberlain's Men, in order to disown the first Quarto. Around 85 lines were omitted in deference to the sensibility of the queen, Anne of Denmark.

The first Folio, probably based on a prompt copy of the second Quarto, appeared in 1623, after Shakespeare's death. Intended as a definitive edition of the plays, it was published by two of Shakespeare's fellow-actors, John Heminges and Henry Condell, who were also, like Shakespeare, shareholders in the King's Men company. It contained a different text, with some additions – several probably by actors; omissions that included the soliloquy 'How all occasions do inform against me'; and numerous verbal variants. It may have been amended by Shakespeare from an original draft, or altered as a result of performance. Its cuts, made as a result of the 1605 Act to Restrain the Abuse of Players, included removing many 'Gods' and 'Amens'.

Hamlet was an immediate success. In 1604 a member of one audience noted that '*Hamlet* pleased all'. The scholar Gabriel Harvey had a different slant on its success: 'The younger sort takes much delight in Shakespeare's *Venus and Adonis*, but his *Lucrece*, and his *Tragedy of Hamlet, Prince of Denmark*, have it in them to please the wiser sort.' This contrasted with the view of many of his contemporaries that he was a hack writer; his fellow-dramatist Robert Greene notoriously called him 'an upstart crow'.

Hamlet continued to be performed regularly at playhouses, at Court, and at Oxford and Cambridge, until the theatres were closed in 1642. After they opened again in 1660 it was one of the first plays to be performed at Lincoln's Inn Fields. The diarist John Evelyn noted: 'I saw *Hamlet, Prince of Denmark* played, but now the old plays begin to disgust this refined age.' But another diarist and regular theatregoer, Samuel Pepys, confessed himself 'mighty pleased with it'. With the coming of Restoration comedy the play disappeared from the stage, until Robert Wilkes revived it at Drury Lane in 1708.

In the eighteenth century the playwright George Farquhar described it as 'the Darling of the English Audience, and like to continue with the same Applause', but Doctor Johnson thought it a 'horrible extravagance', while Oliver Goldsmith labelled the soliloquies 'a heap of absurdities'. In the nineteenth century several of the Romantics claimed Hamlet as their prototype, a man of intense sensitivity: Coleridge declared 'I have a smack of Hamlet myself, if I may say so'; Byron said 'We love Hamlet as we love ourselves'; Hazlitt announced 'it is *we* who are Hamlet'.

The original Hamlet was the leading tragedian in the Chamberlain's Men, 35-year-old Richard Burbage, described as 'a master of subtle speech-music, wit and decorative conceit'; as well as Hamlet, over 1,500 words the longest part in the canon, Shakespeare also wrote for him Richard III, Romeo and Brutus. According to Nicholas Rowe, Shakespeare's first biographer, Shakespeare himself played the Ghost. After Burbage, most leading actors of the day took on the role of the Prince. The first Hamlet after the re-opening of the theatres in 1660 was Thomas Betterton, who played it between the ages of 26 and 70, and reportedly acted 'a man of great expectation, vivacity and enterprise', prompting Pepys to declare that 'above all Betterton did the Prince's part beyond imagination'.

But Shakespeare's plays now began to seem old-fashioned, barbarous, and out of tune with the newly fashionable neo-classical works. Dryden argued in 1679 that 'the tongue in general is so much refined since Shakespeare's time that many of his words and more of his phrases are scarce intelligible, and of those which we understand, some are ungrammatical, others coarse, and his whole style is so pestered with figurative expressions that it is affected as it is obscure'. The plays were often thought to be in need of 'improvement'. David Garrick, who played Hamlet every season until his retirement at 69, omitted the graveyard and fencing scenes, and spared Gertrude. In 1776 he declared: 'I had sworn I would not leave the stage till I had rescued that noble play from all the rubbish of the fifth act.'

The trimming continued into the nineteenth century with Hamlet being tailored to fit the Byronic mould. John Philip Kemble, wearing modern court dress, was a suitably gloomy, intensely introspective Hamlet. Edmund Kean's acting was electrifying and exaggerated, and praised by Hazlitt for 'his extreme boldness'. The child prodigy Master Betty tackled the part in 1805 at the age of 14. William Charles Macready, playing Hamlet first at 18 and finally at 58, was an intellectually eloquent Prince, and an excellent duellist.

At a time when theatre managers thought that 'Shakespeare spells ruin', in 1874 Henry Irving staged an uncut version at the Lyceum lasting five hours. Irving was seen as the scholars' Hamlet, expressive, poetic, dignified and profoundly mesmeric – despite a peculiar gait and a voice 'of querulous, piping impatience, which cannot be reconciled with stage elegance'. His successor Johnston Forbes-Robertson offered the 'sweet prince', unfailingly noble, 'the true classical Hamlet', observed Shaw. Herbert Beerbohm Tree was romantic, erratic and sentimental; his elaborate production ended with a chorus singing 'Flights of angels sing thee to thy rest'.

In 1881 the eccentric William Poel directed and played Hamlet in a two-hour version without scenery or interval, in reaction against the spectacular Victorian productions. In 1899 the great Sarah Bernhardt, aged 54, commissioned a French prose version, and played it in Paris, London and Stratford, boasting that 'so profoundly am I imbued with the religion of Shakespeare that I cut out much less of *Hamlet* than you do on the English stage'. As if in reply, that same year at Stratford the actor-manager Frank Benson staged the 'complete' *Hamlet*.

Notable Hamlets in England in the first half of the twentieth century included the handsome, magnetic American actor John Barrymore, who was, however, said by the critic Herbert Farjeon to have 'little sense of language'. In 1923 came the first modern-dress *Hamlet*: directed by Barry Jackson and

starring Colin Keith-Johnston, it was labelled 'the plus-fours *Hamlet*'. In the
1930s John Gielgud's desperately frustrated and disillusioned youth was
recognised as the definitive Hamlet of his generation; Kenneth Tynan wrote
that 'the voice is thrilling and bears witness to great suffering; an east wind
blows though it'.

The psychoanalytical theories of Freud and his disciple Ernest Jones
had an influence on productions; Jones suggested 'Hamlet's behaviour is
that of a psychoneurotic'; he was said to have an Oedipal relationship
with Gertrude, notably in the closet scene. It was there in 1937 in Tyrone
Guthrie's production, in which Laurence Olivier's fiery performance was
described by the critic James Agate as 'the best performance of Hotspur
the present generation has ever seen'; the actor/director Harcourt Williams
thought it 'a shade too acrobatic, and belonging to that class of Hamlet that
makes it not so easy to accept "How all occasions do inform against me".'
Alec Guinness was a gentle and moving Hamlet in Guthrie's modern-dress
production the following year, while Gielgud played the part twice more in
war-torn London, the last time at 40. After the war Paul Scofield, at 26 the
youngest actor to have played the part in Stratford, shared it with Robert
Helpmann, presenting a romantic, haunted Prince in Michael Benthall's
1948 production, the last major production of the first half of the twentieth
century.

2

The Fifties

Michael Redgrave
Hugh Hunt

In 1950 Hugh Hunt directed Michael Redgrave's Hamlet for the Old Vic Company at the New in London. The production was also staged in Switzerland, Holland, and at Elsinore.

Cast: Claudius: Mark Dignam, Gertrude: Wanda Rotha, Polonius: Walter Hudd, Ophelia: Yvonne Mitchell, Laertes: Peter Copley, Horatio: Michael Aldridge, Guildenstern: Leo McKern, Osric: Paul Rogers.

Michael Redgrave was no stranger to Hamlet. While working as a teacher at Cranleigh School in Surrey he had overseen three productions, for which he was director, manager, designer and leading actor. It was, he recalled, an imitation of his idol: 'My first attempt owed so much to Gielgud's performance in 1930 that I must have seemed like Gielgud's understudy.' Strongly influenced by Gielgud's 'dazzling virtuosity of phrasing and breathing', he avoided seeing any of his later performances, 'knowing that if I were to play the part myself I should want to clear my imagination of his presence'.

He played Horatio at the Liverpool Playhouse, and in 1937 he was Laertes in Olivier's version. At almost 42, he came late to the role. Slim and handsome, an intelligent, stylish and subtle actor with a dignified bearing, he was seen by the critic J.C. Trewin as 'an actor of heroic aspect, who appeared to have every gift, mental and physical'. But in his early years he had been seen as an intellectual actor, cold and aloof. He was, Kenneth Tynan suggested, 'chary of direct emotional statement' and 'unwilling to compromise with minds less subtle than his own', and 'actively hostile to his audience'. But his Hamlet was to mark a new ability to communicate.

His director Hugh Hunt set out his stall. 'Let us leave the professors to bury themselves in their theories, in which pursuit they can only too easily succeed in losing the essential truth,' he wrote. '*Hamlet* is intended for the theatre, and although it may be of interest to the psychoanalyst to place the characters on the operating table, there to measure their motives and impulses, such a process, if carried too far, can land the director and the actors in disaster. It is a great error to confuse the operating theatre with the acting theatre.'

Hamlet was, he believed, essentially a revenge play. 'It is this plot – this story of a man called upon to revenge his father's death – that must never be lost sight of, however absorbed we may be by the many fine passages of verse or telling twists of character.' He criticised the idea of 'the gloomy Dane', arguing that 'there is hardly a character in the whole calendar of heroic and tragic drama who displays more humour than Hamlet'. He added: 'We must avoid the romantic view of seeing the play through Hamlet's eyes. We must not believe everything he says about himself: we must regard him as a man with a mission for revenge who tortures himself because fate, rather than his own nature, does not deliver the victim to him easily.'

Like Hunt, Redgrave rejected fashionable views of Hamlet's character. 'I am quite convinced Hamlet had no difficulty in making up his mind,' he said before rehearsals began. 'At first he was uncertain as to whether the Ghost was good or bad, but once he arrived at a conclusion, he acted without hesitation.' He also opposed the psychoanalytical interpretation of Hamlet 'as in some way the victim of an Oedipus complex, so that I used every possible occasion to stress his love for his father'.

During rehearsals he swung between confidence and anxiety. 'I refuse to look upon my forthcoming appearance as an ordeal,' he told *Theatre World*. 'I have the consolation of knowing that no actor has ever completely failed as Hamlet, just as none has completely succeeded as Macbeth.' But on the day of the dress rehearsal he recorded 'wearing anxiety alternating with complete apathy: Is it all worth it?' After a second dress rehearsal he confessed: 'I feel nowhere inspired, and do not feel I am much good.'

His biographer Richard Findlater approved of his interpretation: 'The soldier, the fencer, the prince, the people's idol, are aspects of Hamlet's complex personality too often sacrificed to the latter-day Byronics of a sensitive romantic misunderstood.' Redgrave, in contrast, offered 'not only the loving son, but also the courtier and the soldier, and a man who would have proved most royally had he been put on'.

His handling of the poetry was widely admired. T.C. Worsley wrote:

> He is beautifully sensitive to the words as poetry and gives us, from the very start, the assurance that he will value at its full worth every nuance of every phrase, every supporting syllable of the whole poetic structure ... It is an exemplary performance as a piece of verse-speaking, without tricks, mannerisms or affectations, but immensely various, always absolutely true, always perfectly in tune.

Joan Plowright, a student at the Old Vic School, wrote after seeing *Hamlet*: 'Those lovely passages of poetry really are poetry when spoken by Michael

Redgrave. He took "To be or not to be" well down near the front of the stage, and so quietly and simply ... he was more moving because of his stillness and intensity.'

Although his was an intelligent, rational Hamlet, some observers felt it lacked excitement and mystery, imagination and fascination, or what Audrey Williamson called 'the tragic ring'. Findlater agreed: 'In spite of his consistent lucidity and intelligence, one missed at times the soaring lyric intensity of Gielgud.' Alan Dent also had reservations: 'It is a beautifully composed portrait, an excellent likeness of the sweet Prince – but it is a portrait without highlights ... It is everywhere highly intelligent and human, but always just a little cold.' Several critics felt he misjudged his reaction once Claudius' crime was revealed by the Ghost. Most felt this 'emotional thunderstorm' – described by Milton Shulman as 'chest-thumpings, floor-poundings, eyeball-rollings, and laryngeal groaning' – was out of key with the rest of his performance.

Hunt compared Hamlet to Shakespeare's other great tragic characters: 'Hamlet is not an epic figure like Macbeth or Timon or Lear, he is not an outsize personality who creates the drama around him. Hamlet is a normal man, albeit a Prince, set against an epic situation ... He represents both what we would all like to be, and in some ways what we all are.'

Afterwards Redgrave reflected on what he saw as his shortcomings. 'I played it too heavily and too romantically,' he suggested. 'I'd like to do it in a much more astringent and conversational style next time – if there *is* a next time.' He would have to wait a further eight years before the opportunity arose (see page 18).

Alec Guinness

Frank Hauser/Alec Guinness

In 1951 Alec Guinness directed himself as Hamlet, with Frank Hauser as his co-director. The production was staged at the New as a contribution to the Festival of Britain.

Cast: Claudius: Walter Fitzgerald, Gertrude: Lydia Sherwood, Ophelia: Ingrid Burke, Polonius: Alan Webb, Horatio: Robert Urquhart, Laertes: Michael Gough, Player King: Kenneth Tynan, Rosencrantz: Robert Shaw, First Gravedigger: Stanley Holloway.

This was Alec Guinness' second attempt at Hamlet. Thirteen years earlier Tyrone Guthrie had offered him the part at the Old Vic, at the age of just 24. Guthrie was taking a gamble: skinny, prematurely bald with prominent ears, Guinness had until now played only minor parts. Guthrie chose to do Hamlet in its 'entirety', which lasted over four hours. Influenced by the Freudian psychoanalyst Ernest Jones, he told Guinness the play was essentially about 'Mummy'. Known as a director more interested in staging than in helping the actors, during rehearsals he let Guinness have his head.

'He interfered with me hardly at all,' Guinness recalled,

> but seemed to be grasping at anything slightly original I had to offer, which wasn't much, and encouraging me to develop it. He knew I could never emulate the pyrotechnics of Olivier, or the classical formality of Gielgud ... Tony helped me to find the confidence to be, so to speak, the stillness in the eye of the storm ... Unfortunately I was over-familiar with Gielgud's manner and timing. For all his loving care, he failed to wean me away from, or even mention, my pale, ersatz Gielgudry.

Guthrie's production had the atmosphere of a Ruritanian palace levee. But it fared poorly at the box-office. 'It's easily the best work I've done so far,' Guthrie wrote, 'and it is a blow to have it fall flat'. Guinness, he felt, found it hard to weather the half-empty houses: 'The actor's position to success or failure is so terribly personal. The work of art is inseparable from himself. It's *him* they like, or fail to like.' Yet he thought Guinness 'much, *much* better than Olivier, but Larry with his beautiful head and athletic sexy movements and bursts of fireworks are what the public wants'. He recognised Guinness' virtues – 'His youth, combined with rare intelligence, humour, pathos, realised a great deal of the part' – but admitted 'he had not yet quite the authority to support, as Hamlet must, a whole evening, or to give the tragedy its full stature'.

Guinness described himself as 'a fairly negative Prince'; the veteran critic James Agate agreed: 'This young actor is obviously not trying any of the things in Hamlet which are the ABC of the part. He attempts neither play of feature nor gesture. He rejects mordancy.' Others praised his quiet, gentle, unshowy Prince: 'Guinness was the youngest, quietest Hamlet I had known,' J.C. Trewin wrote. 'He had a sure pathos and no clamour of staginess for its own sake.' Harold Hobson confessed he had 'never seen a better young Hamlet', while Audrey Williamson observed: 'Intellectually he showed much imagination, bringing to the part many thoughtful details and a touching naturalness of gesture.'

By the time he came to play Hamlet in 1951 Guinness, now 37, was an established film star, and had complete control of casting, design and direction. But this proved a costly mistake. In the principal roles he mostly cast actors with little experience in Shakespeare. Bizarrely, he chose Kenneth Tynan to play the Player King, his single professional stage performance (though he had played Hamlet at school). Tynan saw this as an example of Guinness' 'exuberant oddness' in his choice of actors.

His co-director was Frank Hauser, a young former BBC Drama producer with no experience in the theatre. But the divided responsibility resulted in each director deferring to the other, with no clear-cut decisions being taken, rehearsals drifting rudderless, and the actors becoming insecure. 'Relentless direction might have extracted more from the players,' Tynan suggested. Guinness gave designer Mariano Andreu the brief to carry out 'a reaction against permanent, semi-permanent and realistic sets in Shakespeare'. As Tynan aptly observed: 'If you react against these, what is there left to support?' Andreu opted for a simple set without any rostra, declaring: 'Apart from cluttering the stage, they tend to produce a one-foot-up, one-foot-down sort of acting which I find peculiarly dispiriting.'

The first night was a fiasco. The newly installed lighting system went disastrously wrong: the lighting plot was several cues off, so the ghost scene was flooded with light, while subsequent scenes were plunged into darkness. At the curtain the gallery booed. Guinness told the company: 'It was my fault. Don't blame yourselves. I gave up after the first act.' Tynan concluded: 'It was a failure born of indecision, and fostered by the cancer of Guinness' humility. Unwilling to work within the framework of tradition, he was fearful of abandoning it entirely. This bred a fatal ambiguity, both in the production and his performance. Having cut himself off from safe Shakespearean tradition, he resigned the tiller and left the production becalmed. It was *Hamlet* with the pilot dropped.'

Harold Hobson said that, Guinness apart, you would never hear of the actors again. J.C. Trewin wrote: 'The world's most exciting play failed to excite. I felt that nobody, or hardly anybody, in the cast was in tune with *Hamlet.*' Beverley Baxter, in a review entitled 'The Worst Hamlet I Have Ever Seen', wrote: 'Mr Alec Guinness is a brilliant actor whose career will not be halted by this failure. But what in the world decided him to play Hamlet with a moustache and a goatee?' *The Times*, however, felt his low-key interpretation 'in its modern way was intensely alive, intensely accomplished, and so spoken as to be intensely lucid'.

Guinness was deeply hurt and shaken by the opening night and negative reviews. 'I made a balls-up of Hamlet,' he admitted later. 'I was sick every night. I was overcome with nausea.' Yet he showed a surprising reluctance to improve the production: he called no further rehearsals, although he did shave off his beard for the last week. The experience forced him to abandon hope of becoming a great Shakespearean actor.

Richard Burton

Michael Benthall

In 1953 Hamlet, *starring Richard Burton, marked the beginning of a five-year plan by the Old Vic's artistic director Michael Benthall to stage all 36 of Shakespeare's plays in the First Folio (*Pericles *was omitted). The production began at the Assembly Hall in Edinburgh, moved to the Old Vic, and the following year visited Elsinore.*

Cast: Claudius: Laurence Hardy, Gertrude: Fay Compton, Polonius: Michael Hordern, Ophelia: Claire Bloom, Horatio: William Squire, Laertes: Robert Hardy, Osric: Timothy Bateson, Fortinbras: John Neville.

Although Richard Burton was already an international film star, he had attracted praise for his Prince Hal and Henry V at Stratford two years previously. Before rehearsals for *Hamlet* began he woke in a sweat, thinking of the daunting task to come. He confessed to being 'a little nervous', adding that the stage was 'more nerve-wracking' than films. Like Guinness and Redgrave before him, he was haunted by Gielgud's wartime Hamlet. Although he had seen many others, he still thought it the best.

As he observed later, Shakespeare 'put on the stage in one character virtually every emotion of which a man is capable; pity, terror, fear, love, lust, obscenity, virtue, courage, cowardice'. Having worked on the part with his adoptive father and mentor Philip Burton, he arrived at rehearsals word-perfect. So Benthall avoided directing him in the soliloquies. According to Philip Burton, whenever they came to one he'd say: 'OK Richard, that's yours; now let's get on with the scene.'

The stage at Edinburgh's Assembly Hall was a long rectangle jutting out into the audience, who sat on three sides. There was no scenery, and only a set of looped curtains and scattered heraldic shields decorating the back wall. This gave the production what *The Times* called 'something like an Elizabethan intimacy of playing'. Burton played the whole of the Ghost scene with his back to his father's Ghost, waiting until he moved away before turning and responding to him. This break with tradition was widely commented on by the critics.

Benthall's productions were straightforward and vigorous, though sometimes unpoetic. This one proved no exception. As W.A. Darlington put it:

> This well-graced and most promising young actor gave us a Hamlet full of fire and passion and instinct with intelligence, yet not fully moving … Time and time again the great poetical passages were taken at a pace which prevented any emphasis from being laid on their musical quality, until it seemed as though the actor was deliberately playing down the well-known passages for fear they should sound like quotations.

Another reviewer thought Burton looked and sounded like Olivier, his passions running away with him, his voice 'close to hysteria'. The *Punch* critic, quoting T.S. Eliot's poem 'The Love Song of J. Alfred Prufrock', wrote: 'No! I am not Prince Hamlet, nor was meant to be.'

For the Old Vic the production was revised, seemingly to good effect. T.C. Worsley admitted: 'I had not expected Burton's performance would transmute itself from a valiant attempt to a sure achievement. But it does. All other considerations are secondary, when passion and power combine to carry us out of ourselves into the living and suffering centre of poetic tragedy.' But there was still criticism of his speaking: 'He lacked a communicable sense of

poetry: the words were noble, their delivery painstaking and often unvaried,'
J.C. Trewin noted. Others highlighted more positive qualities. David Lewin
described Burton as 'a rugger-playing Hamlet – an uncomplicated Prince ...
He plays the part with dash, attack and verve, not pausing to worry about
psychology.' Burton's fellow-Welshman Emlyn Williams confessed: 'He was
so young, so vital, I was in tears.'

Burton sometimes misbehaved. At one matinee, which coincided with
a Welsh international rugby match, he often moved close to the wings, to
catch the score on the portable radio playing there. Other actors were asked
to bring on the score as the game progressed; it was said that Gertrude
brought on the final result. At another performance, he later confessed to
Tynan, 'I played it as if I would like to be John Gielgud'. Benthall gave him
a severe warning not to repeat this ill-judged imitation.

Burton played Hamlet again in 1964 in America, directed this time by
Gielgud, to mark the four-hundredth anniversary of Shakespeare's birth.
Later he wrote caustically:

After ten weeks of playing Hamlet on the stage one's soul staggers with
tedium and one's mind rejects the series of quotations that Hamlet now
is. Has there ever been a more boring speech, after four hundred years
of constant repetition, than 'To be or not to be'? I have never played that
speech without knowing everybody settles down to a nice old nap the
minute the first fatal words start.

Paul Scofield
Peter Brook

*Peter Brook's 1955 production, which marked Paul Scofield's second Hamlet,
opened in Birmingham, toured to Brighton and Oxford, then visited the
Moscow Art Theatre before arriving at the Phoenix in London.*

Cast: Claudius: Alec Clunes, Polonius: Ernest Thesiger, Gertrude: Diana
Wynyard, Ophelia: Mary Ure, Horatio: Michael David, Laertes: Richard
Johnson, Gravedigger: Harry H. Corbett, Fortinbras: Richard Pasco.

'The more you know about acting, the more you are aware of the pitfalls
and the more nerve-wracking it becomes,' Paul Scofield reflected in his later
years. 'When I was young I wasn't nervous at all. Even doing Hamlet I just
had a go.' His first experience of the play had been in 1942, as Horatio at
the Birmingham Rep. Six years later he took on his first Hamlet, alternating
the part with Robert Helpmann at Stratford, the production co-directed by
Michael Benthall and Tyrone Guthrie.

In 1955 he returned to the role under the direction of Peter Brook. Looking
back over half a century later, Brook was critical of his first production of

Hamlet. 'Full of awe and respect for this great challenge, I closely studied all the detailed analyses I could lay my hands on. As a result intuition had no place, and the production was dull, except for Paul Scofield, who refused all discussion and analysis. He went his own way.'

Critics of the day endorsed this view. 'Brook's first attempt at a major tragedy seems to have over-awed him,' Tynan wrote. 'His direction is oddly tentative, with niggling cuts and ear-distressing transpositions.' Caryl Brahms noted: 'Pace has outdistanced poetry. If speed is Mr Brook's presiding genius, it is also his besetting daemon.' Gielgud was even more severe, describing the production as 'really disgracefully bad – not even a correct text spoken, and not one decent performance'.

Scofield admired Brook hugely, but in his early years was overawed by him. Later he described the director's

> very acute, perceptive, imaginative approach towards the plays. In a way working with him was quite traumatic. One was suddenly thrown up against a directorial influence which was so demanding of whatever intellectual powers one possessed – which were so undeveloped – that I suddenly found the business of being an actor was something quite different from what I had perceived ... We were supposedly joint directors and we used to 'consult', but with Peter that meant he decided what to do, and I agreed.

Scofield outlined his approach to rehearsals:

> Sometimes things happen very fast and sometimes one has to take one's time. I'm very careful not to let any kind of pattern emerge too soon ... I find that energy in rehearsal, the early part of it, has got to be devoted entirely to thinking, and that my equipment – my voice, and what I'm doing, sitting, standing, or whatever – has got to be completely in abeyance, forgotten about, lost. I don't waste energy on that because I don't yet know what I'm doing with them, so I must leave them to be idle, and get on with it mentally. It's only gradually and in the last stages of rehearsal that one can use the kind of physical energy that is needed in a performance, because then the whole man, as it were, of the character is functioning along the right lines.

Tall and spare, with a memorably craggy, high-cheekboned face prematurely lined, and a melancholic, arresting demeanour and powerful stage presence, Scofield was already a leading player. The scholar Stanley Wells describes his unmistakeable voice as 'gravelly with a nasal twang, baritonal but ample in range, subtle in inflection, capable of resonance and an almost unworldly tenderness, the consonants precisely articulated even to the point of creating infinitesimal pauses between words'. Simon Callow admired 'an organ with limitless stops, from the mightiest of bass rumbles, through light tenorial lyricism, to falsetto pipings; he seemed to be able to sound several notes at once, creating chords which resonated to the most remarkable effect, stirring strange emotions'.

His Hamlet garnered mixed reviews. J.C.Trewin wrote: 'I have not met a performance less externalised than Scofield's, able to communicate suffering without emotional pitch-and-toss; he had that within him which passeth show.' Caryl Brahms was also impressed: 'This Hamlet is precisely and decisively played, stylishly enacted, beautifully spoken. His movements are purposeful and swift, his frenzies carefully considered.' Others were more critical. Philip Hope-Wallace noted 'a curious, moth-like fragility', while Anthony Hartley held that 'the demonic, brutal character of the Renaissance Prince was much under-played, and we were left with Renaissance melancholy'. Richard Findlater argued that 'his second Hamlet was gabbled, dull, monotonous and actorish', a point also made by Kenneth Tynan: 'Mr Scofield's outline is impeccable. What is surprising is the crude brushwork with which he fills it in. Vocally and physically he is one long tremendous sulk ... Too many speeches are mechanically gabbled; and the actor's face is a mask devoid of pathos.'

Scofield himself had reservations:

The second time was more difficult, the problems of the play became more painful to try to solve. I found myself almost out of sympathy with the character, and that the dominant note of revenge, of vendetta as it were, is something which doesn't really communicate to modern audiences ... One has to work very hard to make an audience sympathise with a planned revenge. So Hamlet seems very self-absorbed, and that's not what Shakespeare intended.

The company's visit to the Moscow Art Theatre marked the first English production to be staged there since the 1917 revolution. At the end of the first night, attended by Chekhov's 86-year-old widow Olga Knipper-Chekhova, an enthusiastic audience gave the actors 20 curtain calls. As Brook, whose family originated in Russia, remembered: 'In Moscow the audiences, so accustomed to elderly Hamlets' laboured interpretations in ponderously long productions, were completely bowled over by the clarity and speed.' Tynan wrote: 'Accustomed to constant changes of scenery, they were baffled when the curtain rose again and again on the same grey permanent setting. Nor, in a theatre where doubling is unknown, could they comprehend why so many of the cast were playing more than one part.'

Scofield later spoke appreciatively of the audience's response: 'They followed every nuance of our performance; in terms of artistic endeavour and human compatibility they made the great ideological divide between Eastern and Western Europe seem unimportant. It was an experience of kinship, the breaking down of barriers, and an awareness that we are none of us as our political leaders proclaim us to be.'

Peter Brook directed Hamlet *again in 2000, with Adrian Lester as the Prince (see page 85).*

Michael Redgrave
Glen Byam Shaw

In his second Hamlet in 1958, Michael Redgrave was directed by Glen Byam Shaw, director of the Shakespeare Memorial Theatre. After Stratford the production visited Moscow and Leningrad.

Cast: Claudius: Mark Dignam, Gertrude: Googie Withers/Coral Browne, Ophelia: Dorothy Tutin, Horatio: Ron Haddick, Polonius: Cyril Luckham, Laertes: Edward Woodward.

When Michael Redgrave played his second professional Hamlet he was 50 years old. Some critics felt he was too mature and cool-headed for the role. T.C. Worsley wrote: 'Every age can sympathise with the self-dramatising of the very young; it is even part of their charm. But to a man patently old enough to work through it we cannot feel quite so indulgent.' Kenneth Tynan was crueller, stating: 'The actor sometimes less resembles a youth approaching a murder for the first time than a seasoned Commando colonel suffering from battle fatigue.'

His age created a difficulty with his relationship with Gertrude, since Googie Withers was nine years younger than him. In the notes she kept, she saw the queen as 'a kindly, slow-witted, self-indulgent woman, in no way emotionally or intellectually the equal of her son'. As a result, Hamlet assumed the authoritative role in the key closet scene.

In his book *Mask or Face*, published to coincide with the opening at Stratford, Redgrave rejected Olivier's idea in his film of *Hamlet* as 'a man who could not make up his mind'. *The Times* observed this interpretation in action: 'His tragedy springs not from his infirmity of will, but from a situation which surrounds him with problems so many-faceted in their subtlety that only the stupid brain or the blunted moral sense could solve them satisfactorily.'

Redgrave, a confessed slow starter, loathed and feared opening 'cold' – at this time there were no previews at Stratford. Yet the critics praised his complete intellectual grasp of the part. 'Age seems to me irrelevant when it comes to Hamlet,' Michael Billington later argued. 'What I recall is the completest interpretation of the role – one that embraced Hamlet's passion, intellect, violence and ultimate resignation.' It was 'one of the greatest pieces of acting I have ever seen, because of the abundance of insights the actor offered us into the character, and because intensity of feeling was combined with intellectual volatility.'

Other critics saw his second Hamlet as romantic, sensitive, virile and humourless. Some felt he remained aloof from the rest of the cast. Yet Dorothy Tutin, as Ophelia, found working with him exhilarating, even when he varied his performance on certain nights: 'It was impossible to get stale with Michael,' she said. 'It wasn't frightening when things were different – the groundwork of the scene had been well laid so you still felt absolutely safe, no matter what had changed. He always acted *with* you, it was always *mutual*.'

Tynan thought his Hamlet 'much richer in detail than the one he gave us eight years ago', and his biographer Alan Strachan agreed:

Michael's reading was infinitely more subtle and rich than his Old Vic performance ... He retained that sense of a near-paralysing grief at the loss of an obviously adored father in the early scenes, but now it was noticeably yoked to a more active, participatory perspective on elements in Elsinore. The essentially sceptical side of Hamlet's intellect was also considerably more in focus; this was perceptibly the quickest brain in Elsinore.

His son Corin Redgrave remembered: 'A stillness and a melancholy in the first scene; a directness about his soliloquies, such as he seemed to be both thinking aloud and, for the first time, talking to the audience as to a friend, but also observing always the line of the verse.' J.C. Trewin thought him 'a touching and nobly imagined Prince' who 'appeared throughout to be two moves ahead of everyone else'. The fact that the production lasted four hours he ascribed partly to Redgrave's pace: 'Swift though his intuition was, he took longer than in the past to explain it to us. He was dilatory because he had to dissect any phrase, a tireless searcher.'

The labelling of him as an intellectual actor was refuted by his daughter Vanessa Redgrave: 'I never saw an actor, except perhaps in the Moscow Art Theatre company, who possessed such capacity for emotion and the appropriate form of that emotion,' she said. 'Perhaps it never occurred to those critics that only an actor who can think can also feel, to the extent demanded by Shakespeare's tragedies and histories.' The poet Siegfried Sassoon concurred, writing to Redgrave: 'Thank you for a lovely Hamlet, magnificently sustained and real and true in feeling.'

Glen Byam Shaw's high Renaissance production was conventional, devoid of tricks, but criticised for being old-fashioned and uninspiring. Strachan described it as 'sadly routine, and surprisingly poorly designed by Percy Harris. The costumes were fine, but the stage was often reduced to an enormous bare space ... There was little sense of a world within Elsinore, with static groupings like an old-fashioned opera production.'

That winter the company took the production to the Soviet Union. The performances in Leningrad represented the first visit there of an English company since the revolution. The enthusiasm was tremendous, the final performance of *Hamlet* provoking 14 curtain calls. In Moscow the last of the 15 performances was relayed live on television on Moscow's Channel 1 to five million viewers.

Michael Redgrave later played Claudius to Peter O'Toole's Hamlet in Laurence Olivier's 1963 National Theatre production at the Old Vic (see page 22).

3

The Sixties

Jeremy Brett
Frank Hauser

The 1961 Oxford Playhouse production, starring Jeremy Brett and directed by Frank Hauser, visited the Cambridge Arts before moving to the Arts in London.

Cast: Claudius: Joseph O'Conor/John Maxin, Gertrude: Helen Cherry, Horatio: William Abney, Polonius: Robert Eddison/Robert Bernal, Laertes: Ronald Hines, Ophelia: Linda Gardner.

When Jeremy Brett played Hamlet at 27 he was one of the youngest actors since Gielgud to land the role. Like others he was acutely aware of his predecessors: 'To take on Hamlet is humbling, because of the history that comes with it,' he said. 'The ghosts of the past are very close.'

One critic suggested 'the incestuous bed' was at the centre of Brett's performance. More than 30 years later the actor, who had a tormented personal life, explained:

> I was very rough on Gertrude, I mean physically rough. I was angry at that time. My mother had been killed in a car accident in 1959, and I was very angry about that, because my son, when she was killed, was only three months old. I felt cheated, I felt my mother had been cheated, and the rage of that came through.

He was also brutal to Ophelia, which may have reflected, unconsciously or otherwise, the fact that his marriage to the actress Anna Massey was breaking up.

Quietly spoken, affable, tactful and shrewd, Frank Hauser, director of the Oxford Playhouse, presented the play on an almost bare stage. Some critics expressed their relief, having disliked a recent production at Stratford. Frank Dibb admitted: 'It came like a fresh cooling draught after our recent agonised wanderings in the desert of the Ian Bannen–Peter Wood *Hamlet*.' Bamber Gascoigne also approved of Hauser's direction: 'Each of his new touches sits so neatly in its context that one feels that, from Burbage to Brett, it must always have been so.' But J.C. Trewin qualified his praise: 'Frank Hauser had been more helpful than some other directors who are governed by a persistent whim,' he stated, but decided 'the performance remained nevertheless an accurate diagram rather than a living experience'.

Brett recalled:

> There were times when I used to move into the third movement and the return from England and I used to feel absolutely as though I was in a serene space, because if you've won the audience by then – you really should win them at the end of the first movement when you say 'O cursed spite.' You should have captured them by the end of the second movement, for the return from England. And then you glide on a most wonderful plateau of serenity right through to the end, with one or two little hiccups. But Hamlet is on a line, he's found himself, and that's very beautiful for an actor to feel.

His performance attracted a spectrum of reviews. Gascoigne suggested his Hamlet was 'as intelligent and straightforward as the production. He plays those qualities which a modern reader finds in Hamlet – his probing student intelligence, his taste for gloom, his bouts of ineffectual self-criticism, his exhibitionism, his talent for sudden and unexpected bursts of affection and, above all, his exuberance.' For Dibb, 'Here was a Hamlet youthful, princely, embittered, passionate … a man who suggested in voice and mien a royal personage. His speaking of the language had a consistently fine and expressive musicality.' Peter Carthew had more mixed views: 'He managed the comedy and the mock-madness scenes extremely well; this was a Hamlet with a sense of humour. But he failed to do justice to the soliloquies, displaying at times a tendency towards ranting and impotent mouthings.'

Brett was later critical of his performance: 'I don't think I was very good as Hamlet, because I was too young in many ways: too young intellectually, too young philosophically. I was Byronic, I was very handsome, I had qualities – but I'd have much rather seen other people's Hamlet – I wasn't convinced by me.'

Peter O'Toole

Laurence Olivier

In 1963 Laurence Olivier, director of the National Theatre, staged the play as the theatre's inaugural production in its temporary home at the Old Vic, with Peter O'Toole as Hamlet.

Cast: Claudius: Michael Redgrave, Gertrude: Diana Wynyard, Ophelia: Rosemary Harris, Laertes: Derek Jacobi, Polonius: Max Adrian, Horatio:

Robert Stephens, Ghost: Anthony Nicholls, First Player: Robert Lang, Fortinbras: John Stride, First Gravedigger: Frank Finlay.

Having recently completed two years of filming *Lawrence of Arabia*, Peter O'Toole was now an established international star, and thought by some to be the most exciting actor of the day. But Olivier's decision, based on advice from the theatre's newly appointed *dramaturg* Kenneth Tynan, met with opposition from within the National Theatre. Of the two associate directors Olivier had brought in from the Royal Court, John Dexter was ambivalent about the star system, while Bill Gaskill was irrevocably opposed to it. The casting – Tom Courtenay was pencilled in as a possible alternative – also went against Olivier's vision of creating an ensemble along the lines of the Berliner Ensemble or the Moscow Art Theatre company.

O'Toole had no desire to repeat the role after playing it in 1959 at the Bristol Old Vic, but Olivier won him over. 'He was the most persuasive bastard ever to draw breath,' O'Toole recalled. He had wanted the production cut to two-and-a-half hours, and to play it with a beard and his own hair. 'Why should I be the only man in Elsinore with a razor blade?' he asked. But three weeks later: 'There I am on the stage, clean-shaven in a Peter Pan suit with my hair dyed white. Such is the power of Olivier.' He had also agreed to a full-length Hamlet running to four-and-a-half hours, and to be paid just 30 guineas a performance.

Olivier outlined his view of Hamlet in a programme note drafted by Tynan: 'The play deals with a man who says no to official obligations and feudal oaths – in fact, to anything outside himself, any external force that tries to tell him how to behave. He is the permanent rebel and nay-sayer, and would be the same in any society or period of history. He works out his morality as he goes along, taking nothing on trust, and approaches life like an actor, always trying on new characterisations to see if they fit.'

> It also makes him something of a crank, a sore thumb, and a source of nagging embarrassment; and here he joins hands with such latter-day rebels as Jimmy Porter in *Look Back in Anger*. He abhors the world in which he lives, and is forever doubting its values, testing its honesty, and deriding its pretensions. In short, he is not a good social animal but a dangerous outsider, a nuisance and a threat, often unpleasant and downright offensive; and it is thus that we should regard him, not as a romantic weakling or a paragon of charm.

Privately to designer Desmond Heeley he confessed to doubts about taking on the play again:

> It is terribly difficult ... to feel glossy ... about it when one has done a thing more than once, and then made a film ... I do not think it is any good my trying to join the Brechtian ranks in my presentation; that would only be a lame follow-on to a trend. The [*Hamlet*] aura which still

exists with me is what would be thought today a romantic one – with O'Toole as the principal it would be hard to think of it otherwise.

Rehearsals went well at first; O'Toole initially viewed Olivier with awe: 'He's done it; he's sat on the top of Everest and waved down at the Sherpas,' he stated. Olivier was convinced O'Toole was going to do everything he asked of him. But although the actor came to the read-through word perfect, relations between the two soon deteriorated. They were probably not helped when Olivier said: 'I know my way about the map of *Hamlet* much more than you can possibly do.'

Robert Stephens recalled O'Toole's behaviour: 'He shambled about at rehearsals, smoking a cigarette and telling jokes.' Michael Gambon, then an extra, remembered him turning up for one rehearsal in evening dress, having been out drinking all night. Derek Jacobi remembered: 'Peter worshipped the very ground Olivier trod on ... but it hardly stopped him being defiant. Rehearsals were bumpy and unpredictable, and somehow a good rapport between Olivier and Peter failed to get off the ground.' Rosemary Harris recalled that 'they did cross swords a few times ... Peter pretty much stuck to his guns and did what he was comfortable with, and Sir Laurence in the end shrugged and gave up.'

O'Toole ignored much of Olivier's direction. Gaskill pinpointed the problem: 'Larry tried to make O'Toole act Hamlet as *he* would have done.' While Olivier wanted a variation on his 1948 film performance, O'Toole was keen to re-visit his Bristol Old Vic interpretation. Later he referred disparagingly to Olivier's 'grey-eyed, myopic stare that can turn you to stone', suggesting he belonged to the actors' stable, and had little to contribute as a director. One exchange, remembered by Gaskill, suggests vividly Olivier's attitude to the critics as well as to O'Toole. As the curtain was about to rise he grabbed O'Toole in the wings. 'Are you ready?' he asked. 'For what?' O'Toole replied. 'For them. They're out there with their machine guns. It's your turn, son.'

The uncut version, playing six nights and two matinees a week, which meant nine hours on matinee days, put enormous demands on O'Toole. He recalled the first night as 'the most humbling and humiliating of my life ... As I went on I suddenly knew it was not going to be any good ... I wandered amazed among scenic flyover and trumpets: I didn't know where I was.' One matinee, having been picking racing winners from *Sporting Life* with the stage hands in the wings, he went on still unknowingly wearing his glasses, provoking giggles from Noël Coward and others in the audience. Later he remarked: 'If you want to know what it's like to be lonely, really lonely, try playing Hamlet.'

According to Stephens: 'Peter simply walked through the role, and didn't really bother with it. He was terribly out of condition; he kept losing his breath, so he played most of it standing stock still. You have to have some muscle on you to play Hamlet. So it was all ghastly.' Sometimes, with drink inside him, he terrified Jacobi in their duel. 'If he gave me a wink, and he usually did, this wild Irishman, it meant a very hard fight. It was even dangerous to be sitting in the front row when he flashed out his sword like Douglas Fairbanks.'

Olivier suggested O'Toole had wilfully departed from his carefully plotted moves, introduced 'silly and impractical ideas', and 'indulged his emotions extravagantly … It was tragic actually. If O'Toole had given on the first night the performance he gave on the last dress rehearsal it would have been an absolute sensation. Somehow, when it came to performances, he either didn't do it, or he was being much too free and brave in changing the pace of whole scenes.'

Within the profession the verdict on O'Toole's playing was harsh. His wife Siân Phillips, to whom Olivier had offered Ophelia, called it 'a pale shadow of his Bristol Old Vic performance'. Gaskill thought it 'dreadful, absolutely terrible', while Michael Redgrave, who received good notices for his Claudius, referred to 'a ghastly production'. Some reviews were respectful, though welcoming the National's existence rather than the performance. 'After a wait of a hundred years, this will do for a start,' Bernard Levin wrote.

But O'Toole was generally seen as too angry and rebellious a Prince, lacking poetic reflection. T.C. Worsley thought him badly miscast, suggesting it was 'hard to think of a young actor less able to imply impotence'. J.C. Trewin felt he was 'a tormented spirit who did not always communicate his torment. A recognisable portrait in its harsh way, but without much warmth … The passion was barely more than external, seldom inflammable.' *The Times* thought the production contained good things, but 'bears the stamp of having been put on as a means of exhibiting a number of big names in the most famous and popular work in the classical repertory'.

Olivier was scarred by the experience, telling Rosemary Harris: 'If you're opening a theatre, never, ever direct the first production. And when you're opening the National Theatre after a hundred years of waiting, you put on your strongest suit of armour and wait for everybody to shoot you.' He described the production as the worst one of anything he had ever seen, and when Stephens asked him why, he replied: 'Because I don't have a Hamlet.' O'Toole characteristically later described *Hamlet* as 'the worst bloody play ever written. Actors do it out of vanity. I only did it because I was flattered out of my trousers.'

David Warner

Peter Hall

In 1965 Peter Hall, director of the Royal Shakespeare Company, staged the play at Stratford, with David Warner as Hamlet. The production moved to the Aldwych in London, and returned to Stratford the following year.

Cast: Claudius: Brewster Mason, Gertrude: Elizabeth Spriggs, Polonius: Tony Church, Ophelia: Glenda Jackson/Janet Suzman, Horatio: Donald Burton, Laertes: Charles Thomas, Ghost: Patrick Magee, Fortinbras: Michael Pennington, Rosencrantz: Michael Williams, Guildenstern: James Laurenson.

By this stage in the 1960s it was expected that a director would define the overall concept and atmosphere of a production. On the first day of rehearsal at Stratford, Peter Hall outlined his personal vision of *Hamlet*.

'For our decade I think the play will be about the disillusionment which produces an apathy of will so deep that commitment to politics, religion or life is impossible.' He continued:

> To me it is extraordinary that in the last fifteen years the young of the West, and particularly the intellectuals, have by and large lost the ordinary, predictable radical impulses which the young in all generations have had ... There is a sense of what-the-hell-anyway, over us looms the mushroom cloud. And politics is a game and a lie, whether in our own country, or in the East/West dialogue which goes on interminably without anything very real being said. This negative response is deep and appalling.

Hoping to attract the younger generation, he cast the relatively unknown 24-year-old David Warner as the Prince. Warner had played Henry VI for Hall in *The Wars of the Roses*, a performance the director thought 'mesmeric'. Stanley Wells observed that as Hamlet 'his costume and physical appearance seemed clearly designed not just to evoke the student at Wittenberg, but to link him with the modern student'. For Hall he was 'the very embodiment of the 1960s student – tall, blond, gangling. He was passive, yet had an anarchic wit.' Such students were making their presence felt in British theatre through the growing fringe movement, culminating elsewhere in 1968 and beyond in the student revolt, the anti-Vietnam War protests, and the 'flower power' movement.

With this, his first production of the play, Hall was influenced by the Polish scholar Jan Kott's *Shakespeare Our Contemporary*, which linked Shakespeare to Beckett and the fashionable Theatre of the Absurd. Shakespeare, Kott argued, is the mirror of our own age as it has been for every other one, but we have to be alert to the new images that can express him. Hamlet 'was a youth deeply involved in politics, rid of illusions, sarcastic, passionate and brutal; a young rebel who has about him something of the charm of James Dean'.

Frail, gauche and scruffy, and prone to extremes of behaviour, Warner played Hamlet as an immature young undergraduate, wearing a moth-eaten black gown and red scarf. Hugh Leonard observed 'a gangling young swine in an Oxbridge scarf, who spreads woe and disquiet around him with such prodigality as to make Claudius seem endearingly put-upon'. *The Times* suggested: 'He is temperamentally a neurotic intellectual ... patrolling the corridors prematurely haggard like Chekhov's eternal student, wearing a shabby old gown and steel-rimmed glasses.'

Warner denied he deliberately played against tradition. 'There was no question of trying to be new, but just truthful to what Peter Hall wanted. The part grew very slowly, things came out instinctively, they weren't planned. I never went into it with any preconceptions, or thought about it before. I never had the ambition to play Hamlet like a lot of actors do.' He also rejected the idea of creating a Hamlet for the age: 'I didn't really think of it as a Hamlet for our time, it was just that people labelled it as that. I think modern, younger audiences appreciate this Hamlet, because it has the nasty side as well as the sympathetic side. He's a Prince at one moment, and an ordinary man the next.'

Hall cut 730 lines from the text. Before the opening he warned Tony Church:

> The notices are going to be dreadful, because we're doing things the critics won't like, because they haven't seen them before and won't understand. For instance, they will not understand why David addresses all Hamlet's soliloquies directly to the audience. This is not the tradition; they've always been done as 'thinks' as Olivier does them in his film, which is a romantic tradition. That would have been impossible in the Globe theatre.

Warner spoke the soliloquies from the front of the stage, in an unrhetorical manner. Ronald Bryden praised the idea:

> This is a Hamlet desperately in need of counsel, help, experience, and he actually seeks it from the audience in his soliloquies. This is probably the greatest triumph of the production: using the Elizabethan convention with total literalness. Hamlet communes not with himself, but with you. For the first time in my experience, the rhetoric, spoken as it was intended to be, comes brilliantly to life.

But Warner's technique was under-developed, his verse-speaking tending towards a monotonous mumbling, as several critics noted. J.C. Trewin, who found him occasionally inaudible, described his voice as 'brusque, nasal, grating', one which could 'linger monotonously on the note'. Philip Hope-Wallace wrote: 'The language is treated in the most prosaic, flat and unprofitable manner wherever possible.' Julian Holland criticised 'a performance in which the verse is spoken so execrably ... He butchers the rhythms, stresses unimportant words, and affects new and strange ways of speaking the English language.'

His Hamlet was also said to lack the qualities of a Prince, which was certainly the case, but deliberately so. Bryden fully approved of this quality: 'Warner is the first Hamlet, surely, who is young enough to play the Prince as a real student, learning as he goes along. It's this that gives the production its marvellous new life: he feels each line back to freshness, lives each scene for the first time.' The actor Robert Speaight suggested he effortlessly fulfilled the most important criterion for a Hamlet, that he be 'a misfit about whose fate we must care passionately from the beginning to the end'.

This was a Hamlet obsessed with his father, an aspect of his character underlined by Hall in his decision to create a puppet apparition for the Ghost. He wanted it to be colossal and terrifying, and to appear in several places ('Tis here ... Tis gone'). So he had three 10-foot Ghosts built on wheels, and had them breathing smoke. There was a platform halfway up each one on which the actor stood, with a second actor behind him manipulating the figure. While the puppet Ghost folded the now-diminutive-seeming Hamlet in his enormous arms, his words were spoken by the sonorous recorded voice of Patrick Magee.

Glenda Jackson presented an unusually harsh, turbulent and rebellious Ophelia, who strummed a guitar and turned her mad melodies into protest songs directed at the audience. It was a controversial interpretation which offended many critics, who described her disparagingly as 'very strong-willed', a 'tough strident miss' and 'frigidly spinsterish'. But the sole female critic, Penelope Gilliat, praised the deliberate blurring of the traditional gender boundaries, and thought she was the only Ophelia she had seen who was ready to play the Prince. (Jackson later turned down the part.) Her brittle performance was so overpowering, one critic suggested the play's title be changed to *Ophelia*.

In his autobiography Hall observed: 'The production lives for many people as the moment when they realised that Hamlet is always our contemporary.' He then appeared to forget the talk he had given to the cast on the first day of rehearsal. 'I did not try to make this happen. I had no overall theory of the play to take into the rehearsal room. I worked with the company to find the meaning of each scene and to express it as best we could.'

Despite the critical reservations, the production was a box-office success. It was especially popular among the younger generation; scores of teenagers queued all night round the block for balcony seats, or came night after night to stand at the back of the auditorium, in order to see this classless, disaffected student Prince who mirrored their lives. As Michael Billington stated: 'It was a performance that redefined the role for a generation, an expression of 1960s culture where youth and age were locked in combat.' Warner concluded: 'I don't know whether I learnt a great deal about Hamlet, but I learnt an awful lot about myself.'

Nicol Williamson
Tony Richardson

Tony Richardson's 1969 production, starring Nicol Williamson, was staged at the Roundhouse in Camden, north London. It then toured the United States before coming to Broadway.

Cast: Claudius: Anthony Hopkins/Patrick Wymark, Gertrude: Judy Parfitt/ Constance Cummings, Polonius: Mark Dignam, Ophelia: Marianne Faithfull/Anjelica Huston/Francesca Annis, Laertes: Michael Pennington, Horatio: Gordon Jackson.

Tony Richardson saw *Hamlet* as the seminal work of Western European culture: 'For all its revenge-theatre setting, its world is the everyday world of power: the forum, the market-place, the palace; and its limits are the limits of political endeavours and possibilities.' He argued that the key to a successful reinterpretation of Hamlet lay in understanding his sense of irony, 'irony of mind, thought, feeling, language, action. Other great characters engulf us in their feelings; Hamlet makes us always assess, re-examine our choices. And his irony is pure – not born out of bitterness, or over-coloured by emotion, but the result of an ability to stand back and detach himself; to see clearly even when he acts wilfully, violently, playfully.'

It was this irony he believed Nicol Williamson was best placed to embody as Hamlet. The Scottish actor had recently been celebrated for his work in John Osborne's *Inadmissible Evidence*; Osborne had described him as the greatest actor since Marlon Brando, while Samuel Beckett, after seeing him in a revival of *Waiting for Godot*, suggested he was 'touched by genius'. But though he was hugely talented, he had already gained a reputation for unpredictability that was to last throughout his career.

Richardson wanted a simple staging, so he and his designer Jocelyn Herbert built a low, semi-circular stage with seats on three sides, a half circus ring within a circle which required no scenery. 'Our approach was to do a classic performance that allowed total freedom to the actors and the text,' he said; he believed that 'a new revolution needed to destroy, finally and completely, the form of the proscenium theatre and the social habits that go with it'.

He spent a fortnight discussing the play with the cast, discovering its themes and sub-text, and cutting it heavily to three hours. Williamson emerged as an iconoclastic, splenetic, snarling Hamlet, nasal and rasping in tone, harsh in demeanour and, like David Warner, the rebel outsider. It was a mesmeric performance which won him Best Actor at the *Evening Standard* Drama Awards. During the run the play was filmed in the building during the day, in a version cut down to two hours, and mostly filmed in close-up.

The production was a box-office success, and attracted mostly positive reviews. Harold Hobson stated: 'Mr Richardson's production, like those pictures in the National Gallery, is so bright, clear and vivid that one has the impression of seeing both it and them for the first time.' *The Times* noted that 'Richardson's production has a savagely cut text, but it has a justification of force and fluid movement'. Others were less impressed: 'Williamson's Hamlet was born sneering; excessively ill-tempered, it prickled with awkward vowel sounds', J.C. Trewin wrote, while Benedict Nightingale referred to a 'dour, implacable puritan, stalking through the Danish flesh-pots'.

Williamson reinforced his unpredictable reputation. On the first night he stopped in the middle of 'To be or not to be', swore, and walked off stage. He did this with increasing frequency during the ten-week run; people even bought tickets in the hope of seeing a display of temperament. During one performance he stopped and said: 'I can't go on, I am simply exhausted, and I'm not giving my best. In fact I'm fucked,' and then walked offstage.

Later Richardson wrote: 'Nicol was recognised as his generation's Hamlet; without illusions, yet humorous and ironic, capable of instant rage and mockery, and with a sad, existential resignation.' But at the time they fell out: 'He was way over the top in his acting and reckless of other people's feelings. Soon after the opening he was already overacting shamelessly, although he didn't know it. I attacked him for it. He never forgave me.'

In America the production toured to Boston, Philadelphia and elsewhere, before reaching the Lunt-Fontanne Theatre in New York. The tour then continued and ended in Los Angeles.

4

The Seventies

Alan Howard

Trevor Nunn

In 1970 Alan Howard played Hamlet at Stratford, under the direction of Trevor Nunn. The production moved to London, first to the Aldwych, then the Roundhouse.

Cast: Claudius: David Waller, Gertrude: Brenda Bruce, Ophelia: Helen Mirren, Polonius: Sebastian Shaw, Laertes: Christoper Gable, Horatio: Terence Taplin, Player Queen: Frances de la Tour, Osric: Peter Egan.

In 1968 Trevor Nunn had taken over as director of the Royal Shakespeare Company from Peter Hall. In contrast to Hall's preoccupation with politically charged productions, Nunn was more interested in 'the human personalities of a king or queen rather than their public roles', and in *Hamlet* 'the working out of Hamlet's final confrontation with Claudius and Horatio' rather than the question of Fortinbras and the future of the state.

This was not his first *Hamlet*. At 17 he had formed a theatre company. The Ipswich Drama Group's production of *Hamlet* ran for five hours. 'It was the first thing I ever directed, an astonishing act of hubris,' he recalled. Now almost 30, in his first talk with his Stratford company he announced: 'Hamlet is a study in alienation: the gulf between thought and will, will and performance. By the Players, Hamlet the thinker is taught how to feel and perform, to bridge the gap between inner and outer worlds in action.'

His Hamlet was Alan Howard, an established Shakespearean actor with the RSC, who that season also played Oberon and Theseus in Peter Brook's ground-breaking *A Midsummer Night's Dream*. Ronald Bryden observed his Hamlet in rehearsal: 'Alan Howard has always been one of the most fascinating of the RSC actors, intelligent to a fault in his refusal to take the simple, unambiguous line of direct feeling through any role. He is a brilliant elaborator, an infinitely fertile inventor of ironies, jokes and defensive strategies for implying emotion by denying it.' He saw Howard creating Hamlet as 'a glittering, sardonic concealer of his genuine feelings, the most

adept Machiavellian in a Machiavellian court'. Although 32, he seemed to
be aiming for a youthful Hamlet: 'His performance grew more and more
still, and as it did so, amazingly younger. It was as if he was stripping from
himself not only years, but the defensive armour, the competence to hide the
child in the adult.'

Howard explained:

> Every actor is able to identify with some aspect of Hamlet's character – but
> this is often done at the expense of the whole, the complete personality.
> I became involved in the many facets of the man, the incredible range
> of his intellectual and emotional life, his magnificent and very proper
> inconsistency. I found Hamlet could only face the situation he is in by
> being an actor, constantly changing his masks and various personae. He
> responds above all to immediate situations – it's this rather than reflective
> detachment which makes him unique. He takes every situation to the
> furthest point it will go – the breaking point.

In view of the recent student protests of 1968, it was not surprising
that Howard's Hamlet should be the archetypal student rebel: long-haired,
tattered and scrawny, sitting on the floor and blowing raspberries. Violence
was always threatening: his madness was not a political decision, but the
behaviour of a man under pressure. One critic saw 'a Hamlet as palpably
mad as a March hare, from the distracted bolting-eyed moment when he
meets his father's Ghost to his own death. A mad, wild Hamlet, who stabs
Polonius not once but twenty frenzied times.'

Howard told the writer Marvin Rosenberg that he felt Hamlet's
transformation began when the Player King's speech showed him the way to
release himself, then continued in the loosening of pressure after *The Murder
of Gonzago*, and finally in the trip to England, where he 'went through his
Gethsemane. At first Hamlet was close to madness: but when he came back,
the rest of the court is maddened, and he is sane.'

Nunn's setting focused on the madness. The set, a bare stage roofed and
walled with Venetian blinds, resembled a white slatted box: lit directly from
above, it suggested the sterility of a psychiatric clinic. The costumes were
emblematic: they were all white except for Hamlet's and, later, Ophelia's,
whom Nunn saw as 'prickly outsiders' in black – a decision leading some
observers to see an overly schematic simplification. He also emphasised the
theological aspect. Hamlet and Horatio wore crosses; Hamlet consigned
Ophelia to a nunnery in a chapel, overheard by Polonius and Claudius
eavesdropping in two nearby confessionals; hooded monks filed past ringing
bells; at the end of the closet scene Hamlet escaped in a monk's costume
taken from the Players' property basket.

The production was received with respect rather than acclaim.
Howard's Hamlet was recognised as intelligent and capable; the reviews
were generally positive. Peter Thompson typically wrote: 'His voice is

neither strong nor resonant, but surprises by its range and suppleness ... Not a great Hamlet, but not a negligible one.' Irving Wardle offered a theatrical interpretation: 'By turns a simpering child, a smooth courtier, a slack-jawed idiot and an exultant conspirator, he never shows more than a succession of masks ... He is, in short, an actor improvising from one moment to the next, play-acting as much in soliloquy as in contact with other characters.'

Over thirty years later Nunn reflected: 'My actors were superb, but I was trying to solve all the contradictions of the play, and it's not possible; a kind of paralysis occurs. I didn't make it live.' However, after performances in Stratford and the Aldwych, the production was performed at the Roundhouse in north London, without decor and in rehearsal clothes, where to Nunn's delight it emerged with a startling new clarity: 'It was the experience that gave me the greatest pleasure of the whole year, forgetting about design and presentation altogether. The *Hamlet* was free; it was thrilling.' It sowed the seed for his much-admired intimate 1976 production of *Macbeth* at the Other Place, with Ian McKellen and Judi Dench.

Ian McKellen
Robert Chetwyn

Robert Chetwyn's production for the Prospect Theatre Company, starring Ian McKellen, opened at the 1971 Edinburgh Festival, then toured the UK and Europe, ending at the Cambridge in London.

Cast: Claudius: Ronald Lewis/John Woodvine, Gertrude: Faith Brook, Laertes: Tim Pigott-Smith, Horatio: Julian Curry, Ophelia: Susan Fleetwood, Polonius: Geoffrey Chater/James Cairncross.

'I suspect a lot of people hate me as an actor. I fully expect to get the worst notices of my life.' Ian McKellen voiced this fear as he prepared to bring his Hamlet to the West End. It followed an opening night in Edinburgh at which his performance had been greeted by a critical chorus of derision. Since then the production had toured home and abroad, to more mixed notices.

Harold Hobson was one of the most hostile critics: 'Mr McKellen appears to lack any compulsive conception in his performance. The whole evening in fact created the impression of a Wolfit production without Wolfit.' Later he added: 'The best thing about his Hamlet is his curtain-call.' Irving Wardle wrote: 'The depressing factor in his performance is his uncontrolled development of personal mannerisms – the ostentatious shows of distress, abrupt village-idiot grins, the tousled explosions of passion, and the disconcerting Lancashire cadences that appear at key points, even in the very last line.'

Gareth Lloyd-Evans thought his performance lacked genuine feeling:

> Mr McKellen's acting takes us back many decades to the extrovert,
> mannered days of the old touring companies and matinee idols. His
> acting is less a committal to the part than a demonstration of personal
> idiosyncrasies ... His speaking is constantly listening to itself, his diction
> has moments of incredible eccentricity, his movements disguise a basic
> awkwardness by being incessant and exaggerated. Mr McKellen is a
> nineteenth-century star actor – what he lacks is anything that seems natural,
> truly felt, interpreted. His is the triumph of artifice over anything else.

McKellen had recently been acclaimed in the title-roles in *Richard II* and
Marlowe's *Edward II*. This had led to him being labelled 'the Olivier from
Wigan' and 'the greatest Shakespearean actor alive'. Such extravagant praise
may have contributed to the hostility about his Hamlet. He himself partly
blamed the surfeit of Hamlets that year, describing the experience as being
'like climbing Great Gable in the Lake District on Bank Holiday Monday'.
He felt the critics were sick of the play, a feeling reflected in the suggestion by
one that there be a ten-year moratorium on productions. McKellen argued:
'Critics may well be right when they say that a performance has failed (or
succeeded), but they are invariably hopeless in analysing why.'

His director was Robert Chetwyn, for whom he had played 15 roles when
Chetwyn was running the Arts Theatre in Ipswich. For *Hamlet,* McKellen
explained,

> Robert persuaded me that we shouldn't tell the Olivier story of a man
> who couldn't make up his mind. Our Hamlet was a boy who knows
> exactly what has to be done, but lacks the manly resources to do it ...
> The production was all about youth culture against middle age. The play
> is about a young person's search, and that is why the play has always
> fascinated young people.

Chetwyn recalled: 'Ian and I went through the text three or four months
beforehand, word by word, and talked over the meaning of it thoroughly.
We would be seen on tour by school kids, audiences who had never seen a
Shakespeare play before, so we strove for clarity.'

Aged 31, McKellen came up with a romantic, neurotic, emotional young
Hamlet, an unkempt university drop-out, with a costume embracing a range
of periods from Elizabethan to modern, with more than a hint of hippie –
shaggy hair, a fringed jerkin, a medallion on a chain, and dirty boots.
Chetwyn recalled his set and his novel treatment of the Ghost:

> The set was all mirrors, for it seemed to me this was a recurring image in
> the play. And it made some good effects. We had three ghosts, all reflected
> time and time again, so the stage was covered with ghosts ... I suddenly

thought that there wasn't a real ghost, but that it was all in Hamlet's mind. So the voice was done electronically by James Cairncross.

The London notices were scarcely better than those in Edinburgh. Nicholas de Jongh thought the production had got worse, but Wardle thought McKellen's performance much improved: 'Many of his vocal oddities have been corrected, and there is no trace of his unconscious Lancashire inflections. Gone too are the slack, village-idiot's jaw and the gangling stance. The performance has more authority, more economy, and more detail that really tells.'

Looking back, McKellen thought he had rushed at the part, going too much for angst and bewilderment and pain, and not finding Hamlet's humanity: 'So much of the play encourages you to be self-obsessed and neurotic,' he said. He also decided that 'any actor more than thirty is dreary – Hamlet should be eighteen – a kid – otherwise his behaviour is inexcusable'.

Following the end of the London run, the production was filmed for television, directed for the BBC by David Giles. McKellen was critical: 'It didn't work on television. I was running alongside the character telling the audience this is how you do it.'

Albert Finney
Peter Hall

Hamlet, *with Albert Finney in the lead, was Peter Hall's choice to open the new National Theatre. But since the building was not yet ready, the play started at the Old Vic in December 1975, the National's last production there, before opening the Lyttelton in March 1976.*

Cast: Claudius/Ghost: Denis Quilley, Gertrude: Angela Lansbury/Barbara Jefford, Polonius: Roland Culver, Laertes: Jim Norton, Ophelia: Susan Fleetwood, Horatio: Philip Locke, Rosencrantz: Oliver Cotton, Player King: Robert Eddison, Osric: Gawn Grainger.

In 1973, the year before he took over from Laurence Olivier as director of the National Theatre, Peter Hall suggested the theatre should stage *Hamlet* every two years, with Ronald Pickup or Alan Bates as candidates for playing the Prince. Then he was approached by Albert Finney, who was determined to play the part.

A burly, ebullient actor and an international star on screen, Finney had not appeared at the National since playing in Feydeau's farce *A Flea in Her Ear* in 1966. 'He wants to try and examine a rougher, more instinctive form of classical acting,' Hall noted in his *Diaries*. 'He wants to take on bigger parts.' Finney himself was ready for the challenge, stating: 'You have to have a go at the big classics to see if you can do them.' Although some of Hall's

colleagues doubted Finney's abilities as a classical actor, Hall wanted a star
on board.

He was reluctant to direct the play himself: 'I can't say I have an
overwhelming passion to do *Hamlet* again.' Initially he gave the job to
his associate Michael Blakemore, who decided to stage it in the smaller
Cottesloe theatre. But when Finney became available earlier than expected,
and Blakemore was already engaged for another production, Hall took over
himself. In contrast to his 1965 production with David Warner, he wanted
to use the uncut 'Hamlet in its eternity'. The idea met stiff opposition within
the National.

'There is enormous pressure on me from my colleagues not to do it as I
want to, full-length,' Hall wrote.

> We simply can't afford it, they say. Overtime, and the impossibility of
> matinees, with the consequent loss of revenue, would put another £50,000
> on the budget ... I took on *Hamlet* as a gesture of trust to Albert. I didn't
> much want to direct it. But now I have a line, an excitement, something
> to get the adrenalin going, I don't want to *interpret* the play by cutting it.

He reflected further: 'We still cut the text like barbarians. Do we know *what*
we cut? And don't we normally cut either to fit some preconceived theory
for the production, or because we simply can't make the passage work?' His
view prevailed, and he used the unabridged second Quarto. It was the first
uncut *Hamlet* since the Guthrie/Guinness version in 1937, and set a fashion
for playing Shakespeare as written.

Finney, now 39, spent months working out in a gym. On the first day
of rehearsals Hall was thrilled by his appearance, noting: 'Albert looks
wonderful with his beard: a powerful, passionate, sexy Hamlet, glowering
with resentment.' As work progressed and they came to Hamlet's most
famous soliloquy, he observed: 'When Albert walked on to the stage and
launched into the current problem of Hamlet – was he to be or not to be? –
it was electric and urgent, not introspective. I'm sure that's right.'

With the closet scene he broke with tradition, cutting out the bed on the
grounds a closet was a place for disrobing, not a bedroom. 'A bed is not
what the scene is really about. You rapidly get to Freudian images. Instead
I put two chairs on stage and had Hamlet and his mother confronting each
other. The scene was immediately more alive.' He subsequently mused on
a problem that had long puzzled him: 'In the second half of the play the
soliloquies cease and it's no longer the public discussion of morals and ethics
that the first part was ... Where is the tragedy?' He thought he saw a solution:
perhaps the soliloquies *needn't* cease? 'I am sure Hamlet should *continue* his
dialogue with the audience – particularly with the graveyard scene. If Hamlet
addresses a good deal of his graveyard humour to the audience – so that the
lawyer, the politician, and my lady painted an inch thick are out there, in the
audience – then the contact continues and the play goes on building.'

Before the opening night, life offstage intervened. Finney's father had been unwell, and while this saddened him, he felt it gave him an insight into the part. Then during a dress rehearsal his father died. Finney was compelled to carry on, playing three previews and the first night before being free to go to his father's funeral. 'It was difficult to get the words out,' he confessed later. 'Even after six months it was tough to get through it.' Yet he seemed in control, telling Hall after the second preview that he was experiencing 'a sense of ease, of freedom, of oneness with the audience'. After the third preview Hall too was positive: 'The actors are in a marvellous state, like a trained orchestra who can play the piece and will move it in any direction the conductor wants. Albert is flexible and eager to live dangerously.'

The play was staged not in the still-unfinished Olivier theatre but in the proscenium-arched Lyttelton. Hall was influenced by John Russell Brown's book *Free Shakespeare*, which argued the plays should be staged in quasi-Elizabethan conditions, avoiding elaborate sets. John Bury's stark set was suitably spartan: a bare horizontal wall upstage with a large door within it, with most of the action taking place in a white painted circle. It was reminiscent of the type of setting for a Greek tragedy.

The play was taken at considerable speed; at over four hours it was only five minutes longer than Hall's 1965 production, despite the fact that at Stratford he had cut 730 lines. That night Hall expressed his satisfaction: 'All in all it was our best performance. The last scene has never gone better, and I felt an actual purgation in the house. The reception was really thunderous.' But he foresaw 'a contentious press', and he was proved right.

The critics' comments ranged from 'dreadful' to 'the best Hamlet since Redgrave's'. Some critics admired Finney's heroic, rough-hewn, energetic Prince, who rushed on stage threatening to commit hari-kari for 'To be or not to be'. Robert Cushman was one: 'His timing is marvellous; he can detonate a famous phrase before you have time to duck away from it.' Michael Billington was another: 'Finney roams the perimeter of the stage, at times "playing" the house like an old-style comic, and at others fixing the audience with the unrelenting stare of the savage moralist ... I unrepentantly admire his performance, because it restores something long missing from the play: a sense of danger.'

Others described his Hamlet as 'insensitive', 'rasping like a buzz-saw', 'petulantly eccentric', 'monotonous', and offering 'a rant without emotion'. John Elsom felt 'he sometimes seemed to stress the bitterness of the part at the expense of its other aspects'. Harold Hobson was especially harsh: 'In an age which puts a low value on grace, style and subtlety, Mr Finney is an appropriate enough choice. His voice is monotonously rasping, his mind does not respond to the text, and his way of taking curtain calls suggests an unsufferable conceit.'

Hall's production also came under fire for creating static groupings, and for having the courtiers speak in unison like an opera chorus. Irving

Wardle wrote: 'Ten years ago when Mr Hall directed the play at Stratford ... the tragedy swung round and confronted us like a great dark mirror ... Whatever the claims of the new version, it throws back no reflection of that sort. It is a ponderous cultural event which will attract the star-following public, and gratify spectators of the "Shakespeare intentions" school.'

Hall pondered the reviews: 'Some critics are wonderful, some are dreadful. Why are they, the bad ones, so angry? I suppose because this is a different kind of Shakespeare, undecorated, and in some sense uncomfortable.' Having originally felt Finney was five years too old for the role, he now disagreed with those who thought so: 'I always think that Hamlet is 18 or 19 at the start of the play, and 35 at the end ... Albert was unforgettable in the fifth act.'

In the spring the play was out of the repertoire for a month. During an extra dress rehearsal, Hall criticised Finney for playing 'just too bloody fast to investigate the text', and begged him to slow down. The next night he obeyed, and the first act was seven minutes longer. Finney felt he had unblocked something in himself, and Hall agreed: 'What we'd had before was energy, ferocity and agility. What we had tonight was a man exposing his own heart.'

Gertrude was Angela Lansbury's first Shakespearean role, and she had felt miscast. 'I had to play her as a rather annoying, pudding sort of woman, and I wasn't ever comfortable with that,' she said later. She saw the production as 'an extremely Anglo-Saxon sort of *Hamlet* ... It was very, very spare. At times Albert resembled a kind of black-clothed paratrooper, while I felt like a rather roughly hewn chess-piece as the queen – chained to the ground.'

Despite the critical brickbats, Hall was pleased:

This is the closest I have reached to the heart of a Shakespeare play ... it is the production which has the least gap between my hopes and the facts on the stage ... and the closest I've ever got to a unified style of verse-speaking which is right. I feel now I know how the verse should be treated. In Stratford days what I did was intellectual. Now I have found a way of doing it which is based on feeling and passion.

Ben Kingsley
Buzz Goodbody

Buzz Goodbody's 1975 production of Hamlet, *with Ben Kingsley as the Prince, opened at the Royal Shakespeare Company's small-scale theatre The Other Place. It then played in London at the Roundhouse in Camden.*

Cast: Claudius: George Baker, Gertrude: Mikel Lambert, Ophelia: Yvonne Nicholson, Polonius: André Van Gyseghem, Horatio: Sid Livingstone, Laertes: Stuart Wilson, Player King: Bob Peck.

Until 1974 The Other Place at Stratford was a run-down, corrugated-tin hut used to store costumes, situated across the road from the Royal Shakespeare Theatre. It then became a home for radical experiment which compelled the RSC to embrace new ideas and styles of acting. This was a tribute to the vision of the young, hugely talented Buzz Goodbody, the first woman to become a member of the RSC's directorial team. Her previous productions had been controversial and attacked by the critics, partly because of their startling modern cultural references. But her *King Lear* in The Other Place, while dividing the critics, was hailed by *The Times* as 'the most dispassionate re-examination of the play since Peter Brook's 1962 version'.

Her production of *Hamlet* opened the second season at The Other Place in 1975. It seemed to mark the moment when she was fulfilling her great promise as a director. But four days into the previews, aged just 28, she took her own life. The news came as a total shock to those working with her, and affected them deeply. 'I used to hit terrible despair and helplessness and questioned everything,' Ben Kingsley remembered.

A committed feminist, Goodbody had started the first feminist theatre company, the Women's Street Theatre Group. As a member of the Communist Party she described herself as 'a Marxist-Socialist revolutionary'. She made her political intentions clear: 'To me working on a production is a political act. One of the sad things about much work on Shakespeare is that it springs from a mildly left, incredibly hegemonic order over the arts, which has a very distinct bourgeois ideology behind it. That is unfair. I would like to see good Shakespearean productions done by Marxists.'

In 1973 she had sent a memo to the RSC's artistic director Trevor Nunn, arguing for a 'studio/second auditorium' operating on a near-invisible budget, using RSC actors already on contract, and aimed at an audience of locals, factory workers from Coventry and Birmingham, and schoolchildren. As an alternative venue to the main theatre, she saw The Other Place as a first step towards breaking down the economic and social barriers between the RSC and the public that helped finance it. She staged *Hamlet* in modern dress on a shallow platform against plain-white grooved panels, with a Kabuki bridge leading to the rear exit of the auditorium. It shone an intense light on the complexity of personal and family relationships, a clear reaction against the epic style of RSC productions of the 1960s, which tended to highlight the political aspects.

Ben Kingsley, now 31, dark and slightly balding, had played Demetrius in Peter Brook's iconoclastic version of *A Midsummer Night's Dream*. Like other actors, playing Hamlet made him examine his own character: 'I had to mine my own growth as a personality, examine and explore my own fears and my own inspirations,' he said. 'They are the molten metal that you pour into a mould – and that mould is called Hamlet.'

George Baker, playing Claudius, was initially sceptical of the young director's unconventional rehearsal methods, but came to value them:

'We did a fair amount of moving round in circles and touching hands to communicate,' he recalled. 'Sending out positive vibes and negative vibes. I began to feel all sorts of preconceived prejudices falling away. I was gaining a freedom of emotion I had not bothered to touch before.' But he was shocked by one directorial decision:

> Just before we opened Buzz organised a macabre rehearsal. In order for us to realise the magnitude of suicide and burial in an unconsecrated grave, she got permission from Holy Trinity, Stratford's parish church, to allow us to dig a grave in unhallowed ground. Yvonne Nicholson, playing Ophelia, was wrapped in a shroud and put on a two-wheeled trundle. The gravediggers pushed her to the grave, and the scene between the priest and Laertes was played.

Goodbody staged the play with virtually no scenery, creating the impression of the inside of an army barracks or a makeshift prison camp. Her production was fast-paced, with scenes overlapping each other, the actors sometimes spilling out into the aisles. For the play-within-the-play the actors appeared in masks. Denmark was peopled by businessmen in suits, with Claudius addressing the house like a company director at a shareholders' meeting. Goodbody saw him as 'one of the most powerful businessmen in the world, and certainly more ruthless than Tiny Rowland or Robert Maxwell'.

'It is a long time since I have been so gripped by this play,' Irving Wardle wrote. 'However delicate the personal nuance, the overall view is the bleakest I can recall; not only is society poisoned, but neither Hamlet nor anyone else has any chance of setting it right.' For Michael Coveney there was 'a Strindbergian intensity about the production that pays particular dividends in the domestic scenes'. Peter Hall also approved: 'Because this was Shakespeare in a room, it could be quick, intimate and flexible. And how good it makes the actors seem.' Kingsley's angry, unromantic Prince was 'one of the best Hamlets I have seen. His performance is shrewd, ironic, perceptive, paranoid.' The actress Janet Suzman observed: 'Ben Kingsley is a very spiritual actor, but he played Hamlet with such a combination of extreme humour and gut feeling that he was both sunny and moving. I feel I don't need to see the play ever again, it was so marvellous.'

The critics were equally enthusiastic. As Coveney saw it: 'Ben Kingsley, so intelligent and explicit at every turn, builds his fury and resolve as powerfully as he describes the growth by leaps and bounds of his own existential imaginings.' Wardle wrote: 'Ben Kingsley's Hamlet is set apart from the others not by nobility of bearing, but by intelligence,' while Benedict Nightingale stated: 'I can't remember a Prince who found more humour in Hamlet.'

Following Goodbody's death Trevor Nunn supervised the production for the rest of the run. Moving to the Roundhouse, the play was again a critical success. Kingsley was said to be so nervous the night before the opening that a friend of his took him to the top of a tall building to look at all the millions of lights in the city, to remind him that only one of them was the Roundhouse.

Goodbody's innovative production led Nunn to realise he had been 'yearning to do small-theatre productions'. The loss to the theatre from her tragic death was summed up by Wardle: 'The production redoubles belief that the theatre has lost a superb talent at the very moment that it was moving from promise to fulfilment.'

Derek Jacobi
Toby Robertson

In 1977 Derek Jacobi played Hamlet for the Prospect Theatre Company, directed by the company's artistic director Toby Robertson. It toured in the UK and abroad, including Elsinore, and was the first English Hamlet *to be staged in post-revolutionary China.*

Cast: Claudius: Timothy West/Julian Glover, Gertrude: Brenda Bruce, Polonius: Robert Eddison, Ophelia: Suzanne Bertish/Jane Wymark, Laertes: Terence Wilton, Horatio: John Rowe.

This was not Derek Jacobi's first Hamlet: as a schoolboy of 18 he had played the part in a National Youth Theatre production, and again at Cambridge in a university production. In 2014 he looked back at that first attempt: 'It was a very simplistic, black-and-white Hamlet. I was tearing a passion to tatters, to very rags. What I lacked in technique and finesse I made up for in volume, noise, and a lot of gestures. I wasn't a very contemplative Prince.'

By 1977 he was a highly experienced Shakespearean actor, with a reputation for intelligent verse-speaking who, among other parts, had played Laertes in the Peter O'Toole *Hamlet*. Aged 38, he was older than many Hamlets, but looked younger than his years. 'I was on the threshold of 40, perhaps the best age for the most rounded portrayal,' he suggested. 'Hamlet is so many things, so complex a character: he's a universal figure, he's all men, he's everybody's problems ... It's a vast canvas, a huge journey. And any Hamlet can only get some of it right some of the time ... It's very much the particular actor's look, sound, charisma, rhythm, movement. Rather than you becoming Hamlet, Hamlet becomes you.'

He was conscious of audience expectations: 'Audiences are always bristling with preconceptions, prejudices and contradictions. They know what Hamlet should look like and sound like, how he should behave. If they don't accept the actor by the end of the evening, they won't accept that he is Hamlet, *their* Hamlet.' He was also aware of the physical demands: 'Hamlet is on stage for three hours, and has more than 1,500 lines. Unless you learn to pace it correctly, it is the most knackering show ever. I had to find out how much energy I needed to use in each particular scene, so that I did not exhaust myself.'

Toby Robertson had been Prospect's artistic director since 1964. As Michael Coveney observed, he was recognised as having 're-established the good name and reputation of touring theatre in the UK after it had become a byword for second-rate tattiness in the 1950s'. He pioneered a type of production with minimal stage designs that enabled the company to tour effectively to a wide range of venues.

Jacobi reflected on his approach to *Hamlet*:

Although Toby had been at Cambridge he had no overall directorial mission, nor was he an intellectual wanting to impose any reading or interpretation on the part and the play. He was not out to create a style, or prove Shakespeare was our contemporary. He looked more to Shakespeare's universal and timeless appeal ... he was content to let the director take a back seat and leave it up to the actors and the play.

He remembered a moment in rehearsal that reflected this attitude, when Robertson announced: 'I feel the production belongs to the actors now. There are things which will never be quite as I want or would like them to be. But you have to work with your actor, and especially with your Hamlet. This Hamlet is perhaps a more rational man than I saw, but Derek has defined his own interpretation.' Nevertheless, Jacobi acknowledged that 'Toby brought more aggression into my performance than might otherwise have been there'.

He rejected Olivier's idea expressed in his 1948 film that Hamlet was 'a man who could not make up his mind'.

On the contrary, I firmly believe he is a man of great action, and enormous energy. Nor do I believe he is ever quite mad. He uses madness as a cloak, although there are moments when he teeters on the brink of sanity: when he sees the Ghost, in the nunnery scene, and with Gertrude in the closet ... He has an over-abundance of sensitivity, nerves as taut as a piano wire, but I think he remains for the most part the sanest and most sharp-witted man in the court.

Like many actors, he disliked opening nights: 'The first night is the most uptight, nervous and unrepresentative performance I'll ever give. When I've worked more into the play with audiences I'll know more about it. The critics never see those performances. It's so unfair, as judgements are often made prematurely based on first-night performances.' On this occasion he need not have worried: his intelligent, humorous, very physical Hamlet, burning with anger from the start, was much liked by the critics.

The veteran J.C. Trewin wrote: 'Logical, graceful, possibly the most touching Hamlet since John Neville, but fortified always by his fiery spirit, he re-charged my faith in the courtier's, soldier's, scholar's eye, tongue, sword ... To listen to him was like reading the play in a fresh format.' Irving Wardle noted: 'Jacobi restores the figure of the Renaissance Prince, and the masterful variations of tempo and weight that traditionally belong to the part.' Timothy West, playing Claudius, described him as 'a fine Hamlet, intelligent and humorous'.

Robertson's traditional production included unexpected touches. Hamlet addressed 'To be or not to be' to Ophelia, a decision which Jacobi argued was textually justified. During 'I have of late, wherefore I know not' he read the lines from a book, from 'What a piece of work is a man' to 'the paragon of animals', before returning to his own words with 'And yet, to me, what is this quintessence of dust?' He also donned a fierce-looking mask as he invited Claudius and Gertrude to take their seats for *The Murder of Gonzago*.

After two years Jacobi had played Hamlet over four hundred times. 'It's the most wonderful part in the world,' he reflected. 'It calls on an actor's full armoury of craft – vocal, physical, mental, emotional – everything. It can be played in so many different ways and with so many different colours.'

In 1988 he directed Kenneth Branagh as Hamlet in the 1988 Renaissance Theatre Company production at the Birmingham Rep (see page 59).

Frances de la Tour
Robert Walker

Directed by Robert Walker, Frances de la Tour played Hamlet in 1979 at the Half Moon Theatre in London's East End.

Cast: Claudius: Sam Cox, Gertrude: Maggie Steed, Horatio: Robin Soans, Laertes: Matthew Robertson, Ophelia: Judy Lloyd, Polonius: Robin Hooper, Gravedigger/Rosencrantz: Andy de la Tour.

In 1979, in a promenade production at the Half Moon, Frances de la Tour became the first woman to play Hamlet on the English stage since Sarah Bernhardt, the idol of the French theatre, had famously taken on the role in 1899, playing a French adaptation in Paris, London and New York, and a single performance in Stratford.

The tradition went back to the late eighteenth century, with leading actresses demanding to play the role. Those who took on the part included Sarah Siddons in 1775, the first female Hamlet; the American actress Charlotte Cushman in 1661, who also played Romeo and other male roles; and in the 1880s Isabella Pateman. Bernhardt argued provocatively that the role was more suitable for a mature woman – she was 54 – than an immature man, since 'The woman more readily looks the part, yet has the maturity of mind to grasp it.' Critics were scathing, stating that her cocking her legs up on a couch, her 'manly stride' and 'gruff howlings', suggested an 'angry elderly woman' rather than a 'young and emotional man'. In 2014 Maxine Peake carried on the tradition at the Manchester Royal Exchange (see page 116).

In 2016 de la Tour recalled:

I didn't approach the part as a woman, I just studied the role as any actor would. I was dressed in trousers and jacket, so I could be seen as androgynous. My hair was long and curly and I wore no make-up, so I was just a young person. I think audiences readily believed this from the first soliloquy. I was told later that I became quite feminine when I was with the male actors, for example when I greeted Rosencrantz and Guildenstern. But I didn't know that at the time.

Director Robert Walker explained: 'I wanted a radical re-working of the play, to forge a new language. Frankie was utterly remarkable, it was so powerful what she did. She played it as a woman playing a man, and it was a wonderful embodiment of the role.' Michael Billington agreed: 'She is tough, abrasive, virile and impassioned'; he noted 'a good performance, compact with every male virtue except femininity'. But Milton Shulman was critical: 'She speaks most of the poetry on a one-note nasal pitch and, in her final death throes, tottered about so long she was in danger of being given a breathalyser test.'

As the Half Moon was in the process of moving within the East End, and there were no seats as the new theatre was not yet ready, they staged *Hamlet* as a promenade performance. Three separate stages were placed around the edges, with the actors moving through the audience to the relevant stage, sometimes having to shift people off it before they could start a scene. 'It was a very involving production,' de la Tour remembered. 'The audience could touch us.'

With little money available there was a need to improvise. 'The set was built out of driftwood picked up on the shores of the Thames, and that became the battlements. It looked a million dollars on the outside, but close to it looked manky and rotten – which worked brilliantly with the play.' Iona McLeish, the costume designer, wanted to create a raw feel. 'We got hold of old coats, sheets, any fabrics we could find, from Brick Lane and other markets,' she said. 'Then we slashed them, in order to create an Elizabethan effect.'

Many people from the nearby flats came to the show. In order to further involve the local community, Walker recruited local children to play some of the Players, and invited children from Tower Hamlets, most of whom had never been to the theatre, to come to the production. De la Tour remembered the result: 'When I was waiting by the side of the stage for my next entrance they would come and talk to me. They would ask me questions about the story, such as: "Why did your father die?" and "Why do you want to kill your uncle?" I loved that.'

She was less happy when during one performance a group of 13–14-year-old schoolgirls started to laugh, apparently at seeing a female Hamlet.

> I was holding a pretend candle at the time. I stopped the show and said to them: 'You see this candle. It's not real: I turn it on with a battery. We're pretending, we're telling a story. If it's difficult for you to watch a woman playing a man, I will completely understand. If you would like to go you must feel free to do so, and if you stay that would be great'. It was a risk, but I think it worked – just about.

She felt the rough-and-ready quality of the setting was appropriate: 'The state of Denmark was falling apart, and so was the building, so everything echoed its breakdown. We had a skeleton structure, and rough clothes, even though we were royalty. There was a rebellious spirit, some of the men wore make-up, and Maggie Steed as Gertrude showed her breasts, which was very shocking.' She underlined the experimental nature of the work at the Half Moon. 'They were very special productions, innovative plays being staged in small spaces. Out of that came the Donmar, the Almeida, the King's Head and similar venues.'

5

The Eighties

Jonathan Pryce
Richard Eyre

In 1980 Richard Eyre directed Jonathan Pryce as Hamlet at the Royal Court in London.

Cast: Claudius: Michael Elphick, Gertrude: Jill Bennett, Ophelia: Harriet Walter, Laertes: Simon Chandler, Polonius: Geoffrey Chater, Horatio: Jarlath Conroy, Player King: Christopher Logue.

Even though at 32 he had leading Shakespearean roles under his belt – Mark Antony, Richard III, Petruchio, Edgar – Jonathan Pryce took a while to decide to play Hamlet. 'I wasn't sure I had anything fresh to bring to the part; I didn't think I had anything to say. Then my father died, and the reason seemed to be there.' There was a further factor. 'One day I became convinced he'd appeared to me: only for a moment, but clearly I'd wanted to conjure him back into being … So I approached Hamlet as someone who had seen his own father's ghost.'

At the Royal Court, a venue more famous for staging new work, he used this experience to startling effect. Richard Eyre explained his radical idea: 'We dispensed with the Ghost in search of a plausible means of presenting the spirit of Hamlet's father to an audience (and actor and director) sceptical of paranormal phenomena.' He and Pryce had seen the film *The Exorcist*, and the idea of some kind of possession seemed a powerful one. Pryce then watched documentaries on voodoo and people speaking in tongues, and tried a few ideas out at home. The result was startling, and a mesmerising shock to the audience.

As a projection of his fevered mind, Hamlet was taken over by his father's spirit. Pryce called up the deep, sepulchral voice of Old Hamlet from the depth of his guts in an agonising growl. Harriet Walter, playing Ophelia, described the scene. 'His body writhed and contorted as if some alien creature had invaded him and was kicking at his sides. He belched the Ghost's words from the pit of his stomach, and gasped for air as his own voice recovered enough to answer. His body convulsed, his eyes closed, his head rocking back and forth, he twisted and shuddered in agony, communicating unbearable pain. He seemed to observe himself in horror as he was taken over by his father's words.'

Later Pryce recalled the reaction on the first night: 'You could hear people in the audience saying "What the fuck?", and there was a titter or two; but they seemed to adjust.' In Eyre's opinion, 'Jonathan made the phenomenon of "belly speaking" terrifying and, at the same time, touching.' The absence of the Ghost inevitably affected the closet scene. It meant that when Hamlet broke off from his aggressive onslaught on Gertrude he went into a spasm, started talking to an empty space and growling in reply, and gave every appearance of madness. On his final line, 'The rest is silence', he gave a sudden epileptic shudder, which recalled the possession by the Ghost.

Pryce spoke 'To be or not to be' directly to Ophelia, as Derek Jacobi's Prince had done. Eyre defended this decision, suggesting 'it was stubborn logic that led us to play the soliloquy to Ophelia rather than countenance the implausibility of having her present on the small stage (as Shakespeare indicates) without being noticed by Hamlet'. And after killing Polonius, as Pryce explained, for Hamlet the 'sudden shock and distress', the realisation of the seriousness of what he had done, leaves him distraught.

Walter decided her Ophelia was 'to be no flibberty-damsel, but an intelligent girl locked in her mind by the oppressive rules of the establishment'. She is hampered by the fact that 'she has depended on Hamlet and her brother and father for what flimsy self-definition she has. The one has just denounced her as a whore, the second is abroad, and the third is about to be murdered by the first.' Seeking insights into the text, she found value in the work of the radical psychiatrist R.D. Laing, especially his case-histories of young schizophrenic women, and the mechanisms by which their families inadvertently contributed to their disorder.

She also jotted down notes on Ophelia's situation as an aide-memoire:

Mother is dead and no one mentions her. No known female companion. Only female role-model known to be present in her life is Gertrude, who has too many problems to be of much help … Little experience of love. Duty rather than deep love binds her to her father, and although her brother had been an affectionate companion in childhood, they have been brought up increasingly apart from one another. Her education, such as it is, has been at her father's hands and of a deliberately unworldly nature, while her brother's education was a serious preparation for a public role in life.

Eyre made it clear to her he didn't want 'mad acting'.

I knew what he meant. For Ophelia, her mad scene is an ungoverned artless release; for the actress playing her it can be a chance to show off her repertoire of lolling tongues and rolling eyes, in a fey and affecting aria which is anything but artless. That is the paradox of acting mad. The actor is self-conscious in every sense, while the mad person has lost their hold on self.

The solution, she felt, was to find a method in Ophelia's madness, 'so that I could root her actions in her motivations (however insane and disordered), just as I would with any other character ... I started to see the seeds of her madness had been sown long before the play started, by the workings of a cold, repressive environment on an already susceptible mind.'

The production was a box-office hit, and hailed by some observers as the first definitive reinterpretation since David Warner's Hamlet. Robert Cushman observed: 'For the first time since Warner played the role fifteen years ago, a generation has found and crowned its Prince.' Pryce's Hamlet was highly strung and extremely energetic, liable to erupt into terrifying violence; his attack on Ophelia was particularly nasty. He straddled the boundaries between sanity and insanity, his intensity being at times so overwrought as to seem barely under control. As Eyre described it: 'Jonathan's whole performance walked a knife edge between danger and an almost childlike vulnerability. Madness never seemed far away ... A few critics were ecstatic, a few indifferent, and some patronising ... but the audiences were never less than enthusiastic.'

Robert Cushman wrote: 'If you want to see an actor wrestling vibrantly, wittily and honestly with a great role, then London offers nothing better.' James Fenton enthused: 'This actor is immensely forceful, can hold the attention of the house, and can dominate the stage at will.' Dominic Cavendish wrote: 'Pryce's virtuosic suggestion of a man possessed and channelling his own tormented flesh and blood, coupled with his characteristic sensitivity and intelligence, scored a palpable hit.' Michael Billington thought the possession idea 'a dubious device', but felt 'Pryce carried off his spiritual occupation with tremendous skill. He also restored a quality often missing in more melodious Hamlets – a genuine sense of danger.'

Pryce later commented: 'Though obviously *Hamlet* is a tragedy, it's often very sharp and funny. I never found it draining, even though there was all this difficult stuff emotionally. It was a way to release all that, in a way.' He cautioned any actor embarking on the role.

> I think it's really difficult for a young actor to get up there and do it, with the pressure to find something distinctive. But also you can't think this is the most important role of your life – in some ways it's not even the most important role in the play. *Hamlet* is a real ensemble piece: you have to realise he's just one part of the story.

His performance proved both a landmark in Pryce's career and a benchmark by which succeeding modern Hamlets were judged. But not everyone was in tune with Eyre's radical ideas. After seeing a performance the director Lindsay Anderson told him: 'The play is still there for somebody else to put the record straight.'

Jonathan Pryce won the Olivier Award for Best Actor.

Michael Pennington
John Barton

John Barton directed Michael Pennington as Hamlet for the Royal Shakespeare Company at Stratford in 1980, the production moving in 1981 to the Aldwych in London.

Cast: Claudius: Derek Godfrey, Gertrude: Barbara Leigh-Hunt, Horatio: Tom Wilkinson, Polonius: Tony Church, Laertes: John Bowe, Ophelia: Carol Royle.

'I wanted to go back to the classic tradition of a lyric-poetic-intellectual-princely Hamlet, after twenty years of a British tradition of the boorish, lout Hamlet that I didn't like.'

In his vision for his production, John Barton was in revolt against recent Hamlets, whose interpretations had overtly reflected the social and political turmoil of the last two decades. He was reacting against many 'petulant Princes', such as David Warner's tormented student, Steven Berkoff's skinhead Hamlet, and Jonathan Pryce's volatile Prince. He wanted a graceful and sensitive Hamlet to counter-balance those anti-heroes, and a production concerned more with the breakdown of family relationships than the contemporary political context.

He set out his requirements for Hamlet:

He must have the capacity to be noble and gentle but also brutal and coarse ... he has to be obviously full of passion, but able to stand outside his own passion and be objective about it. He has to have a strong sense of irony, wit, humour. He has to have a *deep* intellectual energy. He has to have a *very* volatile temperament, so that you never know what he's going to be like from one moment to the next. The demands are huge.

His choice fell on Michael Pennington, who had been with the RSC for five years, and already had a good working relationship with Barton, having been first directed by him as Berowne in *Love's Labour's Lost*. Now aged 37, he was very familiar with the play: he had played Hamlet while a student at Cambridge; doubled as Fortinbras and the Ghost in the Warner/Hall version; and appeared as Laertes in the Williamson/Richardson production. An intelligent, graceful and thoughtful actor, he had a fine feeling for the verse, and a deep knowledge and understanding of Shakespeare.

He described Hamlet as the most intelligent character in world literature, at the centre of one of its most exciting adventure stories.

> To pull it off will take the actor further down into his psyche, memory and imagination, and further outwards to the limits of his technical knowledge, than he has probably been before ... The part is like a pane of clear glass disclosing the actor to a greedy audience; playing it changes you for good, and for the better ... It's said that nobody can quite fail in the role, because Hamlet becomes the man (or woman) who plays it. It has certainly been a garment pulled in all sorts of directions; it's so adaptable to your personality.

He stressed that the actor's own mental state should not reflect Hamlet's turmoil.

> His character can only be defined by the action of the play, not by importing a quantity of neurotic or emotional baggage, let alone by a determination to speak for the times; in a sense you have to enter the action naked, with a kind of sweet optimism, and allow the story to be written on you ... You don't act Hamlet because you have an identity crisis or have lost faith in your mother, or because you've had a break-up with a woman. In a phrase, you don't use the play, but instead let the play use you.

Director and actor eased themselves in with weekly meetings three months before rehearsals. 'These produced mostly caveats, a few long-range hunches, and a determination to open the book freshly and forget the past,' Pennington recalled. His starting point was to

> follow the script line by line, trying not to make assumptions about character until the action proves them ... I had to trick myself into being as naive as possible; to grasp simply the A to B of every passage; to try to identify the precise purpose of, say, the closet scene; and to free myself from its famousness in the hope of approaching Hamlet's alienation, his struggle with himself and the others, and his particular bravery, only through what lay in front of me on the page.

Rather than a read-through or company call to launch rehearsals, Barton held small meetings with two or three characters at a time. Keen to stress the 'player' element, he had picked up the references to role-playing and theatricality in the text; in collaboration with his cast and designer Ralph Koltai, this became the central metaphor of the production. The action took place on a small wooden forestage, surrounded by low benches, on which the actors sat. The major theatrical props necessary to the story stood in the background: a crown, a goblet, a table for the swords, a suit of armour (behind which eavesdroppers hid). The players chose their costumes for the play-within-the-play from a large, wicker property basket.

As Pennington observed, Barton was becoming increasingly interested in this theatre image,

> the sense in which the chance arrival of a troupe of players at the court not only provokes action in the dramatic narrative sense, a means to catch the conscience of the king, but also precipitates in Hamlet an inquiry into the validity of his own emotions next to the supposedly counterfeit ones of the actors, into his own role as avenger, and into the appearance of the world as against its corrupt reality.

Initially he was uncertain about Barton's Pirandellian concept, but gradually he took it on board: 'Clearly the distinction between self-dramatisation and real feeling, theatricality and life, runs right through the play, and was beginning to influence my reception of the text; soon the theatrical world itself – hampers, cloaks and property swords – began to appear in rehearsals.' While he and Barton were broadly in agreement about his Hamlet, there remained differences: 'Throughout rehearsals of the earlier part of the play John would be inviting me wherever possible to take gentler options with the part, feeling for instance that I should find restraint and courtesy in the first court scene, albeit under great strain, while I was inclined towards sarcasm and sharpness.'

One difficulty, he discovered, was to get right the mixture of the heroic and anti-heroic elements in Hamlet, of the sweet Prince and the churlish avenger. It became obvious, in rehearsing scenes with Gertrude and Ophelia,

> that alongside the evident generosity and grace of the man there was now a strong current of violence, particularly towards the women in his life, aggravated by a sense of betrayal … In the nunnery scene we moved towards an openly expressed viciousness … It seemed a rich streak for the production to mine, not least because the opportunity for the audience to question Hamlet's morality, and even to project an antipathy back to the stage, is an important counterpoint to the mainly sympathetic appeal on which the part rests.

He and Barton agreed that the Ghost should be as human as possible. Wearing a long Napoleonic coat, there was little about him to suggest a supernatural presence; he simply sat down on a bench with Hamlet and quietly explained how he had been murdered. Normally, when the Ghost reappears in the closet scene, Gertrude doesn't see him. But the question arose, why should everyone else but the queen see him? So when Barbara Leigh-Hunt asked Pennington 'Whereon do you look?' he replied 'On him, on him', and gently turned her face towards the Ghost, at which she fell to the floor in terror and seemed to faint.

Actor and director agreed that Hamlet should have the graceful qualities credited to him by Ophelia, Horatio and Fortinbras, and that the Players were professionals who were good at their job. On the key question of Hamlet's madness, Pennington was clear: 'All the characters talk about it; he himself promises a performance of it after meeting the Ghost; but, apart from a handful of grotesqueries, he talks nothing but searing good sense at all times.'

The critics praised the production and Pennington's probingly intelligent performance. Irving Wardle wrote: '*Hamlet*, everyone agrees, is Shakespeare's most obsessively theatrical work. This production puts that idea to the test of the basic scenic elements, ransacking the text for disguisings and routines, and always allowing the spectator a full view of the concrete instruments that create the sense of illusion.' He noted that Pennington 'encompassed all the part's violence without surrender of its essential goodness'. Michael Billington, however, argued that Pennington erred on the side of caution, so that 'Hamlet's fear of emotional excess seems to be confining Pennington himself, and Claudius never seems to be in a moment's danger'.

But when the production moved to the Aldwych his reservations evaporated, and he placed Pennington's 'sharp-brained and sweet-souled' Hamlet in the first rank. 'What strikes one most is the constant dialectic between passion and reason,' he wrote.

Pennington gave us a Hamlet who was both passion's slave and capable of dissecting the speeches with a postgraduate intelligence. He is not your punk Hamlet, your mad Hamlet, or your Lord Alfred Douglas in tights Hamlet, but a man permanently caught between conflicting emotions ... There is no such thing as a definitive Hamlet; but Mr Pennington gives us more facets than any actor we have seen for a long time.

He was, he suggested, much helped by Barton's thoughtful production. 'What we have, in short, is a *Hamlet* that is not the story of a neurotic misfit at a playing-card court, but one that uncovers all the text's preoccupation with time, death, the workings of the soul, and the very mystery of theatre itself.'

Looking back, Pennington observed: 'On some nights the part felt like slipping on a tailored glove, with others it drove me to frenzy; I daresay I was more violent and unruly than John would have liked.' More generally he stated: 'All that is really necessary for the actor is to be ready each time, to stay on his toes, in the knowledge that things will vary, and that the whole tissue of private references that underpin his performance will quietly change with the patterns of his own life and even the world news.'

He drew attention to the dilemma for the actor: 'Since as Hamlet it is your very nature as much as your skills that are being assessed, it follows that you are unlikely to enjoy it unless you are extraordinarily self-confident.' During the run 'I was beginning to taste the famous isolation of the part, feeling the emotional tides of a man adrift from the behaviour, the humour, the very language of his neighbours: a disorientation that in some equivalent way was beginning to separate me from colleagues and friends.'

More recently he has admitted that he has changed his mind about Hamlet. 'I used to think that anyone of sufficient expertise could play it, that it adapted to the individual actor as Gielgud said it did; but now I believe it needs a particular kind of performer, one who justifies Ophelia's description of him, one with the rare gift of being simultaneously one of us and an archetype.'

Michael Pennington doubled as Claudius and the Ghost in Peter Hall's 1994 production at the Gielgud, with Stephen Dillane playing Hamlet (see page 73).

Anton Lesser
Jonathan Miller

In 1982 Jonathan Miller, with Anton Lesser as the Prince, staged his third production of Hamlet *in London's Warehouse theatre (now the Donmar), and then the Piccadilly.*

Cast: Claudius: Edward de Souza/John Shrapnel, Gertrude: Susan Engel, Polonius: Peter Jeffrey/Alan MacNaughtan, Ophelia: Emma Fielding/ Kathryn Pogson, Laertes: Iain Mitchell, Horatio: John Grillo.

> In all three of my productions my direction has almost entirely been a matter of re-considering the motives of the various characters, and trying to re-design the people so that the same words appear to mean something really quite different on each occasion.

Jonathan Miller staged an austere, pocket-sized production in Elizabethan dress in the two-hundred-seat Warehouse. 'It was a very clear *Hamlet*, with nothing romantic about it,' he recalled. 'There were all sorts of psychological motives which were very clearly delineated.' For example, he decided that Claudius, who describes Gertrude as 'so conjunctive to my life and soul', was moved by overpowering love for her rather than, as is often suggested, by lust.

'I'm very interested in the idea of people whose motives are complicated rather than simple and stereotyped,' he explained. 'I love the idea of people who do dreadful things in the name of quite commendable feelings. I wanted to make Claudius slightly sympathetic. The idea that villainy is a pure, unstructured motive is simple-minded. The idea that this is a lustful monster makes him just uninteresting.' John Shrapnel, who played him at the Piccadilly, agreed: 'By presenting Claudius as an effective and ingenious ruler, you make Hamlet's position much more difficult – he's not just up against some drunken oaf he'll be able to stab after three and a half hours. It's much more interesting and dramatic if you show parallel intellects at work, locked in rivalry.'

Using his medical knowledge as a qualified doctor, Miller argued that people do not go mad as a result of grief, and that Ophelia succumbed to insanity because she was someone who had never known the love of a mother. She was

> surrounded by hectoring, bullying men, who supply her with a self-image, and her character is a reaction to their advice as to what she might or ought to be ... Gradually these portrait painters leave her; they vanish one by one; and Ophelia is suddenly alone with an empty frame in which the painting has been provided by others. It is then that she goes mad.

He added: 'I tried to get her madness to look much less feyly romantic – it usually becomes a sort of Laura Ashley scene. I had her really hallucinating, listening to voices, as well as attempting to force her fingers down her throat.' Kathryn Pogson played with dolls rather than flowers, and gradually became catatonic. Shrapnel remembered the scene as 'very graphic, and accurate in medical detail. It was quite terrifying to behold, almost unwatchable.'

Some critics argued that Anton Lesser's Hamlet lacked any princely quality. But Miller had intentionally made him anti-heroic: more at home in a polytechnic than a university, as one critic observed. He conceived him as a problem child, 'a rather unattractive character, a tiresome, clever, destructive boy, who is very intelligent but volatile, dirty-minded and immature'. He didn't believe Hamlet was mad; 'he feigns madness, he feigns eccentricity and tangential thought, that's all'.

Like several Hamlets, Lesser tackled the role at school, aged sixteen. His Troilus and Edgar were both directed by Miller for the BBC Shakespeare television series. He confessed to being nearly drowned by the flood of Miller's creative ideas when playing Troilus: 'Jonathan would be hugely entertaining, but then I'd try to replicate ... erroneously thinking that was what he wanted.' In playing Edgar he felt more confident: 'I had got the measure of him. I was going through the process of learning to listen but not necessarily replicate.' By the time it came to Hamlet, 'I felt I'd really found the way to do justice to his brilliance, and enjoy the relationship creatively'.

Miller thought him 'wonderful in the role – agonised like a student, vulnerable and intelligent, fastidious and pained'. But the London critics offered mixed opinions. Michael Billington felt Lesser lacked weight and 'a sense of danger', while John Barber praised his intelligence, but questioned his dangerousness and nobility, calling his 'a puny Puck with an angel face ... an exasperated wasp with a quiver of stings who reserves the sharpest for himself'. But Benedict Nightingale found the production full of insights that enhanced rather than distorted the story, and Lesser's performance admirable. 'Lesser is a sensitive, thoughtful, wryly witty, and distinctly immature Prince, who gradually cracks under the strain of his dead father's awesome expectations and his own ceaseless self-doubts. After hearing the Ghost, he blubs like a tot; by the closet scene he is clutching at his mother, making childish faces, blowing raspberries, and sniggering in inappropriate places.'

Critics praised the production for its 'lively action', 'swift pace', 'illuminating detail', and 'felicitous and illuminating touches'. Miller welcomed the chance to stage the play in an intimate theatre. The Warehouse enabled him to achieve powerful but simple effects. According to Shrapnel: 'Jonathan wanted to stage the play in a small space without any fuss – I think he's happiest in small theatres. The Warehouse offered him the intimacy he was looking for, and proved very effective. It was a very good example of his ensemble work: attention would be paid to every corner of the play.'

Roger Rees
Ron Daniels

Roger Rees played the Prince for the Royal Shakespeare Company in Ron Daniels' 1984 production at Stratford, which transferred in 1985 to the Barbican in London.

Cast: Claudius: Brian Blessed/John Stride, Gertrude: Virginia McKenna, Ophelia: Frances Barber, Polonius: Frank Middlemass, Horatio: Nicholas Farrell, Laertes: Kenneth Branagh, Ghost: Richard Easton, First Gravedigger: Sebastian Shaw.

In contrast to Michael Pennington's Stratford Hamlet four years earlier, Roger Rees opted to create an intensely neurotic Prince. The critics wrote variously of a 'haunted', 'sunken-cheeked', vulnerable outcast; 'a haggard, hollow-eyed figure'; 'a neurotic living on the edge of his nerves'; 'a psychotic case, a wild-eyed neurasthenic tortured by a too-intense inner life, over-brimming with emotion and forever waxing desperate with imagination, in the grip of emotions he cannot handle'.

The line between neurosis and full-blown insanity is a delicate one, and although Rees did not think Hamlet mad, this was how many interpreted his behaviour. He would lose himself in frightening tantrums; he wept, he cried out, eyes flashing messages of torment. He banged his chest violently after the Ghost had appeared to him, as if his heart were truly breaking. He slapped a frenzied brow before Ophelia; he hurled himself against the staircase while proclaiming Claudius' villainy; in the play scene he impulsively took over the role of the usurper and kissed the Player Queen; he planted a disgusted kiss on the furious Claudius as he departed for England; and he wept uncontrollably on Ophelia's grave.

Dark, slender and handsome, with a boyish air about him, Rees had been widely acclaimed for his eponymous performance in the company's celebrated adaptation of *Nicholas Nickleby*. Critical opinion of his Hamlet was mixed. Michael Coveney wrote: 'Rees comes through the ordeal with flying colours, presenting a genuine chameleon Prince, whose hesitancy and neurosis is channelled through a series of startling Bedlamite phases, before hardening at the fatal duel into a calm and acquiescent resolve.' In a similar vein Michael Billington observed that 'Rees precisely captures the character's spiritual progress'; he is 'a genuinely distracted Hamlet. It is a fine performance in that it balances neurosis and order.'

Others had reservations: 'What it lacks, surprisingly, is a trace of Hamlet the comedian,' Irving Wardle wrote. 'For all its speed and volatility of mood, you are never allowed to forget for long his inner torment and breaking heart, as emphasised through an insistent tearful catch in the voice.' Linda Joffee was more critical:

This isn't Hamlet: this is Roger Rees adapting Hamlet to his immediately recognizable mannerisms. It is a performance of great energy, but little depth – a tragic flaw which is made all too clear in the second half. When Hamlet metamorphoses from crippling indecision to resolution, Rees does not assume the kind of profound inner stillness needed to counterbalance his frenetic portrayal in the earlier acts.

Before rehearsals for the whole company, the director Ron Daniels met for two or three days with the six principals. According to Frances Barber, playing Ophelia, 'Ron wished to explore three worlds of cosmic, political and domestic implications in the text. The rehearsals developed along the lines of exploring each scene with these three factors in isolation, and then finding ways in which they converged.'

Barber remembered Harriet Walter's interpretation of Ophelia in the Pryce/Eyre production, which, she argued, 'dispelled any traditional images of the weak, stupid girl which may have been lurking in the minds of the audience'. After studying the text she said: 'The first thing that struck me was that she is acutely intelligent and highly perceptive. She recognises the potential repercussions of Hamlet's madness before anyone else in the play ... I had never underestimated the challenge of creating Ophelia; what I hadn't taken into consideration was how very much more there was to her than a couple of mad scenes.'

She explained to Daniels the discoveries she had made: 'She's full of wit and humour and intelligence, she's strong, courageous, emotionally open. She shows her independence when she gives Hamlet his remembrances back, she stands up to her father.' Here Daniels interrupted her: 'You *can't* play her as a feminist, it's not in the text.' Undaunted, Barber went on to describe how Ophelia blames herself for Hamlet's prejudice against women, why she's utterly guilt-ridden, and culpable to a point because she knew Claudius and Polonius were spying on Hamlet, but didn't warn him.

'Refusing to be blown apart by argument or threat, I entered rehearsals with the notion that the play was really called "Ophelia and her Downfall".' She even suggested she should first be seen fighting Laertes on his departure, as a swordswoman every bit as accomplished as her brother. That idea abandoned, she concluded: 'I came to understand why Ophelia is so often seen as weak: it is only in recent years that women have not become afraid of revealing the masculine qualities within them, something Shakespeare has always recognised.'

She described the nunnery scene, in which Hamlet passionately embraced Ophelia, and she responded:

Roger wanted to show Hamlet's disgust at his own ardour, and did so by physically rejecting me, throwing me about the stage and finally to the floor. He even went so far as to slap my face ... As the scene proceeded he clasped my face, spitting out all his accusations against women, implying that women, and particularly her, were the direct cause of his troubled mind.

Kenneth Branagh, playing Laertes, was soon to play Hamlet himself (see pages 59 and 69). During the second week of rehearsal he came up with the bizarre idea that Laertes was mad. 'It took three weeks of foaming, twitching and yelling to realise this might perhaps not work ... But it led me to the discovery that Laertes was thick as the proverbial plank, and that's why he was unstable, frightened, aggressive, and finally vulnerable. He was a little man surrounded by great men and events that were way beyond his comprehension.'

According to Nick Walton of the Shakespeare Birthplace Trust: 'Ron Daniels wanted to suggest there had been a great change in Elsinore since Claudius came to the throne. Gertrude and Old Hamlet were both representative of the court as it had been; fashionable, sensitive, a sense of flair and romanticism in the old world. The new court was loutish, and this was characterised by Brian Blessed's insensitive, bombastic Claudius.'

Moving away from the stark staging of recent RSC productions, Elsinore as designed by Maria Bjornson was a sumptuous affair of chandeliers, stairways and balustrades dramatically placed on each side of the stage at right angles to the audience. Both costumes and set were in shades of silver and grey. The lighting was equally muted, with occasional touches such as scudding clouds, and shafts of illumination from the side or behind. The production, Daniels explained, was set 'somewhere in the vast expanses between heaven and earth – a "cosmic" and imposing *Hamlet* set literally among the clouds'.

Kenneth Branagh
Derek Jacobi

In 1988 Derek Jacobi directed Kenneth Branagh as Hamlet at the Birmingham Rep studio, for Branagh's Renaissance Theatre Company. The production subsequently toured the UK and Ireland, visited Elsinore, then transferred to the Phoenix in London.

Cast: Claudius: Richard Easton, Gertrude: Dearbhla Molloy, Horatio: Richard Clifford, Polonius: Edward Jewesbury, Laertes: Jay Villiers, Ophelia: Sophie Thompson.

Kenneth Branagh began his long association with Hamlet at drama school, playing the role at RADA in 1981. Looking back, he felt he had 'fallen into the trap of ranting through it and running out of steam early on'. His voice teachers thought he played the part too quickly, while the school's principal, Hugh Crutwell, was severely critical on two fundamental points:

First, comedy and humour. There is a difference. You give us comedy in Hamlet. What he has is a deep-seated melancholia producing a black, bleak humour. You give us a sort of gratuitous clowning. Secondly, passion. Hamlet is a haunted man, shaken to his very soul by the deep repulsion about his mother's marriage, and horror at the arrival of his father's ghost. You give us a sort of lively irritability.

Branagh had coveted the part from an early age. Seeing Derek Jacobi's Hamlet in the Prospect production in 1977 provided a spark, as Jacobi recalled: 'He was obviously bowled over by the tremendous pace and excitement of the production; my acting excited his ambition, and he wrote me a lovely note about his enthusiasm, and how he wanted to be an actor.' In 1984, joining the RSC at the age of 23 to take on Henry V, Branagh also played Laertes and understudied Roger Rees in Ron Daniels' production. In 1988 he persuaded Jacobi to direct him as Hamlet on the small stage in the Birmingham Rep studio.

The rehearsals began at high speed, as Branagh remembered: 'Derek wanted a dramatic and highly theatrical production that acknowledged the rich store of theatrical imagery in *Hamlet*. He worked amazingly fast, and knew every single word of the text, so that when anyone dried he was ahead of the stage management in prompting them.' At first he resisted Jacobi's suggestions. 'I was determined not to be hurried and over-awed. There were a couple of days' wariness, and then we both began to trust each other, and went to it with a vengeance. The play was blocked in a week.'

He felt Jacobi directed with great sensitivity:

I had my own instincts and he shaped them. There wasn't an acting problem that he hadn't already faced and analysed himself, and the alternatives he offered me were fascinating. He was also of tremendous help in colouring speeches and knowing when to rest on the lines, which was particularly useful for the closet scene. Derek showed me how to pace myself and find enough breath and energy to get through and make sense of the lines.

In playing his first professional Hamlet, Branagh 'felt crushingly the weight of the ghosts of other performances' and the 'great obstacle course' the role presented. He also acknowledged the strain it created, especially when he had to play the part twice on matinee days. 'The stomach-wrenching sick feeling that overtakes one as the first soliloquy begins is truly terrifying, and it's impossible not to be aware of quite how far you have to go in this Everest role.' He reflected later on the critics' response: 'There were raves, and, as always, there were those for whom I could never be Hamlet in a million years, who found the production an offence to their sensibilities.'

But among the public his Hamlet provoked enormous enthusiasm, as the critic Dominic Cavendish remembered: 'It set the British stage ablaze. It generated a rare degree of populist excitement, with its star's qualities of thin-lipped calculation and quick-mettled charisma coming to the fore ... His was the name on everyone's lips. It was an age when to be young was pretty groovy, but to see the talk of the town giving his Hamlet was very heaven.'

One Jacobi innovation was to have Ophelia enter with the Players, and remain with them during their preparations; to have her present for the recorder scene after the play; and make her visible above the closet scene, to remind the audience of the consequences of male aggression. He also came up with extra entrances, and re-allocated lines for Sophie Thompson's Ophelia and Dearbhla Molloy's Gertrude. During rehearsals he spoke of the purpose of such touches: 'Whatever changes we have made have been in order that the story and characters should shine through, rather than any particular person or the director or designer; and that the play should be fresh and new.'

Mark Rylance
Ron Daniels

Following a UK tour in 1988, Ron Daniels' production of Hamlet *for the Royal Shakespeare Company, with Mark Rylance in the title role, was staged in 1989 at Stratford and then the Barbican in London, before embarking on a tour of North America. The company also gave a performance to patients at Broadmoor Secure Psychiatric Hospital.*

Cast: Claudius: Peter Wight, Gertrude: Clare Higgins, Ophelia: Sylvestra Le Touzel/Rebecca Saire, Polonius: Patrick Godfrey, Horatio: Jack Ellis, Laertes: John Ramm.

This was Mark Rylance's second attempt at the part. Born in England but raised in America, in 1976, at the age of 16, he had played Hamlet in a junior high school production at the University School of Milwaukee, where his father taught English. He went to the Milwaukee Public Library and listened to the play on tape. 'I remember listening to Richard Burton, and thinking it was flowery and fake,' he recalled.

This RSC production was also Ron Daniels' second *Hamlet*, after having directed Roger Rees as the Prince (see page 56). He offered audiences something very different from that cosmic production: 'It was to be much more intimate,' he said, 'rooted in personal relationships, a tragedy set in the heart of a family as well as of a state; the action was to take place in a mansion, a home really, perched on the edge of a cliff high above the turbulent sea.'

His production's abiding image was of Mark Rylance shuffling about the court in striped, vomit-stained pyjamas and long bedsocks, like a patient in a lunatic asylum. It provided a stark and shocking reflection of his disturbed mental state, which remained the focus throughout. He was clearly not just assuming an antic disposition, but descending into a state of real insanity and a troubling, angry adolescence, swift to change mood in a moment from witty banter to wild, self-hating violence. Only on his return from England was his mind restored to tranquillity and maturity, and he achieved what Daniels called 'a curious serenity'.

He was first seen as a pale, hunched, isolated and dejected figure, a boy surrounded by much taller men, standing with a shabby suitcase by his side, ready to depart. As Rylance explained: 'At the beginning you see him in a very public situation, which is very painful to him, in a room that's full of memories of his father who has died, with his mother with another man.' Already on the brink of a crack-up, he toppled over the edge after encountering his father's ghost. After this traumatic meeting he cut his hand with his sword and smeared the blood on his forehead; he was frenetic during the subsequent swearing, and almost collapsed after declaring 'O cursed spite / That ever I was born to set it right'. He 'mooned', he jeered, he virtually raped Ophelia, and spat in her face in order to rub off her make-up; in the closet scene he repeatedly stabbed Polonius in a frenzy, and kissed Gertrude fiercely on the mouth. Sometimes he clutched his head or banged it against the wall; alone, vulnerable and suffering, he often seemed close to tears, and did weep a number of times.

His changing clothes reflected his changing state of mind. Dressed at the start in a long black overcoat, he was in pyjamas for 'To be or not to be' until his embarkation for England; he dressed up for the play-within-the-play, sporting a white dinner-jacket with a flower pinned on and a white scarf; but he soon stripped them off and played the closet scene in an undershirt.

For the duel, with the court all in black, he donned a white fencing jacket. As he observed: 'He's actually reached the state of a Prince at the time that he dies, and you should feel he would make a wonderful king. He's come to some kind of peace, and I guess that's part of the reason that makes the play a tragedy.'

The vertiginously angled set chimed with his state of mind; Rylance likened it to 'a palace tilting into the ocean'. Its expressionist, out-of-kilter walls and sloping floors suggested, in Claudius' words, a world 'disjoint and out of frame', Elsinore as a lopsided sanatorium, the courtiers as its inmates. The sea was visible through the window at the rear, skewed from the perpendicular so that it and the palace around it seemed on the point of slipping into the waves. It was a set that served both to highlight the characters and emphasise their littleness.

This Hamlet was much given to ridiculing Claudius. After the success of the staging of *The Murder of Gonzago*, performed as a shadow play, he jubilantly capered on the bed on which the Players had performed it, the property crown on his head and a pillow about his middle in mockery of the 'bloat' king. At 'Come, for England' he jumped into a tin bathtub and mimed paddling himself in a boat, provoking Peter Wight's enraged Claudius, desperate to locate Polonius' body, to dunk his head in the bathwater, nearly drowning him.

Daniels pointed out a crucial element in Hamlet's character: 'One of the most astonishing qualities is his rigorous and unwavering honesty. Hamlet never lies to himself or to us – the soliloquies are moments of utter truth-telling. There is absolutely no equivocation as he lays before us his most secret doubts and fears.' Rylance stated that when Hamlet comes to moments of confusion, as in 'To be or not to be', 'that *is* a question – *isn't it?*', there must be to and fro between the actors and the audience. He made this explicit during his first soliloquy: when he spoke of his father, 'so excellent a king', he held out a photograph of him, pleading for the audience to agree. Even as he was dying he addressed the lines beginning 'You that look pale and tremble at this chance' to the audience rather than the court.

Critics praised his ability to achieve this kind of rapport with the audience. Susannah Clapp stated: 'He exercised his exceptional gift of seeming entirely rapt in his own mental universe, and yet speaking directly to the audience, as if he were alighting on particular individuals.' Paul Taylor stressed the value of this approach: 'What amazed many of us, though, was the way this bonkers, alternative comedian of a Prince also managed – thanks to Rylance's haunted sweetness of countenance and that intense but wary rapport he can build up with an audience – to project Hamlet's infinite solitariness and injured spirituality better than any contender within memory.'

The power and authenticity of Rylance's performance was underlined when the company took *Hamlet* to Broadmoor Secure Psychiatric Hospital in Berkshire. Afterwards one inmate rushed up to him and said: 'You were really mad – take it from me, I should know, I'm a loony.' Another patient wrote to his local paper: 'Mark Rylance was able to capture every aspect of a person's slip into the world of psychopathic, manipulative paranoia ... Many of us here are able to understand Hamlet's disturbed state of mind because we have experienced such traumas.'

Daniels later defended his decision to concentrate on the personal aspects of the play, arguing that: 'Beyond all the poetry, all the spiritual aspirations and deepest meanings of Shakespeare's plays, the personal relationships between fathers and mothers and their sons and daughters lie at the heart of most of if not the entire canon.' He concluded: 'Bringing these relationships to life in the most intimate and truest way possible is the task that befalls the director and the actors ... These are the very strategies that bring heartfelt immediacy and credibility to the plays, and make them leap off the page and pulsate with life.'

Two years later Mark Rylance played Hamlet with the American Repertory Theatre. In 2000 he repeated the role at Shakespeare's Globe (see page 83).

Daniel Day-Lewis
Richard Eyre

In 1989 Daniel Day-Lewis played Hamlet in the Olivier at the National Theatre, directed by Richard Eyre. The production subsequently visited Dubrovnik, Hong Kong and Tokyo.

Cast: Claudius: John Castle, Gertrude: Judi Dench/Sylvia Sims, Ophelia: Stella Gonet, Laertes: Peter Linford/Jeremy Northam, Polonius: Michael Bryant, Horatio: David Bamber, Player King: Oliver Ford Davies, Ghost/ Gravedigger: David Burke, Osric: Jeremy Northam.

According to Richard Eyre, the rehearsals for his second *Hamlet* were perfectly untroubled. They gave no hint of the problems that would lead Daniel Day-Lewis to leave the stage in the middle of a performance. Eyre's diary confirms this. During the first rehearsal week he wrote: 'Dan is determined and immensely committed'; a few days later he was 'showing flashes of great intelligence and daring'; three weeks later he observed: 'Dan is a thrilling and self-effacing actor: wise, with great beauty of speech and movement.'

Day-Lewis was considered the most exciting of the younger generation of film actors. Famous for taking extreme measures to get inside a character, during filming he insisted on staying in character. However, he had only limited experience of Shakespeare: small parts in *Troilus and Cressida* and *A Midsummer Night's Dream* at the Theatre Royal in Bristol, and Puck, Flute and Romeo in an RSC regional tour.

This was the uncut version of *Hamlet*, lasting nearly four hours. Later Eyre explained: 'I suppose I was thinking I wanted to do this production in a way that honours the play, and not bring spurious elements into it, as you could argue I had done at the Royal Court in 1980.' But while that earlier version with Jonathan Pryce was widely praised for its originality, this one, which opened in March, provoked a mixed response. Many critics found it 'dull', 'bland' and 'devoid of any ideas', while others described it as 'adventurous', 'lucid' and 'thrilling'. In his diary Eyre concluded: 'The reviews weren't sufficiently discouraging to warrant jumping out of the window, but not sufficiently effusive to guarantee lifting the depression that follows opening a play as sure as tonic follows gin.'

His production received several positive comments: Peter Kemp thought it 'a triumph of intelligence, full of attentiveness and inspiration', while Michael Billington extolled it for its lack of clichés: 'It combines wit and intelligence with a grasp of the play's huge Gothic structure.' But Day-Lewis' performance attracted a negative response. One writer observed: 'He seemed to be living in a glass shell.' John Gross suggested: 'He is plaintive when he should have been sardonic, wide-eyed in his indignation when he should have been savage.' He felt the actor missed 'the deep reserves of bitterness and bitter intelligence that make Hamlet a hero as well as a victim'. Others criticised his command of Shakespearean verse and the speed with which he delivered his lines. In Gross' view: 'He hurries into his soliloquies; and while odd phrases and lines strike home, he lacks a feeling for the flow of the verse.'

Day-Lewis was desperately hurt by these criticisms. 'One or two reviews made me seriously consider ... getting a sledgehammer and making a couple of visits,' he said. By early May, six weeks into the run, he was clearly under enormous stress: 'Dan's exhausted, stretched on the rack,' Eyre wrote. 'If it weren't for his pride and his loyalty, he'd be off tomorrow. He's completely lost heart ... For him it's partly the subject-matter ... but it's much more that he's determined to investigate the truth of the part, and he has to do it in a great barn with hopeless acoustics to eleven hundred people. How *can* he reconcile this?'

Eyre then had to tell the cast that Day-Lewis had decided not to stay to the end of the run. 'It was painful and embarrassing,' he admitted. 'I thought Dan seemed obviously uncomfortable, and that really crushed me.' However, some of his performances could still impress his director. In July the production was staged in the open air at the fourteenth-century Fort Lovrjenac in Dubrovnik. 'I watched the dress-rehearsal with something approaching despair,' Eyre confessed. 'It seemed a lifeless, unconnected costume parade. But the next night, the opening, it was coherent and animated, and Dan was incandescent.'

The actor's state of mind came to a head on 5 September. In the middle of Hamlet's scene with the Ghost he suddenly walked off stage, and told the stage manager he couldn't continue. Michael Bryant, poised to make his next entrance as Polonius, recalled: 'I found him in the corridor on the floor, crying his heart out. I took him to his dressing-room and held him like a baby while he sobbed and sobbed.' An announcement was made suggesting 'technical difficulties', and the audience were invited to take an extra interval. Half an hour later Jeremy Northam, playing Laertes but understudying Day-Lewis, took over.

Press reports suggested he had left the stage believing David Burke was no longer Old Hamlet, but his own father, the poet Cecil Day-Lewis, who had died in 1972 when Daniel was 15. A few days later he said in an interview: 'I think this is the year of my nervous collapse. Hamlet's a hard part to live with. It conjured up demons with you ... This has certainly taken me closer to the abyss than anything else. And I've discovered fears in myself, or generated fears, I never knew before – and once they're there, they're very difficult to put away again.' Later he confirmed that his walk-out had been caused by 'communication with my own dead father. But I don't remember seeing any ghost of my father that dreadful night.'

Eyre wrote of his breakdown:

Dan's problem wasn't, as the papers say, his relationship with the ghost of his father, but his relationship with the play and that auditorium: it sucks you dry. He wrestled night after night in the Olivier's vast space with the play's subjects – fathers, mothers, sons, grief, suicide, sex, love, revenge, intellect, violence, pacifism, discipline and death – and if they floored him he was guilty not of neurosis or incompetence, but an excess of ambition to do justice to it.

Judi Dench, playing Gertrude, had not understood his problem. 'I didn't sense him being unhappy at all,' she said.

I thought it was just the way he behaved with the responsibility of Hamlet on his shoulders. I thought that was very much his make-up. It was like somebody with blinkers on – not that he was like that on stage with people. He went like an arrow to the stage and did it and came off and was very much in his own world, which of course he was, as we found out subsequently.

But Dench too had a problem, as Eyre recognised during rehearsals. 'Every time we do the closet scene, we end in a sort of stalemate,' he admitted.

Judi and Dan give it all the energy and attack that one could hope for. The scene should be like a wild, vertiginous argument in a car going downhill, crashing – the killing of Polonius – and the two survivors finding themselves intact and mutually terrified, fired by adrenalin, ascending into an emotional territory that they've never explored before. I fear that the problem is that Judi never quite convinces herself that she's Gertrude. In fact she says so.

Dench confirmed this later: 'I didn't ever feel I was Dan's mother, or that he was the son of David Burke and me. I've never been quite able to analyse it, I just never felt that I was right.' Part of her difficulty was that she couldn't get out of her mind Coral Browne's Gertrude, when she herself played Ophelia to John Neville's Hamlet in 1957. 'Coral was absolutely ravishingly wonderful, and I just couldn't be that person. She was the best Gertrude I've ever witnessed, and I suppose that was very much in my mind.'

Eyre was becoming concerned about Day-Lewis' performance as early as the previews: 'The audience can't identify with Dan,' he wrote. 'They admire him, they are awed by him, but they don't yet love him. He must break their hearts.' A couple of months later there seemed to be no improvement: 'I could see clearly that the audience didn't take Dan to their hearts, because although he does let the audience in, they're intimidated by what they find.'

Eyre's fellow-director Howard Davies described him as the most self-critical and self-doubting director he knew. This is evident in the troubled thoughts he experienced before rehearsals began. 'Why did all seem so much simpler to me when I did the play at the Royal Court?' he wondered. He was particularly anxious about his decision to set the play within its period. 'I think it's caution, not classicism. I convinced myself that to make absolute sense the play had to be set in a world where the court, the religion, the hierarchy, the politics had an exact meaning. But I feel inhibited by it.' After the reviews he continued: 'I was much too cautious; everything in the production should have been much more explicit: the court formality, the militarism, the spying, the politics, the sex.' A month into the run he reflected on the production: 'It had energy, passion and detail, but I'd failed to create a world that was expressively realised. It was too static, too realistic, too solid.'

Devastated by what he had done, Day-Lewis moved to Ireland, and never worked in the theatre again. It was five years before he resumed his film career. Looking back many years later, Eyre was full of praise for his Hamlet: 'I thought Dan was the pre-eminent Hamlet of his generation. I actually loved his performance: I think it had such complexity about it, and such pain. It's among the two or three best Hamlets I've ever seen.'

* * *

By the time of Day-Lewis' collapse a new cast was being prepared, with Ian Charleson taking over as Hamlet. But recently he had been diagnosed as HIV-positive. Eyre was shocked at his appearance when they met: 'He's had pneumonia and he's still got a chronic sinus complaint which gives him large, swollen bags under his eyes. It's barely possible to glimpse the face beneath the swelling, a malicious parody of his beauty.' They didn't discuss his being HIV-positive, although it was present as a subtext. 'We talk about the parts he desperately wants to play – Richard II, Angelo, Benedick – and Hamlet. I offer him the part, more with my heart than my head.'

Only his fellow-actors knew the nature of Charleson's illness. 'During rehearsals he was utterly without reserve,' Eyre revealed. 'There was a deep well of generosity of affection, a largeness of heart, and the only Scottish characteristics that he showed were his doggedness and his persistence.' He and Charleson talked about Hamlet's accommodation with death. Nevertheless, he was unsure whether to let him go on stage, or replace him. After watching the opening night he wrote: 'He looks strange but acts beautifully – he's warm, accessible and vulnerable, but a bit underpowered. Since he's become HIV-positive he's acquired real moral authority: courage, sangfroid, maturity.' Later he watched Charleson perform in what proved to be his swansong: 'His performance was possessed. He wasn't playing the part, he became it. By the end he was exhausted, each line of the last scene wrung out of him. He acted as if he knew it was the last time he'd be on stage. He stood at the curtain call like a bruised boxer after fifteen rounds, battered by applause.'

His notices were uniformly admiring. John Peter noted: 'This is a princely Hamlet, every inch the king he should have been ... He oozes intelligence from every pore, a restless inquisitive rationalist', while Martin Hoyle saw 'a civilized, mature, witty and eminently decent Prince ... for humour, anger and intelligence it is one of the best all-round Hamlets going'. But by now Charleson's condition had deteriorated; he was very weak and pale, and his face was deformed by swelling. He was unable to cope with more than one performance a day, so Jeremy Northam took over as Hamlet for the matinees. He was also forced to withdraw from the production's planned visit to Hong Kong and Tokyo, where Northam again replaced him.

He had managed a total of just 18 performances before being compelled to give up. His courage had astonished his fellow-actors. As Michael Bryant put it: 'He played for three and three-quarter hours every night, dying, and came off joking.' His last performance was on 13 November. Eight weeks later, at the age of 40, he died of septicemia brought on by Aids.

6

The Nineties

Kenneth Branagh
Adrian Noble

In 1992 Kenneth Branagh played his second stage Hamlet, directed by Adrian Noble, first at the Barbican in London, then the following year in Stratford.

Cast: Claudius: John Shrapnel, Gertrude: Jane Lapotaire, Horatio: Rob Edwards, Polonius: David Bradley, Laertes: Richard (later Hugh) Bonneville, Ophelia: Joanne Pearce, Osric: Guy Henry.

Hamlet is such a naked, X-ray role, so inevitably you are using your entire being, your intellect, your sense of humour, your sense of romance or cynicism. The basic material of the play is human nature, you end up discussing his, and in so doing you are discussing yours.

In recent years Kenneth Branagh's own nature had been the subject of much discussion, much of it negative. Acclaimed less than a decade before as the brightest new theatrical star of the age, his reputation had suffered a backlash, and he was accused of promoting himself as the next Olivier. Such an attack drove him away from the theatre, and aroused the anger of close colleagues such as Judi Dench and Richard Briers: 'It makes me so angry, it's all so unnecessary,' Briers complained. 'What does he do? He creates employment, he is dedicated to Shakespeare, he's a workaholic. Unfortunately, it is not uncommon to knock someone who can do these things. In my book, he's heroic.'

The critics had given his 1988 Hamlet at the Birmingham Rep mixed reviews, arguing it was too impetuous, and a falling-off from his previous work. But his new performance for the Royal Shakespeare Company, directed by Adrian Noble, garnered almost universal praise. Charles Spencer's review typified many: 'It's fashionable to knock our Ken, but this was a superbly lucid performance, with a palpable humanity, and a knack of letting the audience right inside the character's mind during the beautifully delivered soliloquies.' Paul Taylor welcomed a 'slower, more reflective and movingly filial prince', while Jack Tinker wrote that, having matured both physically and emotionally, 'Branagh is undoubtedly the greatest Hamlet of our time. I have seen none to match him in many a season ... Those of us who prophesied he had turned the shining promise of a career into a mass-marketing goldmine are having to digest a slice or two of humble pie.'

Branagh subsequently spoke about the appeal of Hamlet:

> The attraction lies in his enduring quality, a man struggling in extraordinary conditions. He's in a very human situation, mourning his father, and you don't have to be a Prince or Danish to relate to that. He's engaged in a struggle to find out how you might achieve some sort of happiness, some level of acceptance of all these contradictory, paradoxical anxieties. There's something very thrilling in his courage in sticking to his task; he never walks away from it. His fearless intellectual curiosity is very inspiring; he has great courage in facing the unfaceable ... I think the play is about preparing for death through understanding how to live, how to look at the world, how to understand one's self, how to be sometimes intuitive rather than intellectual, how one can and might value relationships with parents and siblings.

Noble set the play in a disintegrating Edwardian world, with the focus on the family relationships: for some people this gave it a melancholy, Chekhovian air. His vision was reflected in the sets, which grew more impressionistic as the action progressed, changing from white to red to grey. Unusually, the front of the stage was transformed into a garden where Ophelia picked flowers, and later used for the madness scene and as a graveyard, strewn with wreaths and crosses, for her funeral. From here the spectral-looking Ghost, in a military outfit, emerged before the opening scene, and walked to the rear of the empty stage. This area, beyond the cyclorama, represented the outside world, from where the Players and Fortinbras would arrive.

Ophelia, in a nightdress and bedsocks, was first seen in her bedchamber, which contained a doll's house and a piano. When Laertes arrived she had a cuddle with him on the bed, then played the piano when he left. After the nunnery scene, when Hamlet came close to raping her, she tried to calm herself by again playing the piano, but Polonius closed the lid. Her dependence on, and love for her father was highlighted when she entered the mad scene dressed in his clothes, the shirt bloodstained and the shoes, clown-like, much too large.

Charles Spencer believed Branagh's Hamlet was the finest performance of his career. 'This actor's greatest strength has always been his manifest humanity, his dogged decency. He lets you into his character's mind with a complete absence of guile and showy flamboyance, and at almost every stage you feel you know exactly what he is thinking and feeling.' He admired Branagh's ability to catch the many sides of Hamlet. 'The soliloquies have a conversational clarity, and there is never any doubt that his "madness" is feigned. Branagh beautifully captures sudden moments of soul-sick sadness, but there is a wonderful warmth and humour here, as well as shafts of cruelty, sardonic wit and emotional violence. Yet even in his darkest moments this Hamlet never forfeits the audience's sympathy.'

John Gross highlighted his verse-speaking skill: 'He brings to it some basic virtues which perhaps ought to be taken for granted, but which in today's theatre can't be: he speaks clearly, he has a sense of rhythm, and he gives his words (or most of them) their proper weight.' Jack Tinker felt the youthful-looking actor now had a commanding gravitas. 'The voice can soar the verse to the heavens, or draw us into his innermost thoughts by its quiet confiding. The marvellous set speeches come as newly invented; the dangerous mood-swings, between the wintery grief of his earliest scenes to the tightrope journey he hazards between feigned madness, careful cunning and deeply felt wounds, are expertly charted.'

Among academics, Samuel Crowl compared his new Hamlet with Branagh's previous one: 'He retained the quicksilver mimicry, but now he grounded it in steely opposition to Claudius. He was clearly a political rival and threat to Claudius' reign, not just an unhinged stepson clamouring for his uncle's attention and easy laughs.' But although Peter Holland saw 'a clear superimposition of thoughtfulness, focused, above all, on the profundity of his love for his father', he felt 'the melancholy was too self-evidently performed (by Branagh rather than Hamlet), a disguise laid over his normal style'. He added: 'Only in his delivery of "How all occasions" did the stillness grow out of the character, and the soliloquy as the expression of thought convince.'

Noble used an uncut version, resulting in the play lasting four-and-a-half hours. Branagh was ambivalent on this question: 'The argument against cutting is that in condensing the text it puts the highlights, the soliloquies, too close together.' On the other hand,

> It is hard to imagine there will be another full-length version. I know from my own mailbag that for many students, for many people doing their doctorates, and for people coming to Shakespeare for the first time in reading groups, it can be useful to watch the entire play. In that way you also understand why we have arrived at some versions which are shorter. It is an incredibly strong reference tool for people even if it is not their favourite *Hamlet*, and there is no reason why it should be.

Alan Cumming

Stephen Unwin

In 1993 Alan Cumming played Hamlet for the English Touring Company, in a production directed by Stephen Unwin which ended its tour at the Donmar in London.

Cast: Gertrude: Eleanor Bron, Ophelia: Hilary Lyon, Claudius: Pip Donaghy, Horatio: Roger Hyams, Polonius: Trevor Baxter, Laertes: Mark Anstee.

The play dredged up some awful things with my father, and I realised there were a lot of unresolved issues in my life that I needed to deal with.

During his childhood in Scotland Alan Cumming lived in constant fear of his bullying and abusive father. It was an experience that made playing Hamlet at the age of 28 a particularly demanding moment in his career. It led to him having a breakdown, and brought to an end his eight-year marriage to Hilary Lyon, who was playing Ophelia.

He has written about the demands Hamlet made on him in his memoir *Not My Father's Son*, and spoken of it eloquently in several interviews:

I don't think anyone can play Hamlet without him affecting you in a really primal way. The part deals with such universal and yet personal things: your relationship with your parents, dealing with the death of a parent (and as I felt it, dealing with the death of a parent you didn't like very much), wanting to get away from home and back to your friends, university and your own life, trying to cope with your girlfriend suddenly dumping you for no apparent reason when you are feeling really low – as well as some issues that thinking about or exploring, even on a very superficial level, can be incredibly upsetting and haunting, such as wondering whether or not to kill yourself, and how to deal with your father's ghost coming to you and telling you to avenge his death!

His performance when the chamber production arrived at the Donmar attracted some fine reviews. His strikingly different Hamlet was described by Charles Spencer as 'a brattish, bedsit student prince who has read too much Sylvia Plath and listened to too many records by the Smiths', and by Jasper Rees as 'a waif in black cycling shorts, a "yoof" Hamlet who sacrificed nothing in intelligence'. Rees found it 'a compelling performance full of chirpy zest, butterfly wit and spindly gymnasticism', while Spencer though it 'entirely original', and suggested the actor 'hinted at a greatness he has never quite fulfilled'.

Later Cumming recalled:

I was so scared of going back to the theatre after *Hamlet*. I didn't know if I'd do a play again, because I was afraid of the power of it ... It took me a long time to recover because I was so churned up and maddened by it. But even though it was the biggest challenge of my life to play (and sustain playing) the part, I am so grateful to have had the chance, because it really did change my life. It also eventually made me feel much more relaxed about my work. I feel that if I die tomorrow then I will have done something I am truly proud of.

Alan Cumming won the Martini Rossi TMA award for Best Actor, and was nominated for the Richard Burton Award at the Shakespeare Globe Awards.

Stephen Dillane
Peter Hall

In 1994 Stephen Dillane played Hamlet in Peter Hall's third production of the play, staged at the Gielgud in London. It also toured nationally and internationally, including playing at the theatre on the Acropolis in Athens.

Cast: Ghost/Claudius: Michael Pennington, Gertrude: Gwen Taylor, Polonius: Donald Sinden, Ophelia: Gina Bellman, Horatio: Christian Burgess, Laertes: Tom Beard, Player King/First Gravedigger: Alan Dobie.

Playing the Prince at the newly re-named Gielgud Theatre (formerly the Globe) put Stephen Dillane under implicit pressure to do suitable honour to the century's great Hamlet, whose name now adorned the theatre. In this he certainly didn't disappoint: the critics applauded his very modern, mercurial, sensitive and savagely sardonic Hamlet, in a strongly cast production by Peter Hall that was praised for its boldness, tension and insights.

'I think Dillane is one of the great Hamlets, but not for the usual sense of lonely romantic agony,' John Peter decided.

No, it is the private and public politics of the play that shape this tense, edgy, thrilling performance. He is ironically and bitterly self-critical, as well as intensely alert to others, and his quicksilver reactions suggest a restless intelligence ... His intelligence sets him apart, but it also traps him among people whom he needs to watch and forestall. Thinking and private feelings are the natural mode of being for Dillane's Hamlet: life disrupts this and destroys him.

Hall used a combination of the Quarto and Folio editions, which meant the production lasted over four hours. In his talk to the company he suggested the play was about change, most notably 'the change in Hamlet himself, his attempt to grow up. Perhaps this is why the play has such a compelling fascination. We associate with Hamlet, we want to grow up, to re-define, even when we are long past the age of growing up. The play appeals to the perpetual, hopeful, agonised adolescent in all of us.' He also felt *Hamlet* was about finding one's sexuality. 'It's the inability to do that which drives Ophelia mad; and when she does, everything that has been repressed comes out, and it's violently sexual.' Similarly, 'the inability to come to terms with what his mother has done, and his sexual relationship with her, is what drives Hamlet to pretend to be mad'.

Hall argued that the truest and most honest aspect of the play is acting.

The Players invert the world of artificiality. The First Player takes a piece of Marlovian verse and performs it with complete truth. That's truer than all the things that are going on in the court. The First Player demonstrates truth in a world of hypocrisy and masks. In the play scene itself, the Players use a more primitive and earlier form of theatre, antique theatre, formal and rhymed, so that Hamlet can confront Claudius. When we move to the graveyard, we meet a couple of working men who live by death, and have a reality about them as honest as the Players.

Dillane was described by Paul Taylor as an actor with 'the most wonderful capacity for gentle, understated, yet savagely ironic self-criticism, a kind of turbulent passivity that suits a certain conception of Hamlet'. He was praised for the facility with which he switched from comedy to serious matters and back again. Emphasising Hamlet's keen wit, he indulged in much black comedy. Michael Billington described him as 'a sardonic, hawk-faced joker, who could have been editor of Wittenberg's *Private Eye*'. Some of his clowning was simply playful, as when he imitated a crab walking backwards. He mocked Polonius the character, but also mimicked the rich and fruity style of Donald Sinden, who was playing the part. When Claudius rushed out of the play scene, Dillane grabbed a prop crown, put it on his head, and placed himself in Claudius' seat. On other occasions his antics were gross: he spat at Ophelia, made Gertrude smell 'the rank sweat of an enseamed bed' in the closet scene, and pretended to rape her.

Several reviewers drew attention to his being briefly stripped naked, which inevitably led to such press headlines as 'To Bare or Not to Bare?' There was a general view this nudity was not gratuitous, but underlined Hamlet's vulnerability or his sexual confusion. At the end of the closet scene, having killed Claudius, his clothes were covered in blood. He took them off and stuffed them in a laundry-bag, leaving him naked except for the Player King's crown. Depending on his mood, Dillane either streaked off, strolled off jauntily or purposefully – or, if the moment didn't seem right, omitted to strip at all.

John Peter described Hall's production as

an unforgettable event, a historic occasion, thrilling and moving and majestic ... superbly detailed, but also authentic and agile. This searching, quicksilver production reminds you that four hundred years ago this play was what we now solemnly call New Writing, and that it had to pay its way in a large commercial theatre engaged in cut-throat competition with other large commercial theatres.

He particularly admired Pennington: 'simply the best, the most subtly corrupt, and consummately political Claudius I have seen ... His reactions to the play scene are brilliantly played.' Louise Doughty was also impressed: 'Pennington gives the wretched villain Claudius brilliant psychological depth, in a performance so detailed and complex that it almost overshadows Stephen Dillane's confused, skittish Hamlet.' There were also plaudits for Sinden's politically astute and powerful Polonius: 'This is a shrewd, elegant and magisterial performance,' Peter wrote. 'Sinden knows Polonius is a politician to his fingertips; one of his and Hall's most subtle touches is to show how his authority is whittled away as the play goes on.'

Hall concluded his rehearsal talk to his actors by stating: 'There is no blacker play in the canon. Isn't it an almost terrible joke that all Hamlet succeeds in doing is killing everyone near him and handing over the country to Fortinbras?'

Ralph Fiennes

Jonathan Kent

Ralph Fiennes' Hamlet was directed in 1995 by Jonathan Kent for the Almeida at the Hackney Empire, transferring to the Belasco in New York.

Cast: Claudius: James Laurenson, Gertrude: Francesca Annis, Horatio: Paterson Joseph, Laertes: Damian Lewis, Ophelia: Tara Fitzgerald, Polonius: Peter Eyre, Ghost/Player King/Gravedigger: Terence Rigby, Fortinbras: Rupert Penry-Jones.

When it was announced Ralph Fiennes was to play Hamlet, the demand for tickets was so high the production was moved from the intimate Almeida Theatre to the Hackney Empire in the East End. A vast, once-splendid theatre designed by Frank Matcham, it was now just used for music-hall, pantomime and alternative comedy. The change of venue was partly due to Fiennes' popularity after his Best Supporting Actor Oscar-winning success as the concentration-camp commandant in *Schindler's List*.

Aged 32, he had already gained substantial theatrical experience of Shakespeare, including roles for the RSC. As he worked on Hamlet, he was uncertain which of his many characteristics to focus on. During rehearsals he touched on the complexity of the part and the play.

I am very excited and scared in the same breath, but it is weird anticipating what it is going to be like. We are all punch drunk on how many ways we can play it. We are in the process of saying: 'We know that, but what about this?' ... I cannot say that I am yet – and perhaps I never shall be – completely sorted out with the different states of Hamlet's mind.

We sit around and try to apply reasoning as if it is a modern play, but Shakespeare doesn't quite work like that. He doesn't say: 'Now Hamlet goes off to the kitchen to make himself a cup of coffee.' For example, in the play-within-the-play he uses the power of acting to expose Claudius. But it not only 'catches the conscience of the king', it motivates Hamlet. It is an example of what theatre at best is always about: revealing ourselves to ourselves. So then it is decision time, bang. But Hamlet disappears and when he comes on next it is for 'To be or not to be'. He has gone to a place where he has taken his internal debate even further.

He reflected on the continuing appeal of the play:

> Hamlet's mind is modern, and it is a modern dilemma. On one side there is this code of behaviour which is basically about a primitive blood act, avenging his father's murder. Then there is this Christian debate about being able to kill, but together with all that there is the sexual thing. He senses, in his best soliloquy, the rank nature of the world he is in from his mother's infidelity and incestuousness. Womankind becomes completely tainted and disgustingly corrupted and adulterated.

Fiennes' own mother had died two years earlier from breast cancer, a fact which he admitted was affecting his feelings about the play.

> For me it is about those primal blood relationships. They are the one thing Hamlet's reasoning cannot handle. Not only is his father dead but his mother has been fucking Claudius, and that gets him at a level beyond reason, innately to do with flesh and blood and gut feelings. It is, in that sense, personal to me. I think if you lose a parent it is a big change in your life. Your sense of yourself is completely redefined and you re-evaluate your own mortality and the innate child in you.

Director Jonathan Kent saw in Fiennes a 'sort of natural aristocracy and nobility'. His production was a throwback to a romantic tradition of aristocratic *Hamlets*, set in a nineteenth-century world. Peter J. Davison's set was a dark, labyrinthine Elsinore made up of huge ceilings, heavy brown-stained doors, and large shuttered windows, a geometric design giving glimpses of a series of dark and chilly interlocking chambers, dimly lit, and seemingly at the bottom of a great well.

The excessive pace of Kent's production came in for criticism. 'Lines and scenes rattle by as if the determinant were a three-hour time limit,' Peter Holland wrote. 'There could be no pause here for reflection.' Matt Wolf asked: 'Is this a great *Hamlet*? Not yet. It's too impetuous and uninflected to pack much of an interpretive wallop, but for sheer narrative energy it's in a class by itself.' For Charles Spencer, 'Fiennes brought a princely bearing to the role, but little insight. In a superficial, old-fashioned performance he seemed to be knocking at the door of this great play without gaining admission.'

Fiennes' speaking of the soliloquies also came in for criticism. Holland complained they 'were gone through at a speed which left the audience marvelling at his technique, but never engaging with his process of thought'. John Peter thought 'To be or not to be' sounded 'not like thought moulding itself into speech, a subtle intelligence grappling with a problem, but like an obsession that has already been rehearsed more than once'. Wolf noted that the soliloquy 'emerges without warning as a conversational asterisk, uttered as an aside while Ophelia stands nearby, unaware'. But he also observed that those who recalled Fiennes' earlier theatre work with the Royal Shakespeare Company would find him transformed. 'While he continues to speak verse fluently and well, even in the chasm-like acoustics of the Hackney Empire, he has loosened up on stage. The Gielgudian "voice beautiful" feel of his early RSC work has been discarded in favour of a contemporary, almost throwaway style that nonetheless honours the language.'

His Hamlet used a good deal of sexual violence to Ophelia and Gertrude. In the nunnery scene he pulled up Ophelia's skirt and raped her very quickly from behind. This presumably added to the other stress factors that provoked her to insanity: in the mad scene she had no flowers, and instead chopped off her hair and handed out strands of it, describing them as fennel, rosemary and so on. In the closet scene Hamlet imitated raping Gertrude, causing her subsequently to recoil from Claudius' touch. Holland described her traumatised behaviour: 'Gertrude's control collapsed, and she quivered on the edge of madness. By the final scene she sat with her head twitching, her make-up a terrible mask, her suffering ignored by all about her. I have never seen the consequences of Hamlet's treatment of her so graphically and horrifyingly exposed ... By comparison with the women's suffering, Hamlet's madness seemed only an actor's performance, and his treatment of them unmistakably brutal, callous and self-regarding.'

Fiennes was widely admired when the play moved to Broadway. 'He radiates an elegance of spirit that rivets the audience with its sense of unspoken mystery,' John Lahr wrote. 'He has a mellow, reedy voice that filters Shakespeare's gorgeous complexity and gives the language an accessible colloquial ring. He compels attention by his decency, not by his declaiming.' Vincent Canby was also greatly taken: 'Mr. Fiennes is in command from beginning to end. He's a charismatic stage actor. He has a fine strong voice (and complete control of it) that never becomes monotonously distinctive. His Hamlet is utterly contemporary in execution and concept.' He saw 'an intelligent, beautifully read and set production that serves the new star as much as he serves it'. Lahr however was concerned about the pace: 'The speed favours breadth over depth ... What we have here is a ripping Shakespeare yarn that shows the thrills and chills of the melodramatic elements ... The result is lucid without being moving.'

Canby also picked out Francesca Annis' performance for special praise.

She is lovely and exceptionally moving as the ill-fated Gertrude. She's also the first Gertrude I've seen who seems less predator than victim. In this she's helped in no small way by Terence Rigby as the Ghost. His portrayal of the implacable shade of Hamlet's father suggests Gertrude's first marriage must have been less than the idyll Hamlet remembers. The old king was – and still is – a tyrant. Ms Annis' Gertrude is clearly a woman liberated in her sexuality and her emotions by her union with Claudius.

After opening night Fiennes stated: 'The Broadway audience is not used to hearing Shakespeare, and the quality of their listening has been wonderful. Many of the lines are new to them, so it's a fresh response.' Later, after winning a Tony award for Best Actor, he said: 'I have wanted to play Hamlet for a long time, so it's reward enough just to get to play it. Shakespeare has always fascinated me since I was young, so to receive an award for playing one of his roles gives me a particular kick.'

Alex Jennings
Matthew Warchus

In 1997 it was Alex Jennings' turn to play Hamlet for the Royal Shakespeare Company, directed by Matthew Warchus at Stratford and the Barbican in London. The following year the production was staged at the Kennedy Centre in Washington, and at the Opera House of the Brooklyn Academy of Music, New York.

Cast: Claudius: Paul Freeman, Gertrude: Susannah York, Laertes: William Houston, Horatio: Colin Hurley, Polonius: David Ryall, Ophelia: Derbhle Crotty, Player King/Ghost: Edward Petherbridge, Gravedigger: Paul Jesson.

I know that by cutting the play you could diminish it, but by cutting a couple of courses from a banquet you can make the flavours sharper and richer.

This was Matthew Warchus' argument for his decision to cut around a third of Shakespeare's text for his stylised, modern-dress RSC production of *Hamlet*. Conflating the three existing versions of the play, his aim was to focus on the domestic story, since 'Hamlet is a play absolutely saturated with the words father, mother, sister, brother, son, daughter, uncle'. He further explained: 'I feel that what I am doing is taking the play out of the hands of the academics and intellectuals and bringing it back into the area of relationships', adding that 'more than any other play I have directed, I am doing this with my heart, not my head'.

In this modern Elsinore the two families lived together with their staff in an isolated house. The play began with Alex Jennings' Hamlet holding his father's ashes in an urn at the front of the stage, then scattering them on the ground in front of a screen, on which a black-and-white home movie showed him as a boy, playing in the snow with his father and running joyfully into his arms. Simultaneously the audience heard over the speakers Claudius announcing 'Though yet of Hamlet our dear brother's death the memory be green'.

The screen was then flown away, casting Hamlet into a raucous, vulgar party celebrating his mother's wedding to Claudius, with balloons, fireworks and bridesmaids, with champagne corks popping, pop music blaring, coloured lights flashing – 'a gaudy purple disco' as one critic described it – and Claudius groping Susannah York's smiling Gertrude in full view of the guests. Lurking on the sidelines, Hamlet took polaroid photos of Claudius, which he would later use in the closet scene to show Gertrude the contrasting images of her two husbands. The first scene was cut, the Ghost instead initially appearing at the party in a smoking jacket, speaking to Hamlet about 'murder most foul', then drifting away.

Jennings' disturbed Prince, occasionally drawing on a cigarette, was clearly on the edge of a nervous breakdown. He spoke 'To be or not to be' with a pistol pointed at his head, then carried it around in a paper bag, and considered using it when he came across Claudius at prayer. Soon after he employed it to kill Polonius, and in the final scene, after Claudius had drunk the poison, he fired a bullet into his dying body.

The play-within-a-play provided a striking image: Robert Smallwood described 'the eerie, jerky presentation of *The Murder of Gonzago* as a shadow play on a screen, in front of which Hamlet pranced in a brilliant crimson jacket, white face and painted-on smile – circus master, clown, MC – and the shadow of Lucianus, bending to administer the poison, loomed huge and distorted in front of Paul Freeman's suave, expensively suited Claudius, while Hamlet joined in with sing-song recitation of the incriminating lines, until even the hard-headed self-control of the usurper could take no more'. With Fortinbras and the attendant politics excluded, the play ended with 'And flight of angels sing thee to thy rest'; Horatio's voice was then heard over the speakers announcing 'all this can I / Truly deliver'.

In a diary piece published during the run Jennings admitted: 'I never particularly wanted to play the part. Adrian Noble, the RSC's artistic director, asked me; I was quite surprised, but there was no possibility of saying no – it seemed slightly churlish, and I knew I probably wouldn't get the opportunity again, as I was fast approaching forty.' He also mentioned his recurrent back problem. 'On stage, the adrenalin takes over, but sometimes I notice it. Hamlet is quite physical; you're on stage for four hours and you are knackered by the end of it, physically and mentally.'

After playing the role twice in one day, in a matinee and evening performance, he confessed to being 'absolutely exhausted'.

We have a lie-down between shows, and I get up feeling a bit punchy before the second one. I don't do any special preparation; I just try to empty my head and see what happens, see what the words do. What's so wonderful about Hamlet is that you are never going to be definitive; you just have to try to tell the story in a clear and fresh way. Luckily the play is pretty good, so it supports you, and there's always something else to be mined from it.

His exhaustion found expression that night: 'Something went wrong with the sound system. I broke a prop in a fit of pique in the wings – Hamlet's father's urn. I threw it at the table. I don't usually do that kind of thing.'

There was, Smallwood observed, 'no denying the production's absorbing and exciting theatricality'. He also admired Jennings, who 'spoke with all that intelligent, graceful command of the verse that one has come to expect of him, and made one feel the isolation and pain of Hamlet with unrelenting intensity.' Ann O'Bryan praised him for 'a magnificent tour de force of verse speaking. He's a brilliant master of Shakespeare's verse, and here in a deliberately downbeat conversational tone he makes every thought crystal clear as if newly minted, so that the sense and the beauty of the poetry shine through.' Charles Spencer was less sympathetic: 'Jennings's pistol-toting Hamlet had warmth, charm and a wry self-mocking humour, without ever penetrating the play's depths. This was Hamlet Lite.'

In 1998 the production moved to Brooklyn, as the opening play in a five-play RSC season. It met a harsher critical reception than it had in England. In the *New York Times* Ben Brantley criticised Warchus for providing

> what is less a thoroughgoing interpretation than a series of noisy distractions ... The evening is shot through with adrenalin, and it features a few stunning images, but at the sacrifice of any emotional continuity and often clarity of plot. Tremendous effort has obviously been exerted to bring freshness to familiar scenes and speeches, which are sometimes tossed off at such a speed as to be incomprehensible. The overall effect is one of bright sparks of electricity without any flowing current ... As an interpretation of Shakespeare's most introspective play, it sticks exasperatingly close to its showy surface.

Allan Wallach was similarly uneasy:

> By now, unfortunately, these kinds of modernising devices have hardened into trendy clichés. Here, they become substitutes for a point of view; the production seems to have little on its mind but costumes and cleverness ... With very little heft to the characters, the tragic elements are curiously remote. Even when the lines are impassioned, you don't feel the emotions driving the characters ... While the RSC may be right to strive for more inventive ways to stage a classic, the result here doesn't give the play overall the dimensions it demands.

Paul Rhys
Laurence Boswell

In 1999 Laurence Boswell directed Paul Rhys as Hamlet in a joint Theatre Royal, Plymouth/Young Vic production, which later visited Japan.

Cast: Claudius: Donald Sumpter, Polonius: Robert Soans, Gertrude: Suzanne Bertish, Ophelia: Megan Dodds, Laertes: Christopher Bowen, Horatio: Richard Lintern.

> Every part I've played has been Hamlet in one form or another. The parts have had similar qualities to Hamlet – isolated, disposed, pained, funny – all the qualities you see in him.

Paul Rhys' parts had included his fine Edgar in Richard Eyre's production of *King Lear*, another character who had to feign madness in order to survive. Now the challenge of playing Hamlet was 'to forget the people who had success with the role before. I wanted to be myself and the character at the same time, and accept the consequences. What is needed is a fearless interpretation, and you need to alienate as well as attract. I approach the role in presenting Hamlet as nakedly emotional.' Although he had been asked to play the Prince several times, he had 'never wanted to do it unless it was with an ally'. That ally was Laurence Boswell.

While he was a student at RADA, the principal Hugh Cruttwell had warned Rhys: 'You will always need to be very careful about what you give as an actor. There's a slightly unbounded quality about you. You need to always protect yourself.' An intelligent actor of nervous Welsh intensity, Rhys admits he has

> possibly not always protected myself, and I've learnt the hard way. I rehearse and rehearse and rehearse – like a maniac, like a soldier preparing for war – not just in the theatre, but also at home, non-stop, completely obsessive. It's both brilliant and terrible, going that far. It's thrilling, but it's also hell. All that's ever gone on in my head is, 'It's not enough. Come on. You've got to go further. It's not truthful enough. There's more, there's more.'

This intensity led to a hyper-sensitive, fragile-looking Hamlet full of his many contradictions, which was well-liked by the critics. 'Whether being a weeping student ... or a frantic psychotic, he keeps his lean face open but watchful,' was the *Independent on Sunday*'s verdict. 'As a result his madness is unaffectedly credible.' The *Sunday Times* felt his performance 'pulsates with intelligence and feeling'. For the *Independent*: 'No one since Mark Rylance has transmitted as well as Rhys a sense of the hero's spiritual sweetness, or the fundamental peace he has achieved by the time he has returned from England.' Only the *Mail on Sunday* found fault: 'In Rhys' detailed, beautifully spoken if slightly precious performance, all that's missing is the sexiness.'

Boswell's production contained several offbeat, quirky ideas. At the start the actors engaged the audience in conversation as they took their seats. The Ghost was a masked samurai on stilts; Hamlet donned a wig and a crown of thorns to complement a pair of pyjamas (shades of Rylance), and posed as a crucified Christ to taunt Donald Sumpter's Claudius; rows of tiny terracotta soldiers guarding the stage throughout the second half offered an arresting image of Fortinbras' advancing army; before the duel Hamlet washed Yorick's skull while taking a bath. Designer Es Devlin's bare, black veneer set had a black, wooden platform at each end of the traverse, connected or distanced by a retractable central aisle. The props were minimal, the lighting had a stark clarity, creating substantial pools of darkness on the stage, while the costumes were an idiosyncratic mixture of ancient and modern.

When the production was performed in Tokyo and Osaka, Rhys reflected on the changing styles in playing Shakespeare.

The posing declamatory style of acting Shakespeare is going on somewhere right now in the world, but I'm sure Shakespeare didn't intend that sort of thing. The British are known for their technical ability to bump and grind through anything, and that's necessary. If you don't have the technique you can't do this play. If you ignore the technical elements it's perilous. But to just do that is monstrous.

I think young British actors have moved into more personal investment, and it's changed audience perceptions greatly. There's a backlash against the over-technical and an attraction to the truth. What is expected now on both sides of the Atlantic is a serious commitment to truthfulness in performances. If this is combined with a technical facility then the whole package is dazzling. But you can't have one without the other. It's no longer plausible.

In portraying Hamlet he was judged to have successfully combined these crucial two elements.

7

The 2000s

Mark Rylance
Giles Block

In the year 2000, directed by Giles Block, Mark Rylance played his second Hamlet at the Globe, during his tenure as the theatre's first artistic director.

Cast: Claudius: Tim Woodward, Gertrude: Joanna McCallum, Ophelia: Penny Layden, Polonius: James Hayes, Laertes: Mark Lockyer, Horatio: Geoffrey Beevers.

I have great mood swings, maybe because of playing lots of different characters. I'm like a gymnast whose muscles get too stretched. I've got better at it, but I have a lot of emotional energy.

That energy was greatly in evidence in Mark Rylance's Hamlet, as it had been a dozen years earlier (see page 60). Less intellectual than many Hamlets, his performance was marked by volatile, uninhibited emotions and unrestrained physical responses. He wept, embraced the Ghost fervently, sent Ophelia to a nunnery as if he was genuinely fearful for her safety, and wept again after killing Polonius. He also drew out the humour in the part: 'Hamlet has some very funny lines,' he observed. 'I have no problem with a Hamlet who makes me laugh. People who are always sad are not the most tragic people around.'

In the interim between his two Hamlets his roles in Shakespeare had included Benedick and Macbeth in England, Touchstone in America, and at the Globe Richard II, and Olivia in an all-male *Twelfth Night*. Now aged 40, and midway through his time as the Globe's artistic director, Rylance had become accustomed to the inevitable distractions and obstacles thrown up by the world outside the open-air theatre: 'I find the interruptions of birds or planes or other things all very much help in the spontaneity of the performance and the fact that each time it has to be different.'

During rehearsals, to help the actors develop a sense of the reality of the imagined palace at Elsinore, the company visited Hatfield House in

Hertfordshire, built by Robert Cecil, whose father Lord Burghley, Elizabeth's chief minister, may have been the model for Polonius. In the archives they were shown various documents, including precepts that Burghley had sent to his son in Paris. Director Giles Block recalled: 'As we visited the Great Hall, the chapel, the lobby and the closet, or walked up on the leads beside the great Jacobean chimneys and looked out at the gardens and the graveyard beyond, the story sprang vividly to life.'

They also spent time at the sixteenth-century Otley Hall in Suffolk, where they were rehearsed by Richard Olivier. Scenes of spying and surveillance took place in rooms in the house, to give a sense of how their characters might have felt, in the dark, in a gallery, in a mother's closet. Joanna McCallum, cast as Gertrude, remembered: 'We began right before the play of *Hamlet* started, and we played through the story of Gertrude and Old Hamlet, and the marriage to Claudius. A great deal of work was done; it was very imaginative.' James Hayes, playing Polonius, also benefitted: 'I learnt more about the play, the character, Elsinore and courtly intrigue there than in a lot of the rehearsals in Southwark,' he said. 'I feel the world of the play was to a large extent created there. It was absolutely fascinating. I spied on scenes out of windows and behind curtains. I saw Hamlet and Ophelia in the garden, apparently intimate. There was intrigue, and a lot of that seeped into my head and began to be put into the play.' Uniquely, at Olivier's suggestion, Rylance underwent a burial ritual in a hole dug by the Gravediggers.

The critics admired his performance. Charles Spencer observed: 'Rylance's Hamlet seemed almost physically injured with grief, taking to the stage in an excrement-stained nightgown and creating an astonishingly poignant impression of a once noble mind on the brink of a complete breakdown. Yet there were flashes of warmth and spirituality too.' For Michael Billington, Rylance was 'one of nature's Hamlets: alert, humorous, and capable of combining whimsical dottiness with a troubled inner life ... Despite an occasional excess of vocal virtuosity, he offers us a quick-brained Hamlet intrigued by moral and material putrescence.'

His close rapport with the audience sprang from his decision to speak the soliloquies directly to them. Often he seemed alone with the audience, even when others were present. In contrast to his experience in other theatres, he explained that 'at the Globe I have much more of a sense of the play happening out in the space between the actors and the audience, and that we contribute and pass the ball just as much to the audience as we do to each other'. For instance, he hurled at the audience the line about the 'groundlings' being 'capable of nothing but dumb shows', then added after they reacted vociferously, 'and noise'.

Others referred to positive qualities of the atmosphere. Penny Layden, playing Ophelia, remembered a moment at the end of her mad scene: 'Often when I've finished my last song before I go off, there's a moment when it's completely still and quiet outside. It's like everything has stopped. It's quite magical when you feel six hundred people listening.' The weather was of course a major factor, as Tim Preece, doubling as the Ghost and the Player King, recalled: 'The last performance of Hamlet was marvellous because suddenly it was a very still evening and none of us had to project. The whole performance changed, and had a wonderful bell-like sound ... We did a different sort than we had done for the whole of the season.'

Like most actors, Rylance found playing Hamlet an emotional experience. 'You have to touch on certain things inside you that are very difficult – it's got to be gone through from innocence to consciousness every night.' A decade later he revealed that he hoped to act again at the Globe one day, and indeed couldn't imagine playing Shakespeare anywhere else. 'It wouldn't interest me to do Shakespeare in a divided space, with the audience in darkness and me lit. I don't want to speak to or for or at an audience. I want to speak *with* them.'

Adrian Lester

Peter Brook

In 2001 Peter Brook's The Tragedy of Hamlet, *starring Adrian Lester, played at the Young Vic as part of a world tour, which included visits to America and many European and Asian cities. It had originally opened at the Bouffes du Nord in Paris.*

Cast: Claudius/Ghost: Jefferey Kissoon, Gertrude: Natasha Parry, Horatio: Scott Handy, Polonius/Gravedigger: Bruce Myers, Ophelia: Shantala Shivalingappa, Laertes/Guildenstern/Second Player: Rohan Siva, Rosencrantz/First Player: Yoshi Oïda.

Hamlet is like a crystal ball, ever rotating. At each instant it turns a new facet towards us, and suddenly we seem to see the whole play more clearly. So we can always set off again in search of its truth.

Peter Brook's quest for the essence of *Hamlet* was characteristically radical.

If one can very gently take out of this long, sprawling melodrama those elements which come straight to the heart of everyone's interests and preoccupations, you get a fresh view of *Hamlet*. Take away two hours of the romantic, rhetorical staging, and find in its place a very pure, essential myth in which the essential elements are a father, a brother who murders him, a wife who comes into an incestuous relation with her brother-in-law, and a very pure young girl that the son loves. This is the essential tragic and powerful inter-relation, and this speaks to us directly today without any decoration. It was trying to extract that essential pattern which was a great reason to do this production.

His stripped-down version, his first Shakespeare production in English since 1978, lasted a mere two-and-a-half hours, with no interval. Speeches and scenes were reassigned, roles doubled or tripled. He deleted around a third of the text, including most of Act 1. Out went Polonius' advice to Laertes and Hamlet's to the Players, and several speeches of Rosencrantz and Guildenstern, the Second Gravedigger and Fortinbras. Brook justified losing the political elements on the grounds that the Fortinbras sub-plot was of no interest to Shakespeare, who was merely following Elizabethan convention in creating it.

The simple set consisted of a square, red-orange carpet, two low rectangular benches covered in red cloth and several coloured cushions scattered around the floor. Two smaller carpets were placed on the larger carpet and four candles at its perimeter for the Players to perform *The Murder of Gonzago*. Cushions were put on their sides to create Ophelia's grave. As with other Brook productions, this one had a strong international element. The music between scenes, ranging from muffled bells to the sound of birds in flight, was played on a variety of instruments, many of them unfamiliar, by Brook's long-time Japanese collaborator Toshi Tsuchitori. The cast of just eight players, playing 13 parts, included English, Indian, Japanese and West Indian actors.

His Hamlet, Adrian Lester, the son of Jamaican immigrants, was now an established stage and screen star. He had garnered many awards for his Rosalind in Cheek by Jowl's all-male production of *As You Like It* – a performance which Brook had admired. The director was initially uncertain about whether to cast him or another actor. Lester recalls the moment:

He knew he wanted to do something with the play that went against the traditional way of playing Hamlet. He knew he wanted to engage what he called an actor who had the intellectual understanding, but one that went right through the body. He said that when he left the UK there was a very beautiful-voice, talking-head kind of acting, and he didn't want that. He wanted that technical expertise, but also a real bellyful of passion.

Explaining his reasons for casting Lester as 'the most haunting and enigmatic character in all writing', Brook observed:

Adrian has many special qualities. Above all he is somebody of tomorrow, and the audience immediately recognises that. He uses Shakespearean language, which is not of today, in such a way that you feel it is the language of his own thoughts that he is thinking, and finding the only words that correspond at that moment to his experience. And yet you don't get the false impression that this is an artificial, theatrical version of the language, that only people of a certain cultural education can deliver. This is the false tradition of Shakespeare that has lasted for many hundreds of years all through Europe. At last you have an actor that can be so at ease with this complex language that he can make you feel he is inventing it. That is a great quality.

Lester had a unique way of preparing for the part:

I began with the speeches, whispering them to myself in a very staccato rhythm, just to hear the sound rather than worrying about the sense. When you're whispering you don't use your voice, you resonate the vowel-sounds differently, and so when you're listening to yourself, certain words take on a deeper resonance. Then I added the voice, and began to unpick the sense. I took all the punctuation away, and wrote the speeches out by hand without the rhythm. Then I would read that through, and try to make sense of it.

With 'To be or not to be' he tried an experiment. 'I knelt down on the floor and took my pulse, and as soon as I felt its rhythm, that was the rhythm of the first sentence. I then left it alone. And in performance it was very subtly different every single night.'

Initially he rehearsed on his own with Brook. 'I went to Paris, and rehearsed with him every day for two or three hours. We sat side by side on the carpet in his studio and I began feeling my way through the major speeches, very quietly. He was listening for the thoughts, and then we'd talk about what they were, and how we found them changing.' They talked about madness and feigning madness. 'We concluded that Hamlet is madder in front of the people he cannot trust. So he's as honest as he can be for a person who is under extreme emotional pressure, which in itself brings its own frisson. But he starts to paint images of being mad and foolish in front of the people he has to hide the truth from, such as Polonius, and especially Claudius.'

In rehearsing for three months with the company, Lester was struck by the other actors' attitude towards Brook.

I had heard about Peter being revered while I was at drama school, I'd heard the reasons why, I'd read a book or two, but I hadn't grown up in a culture where the director was God. I had reverence for him, but I wasn't in awe of him. But I was working alongside actors who completely worshipped him – they'd read all the books, listened to the lectures. This had an odd effect on Peter. Somehow he was not allowed to do something and get it wrong, and try something else, because with everything he said, the attitude of the actors was, 'Oh that's the way we're doing it.' So if he wanted to try a different way, there was a confusion that didn't allow for flexibility. He needed to be allowed to try something for a week, and then change his mind. A lot of the actors felt the change meant *they* were at fault, and that was why he was doing something different.

Lester differed from the other actors in another respect:

With this text they adopted, quite rightly, a kind of classical mannerism; there were no colloquialisms or modern shrugs or anything like that. I was the opposite. I wanted my character to be full of that kind of thing. So I used sarcasm a lot, and rolled my eyes, which for me was a way of undermining the stiff, hierarchical, lying nature of the world I was trapped in. So you had a very modern man in the middle of a 400-year-old play. It worked, and Peter felt my dreadlocks helped me to be a Hamlet like no other. The more we left convention behind, the happier he was.

Brook gave the actors freedom to tell the story, and advised them never to repeat an action. Exits and entrances were improvised, blocking was never fixed, and even the fourth wall could be breached. 'Once we had the foundations he let us create the play between us, in many ways however we liked,' Lester says. 'I used the audience, I looked at particular people.' At one performance, noticing a woman following the play with her own edition, he strode into the audience, took the book, and played the rest of the scene reading from it. Each audience prompted him to vary details of his performance, which he found very liberating.

He remembers the spark that lit his way to playing Hamlet's death.

Peter said, I don't know how we do it, but I want to try and see if we can have the audience see Hamlet's spirit, actually see the life-force leave him. He mentioned hearing about a monk who knew he was going to die, went into a state of meditation, and died sitting perfectly still in an upright position. Peter spoke about the way he must have gone to a different plane. I wanted to reflect that kind of death. I pushed Horatio away from me and slowly slunk to my knees. When I said 'The rest is silence' I could see what was coming, and it was silent and beautiful and wonderful, and I was going there. That made me smile. And when I'd gone, I was still left with that expression.

Brook also came up with an unconventional ending. The dead characters rose to their feet, and Horatio spoke his lines from Act 1, 'But look, the morn, in russet mantle clad / Walks o'er the dew of yon high eastward hill'. The play then ended as it began with 'Who's there?' with Horatio looking mystically at the horizon. For Brook this scene of rebirth and mystery held the meaning that 'life goes on'.

Summing up Brook's method, Lester explained: 'He directs you as if you are a big block of stone and the character is inside you and, like any sculptor, he chips away at what is not needed until the character is revealed.' One element of his approach, designed to keep their playing fresh, could be disconcerting.

There were times in rehearsal when we found something that we all thought was good and we liked the way it worked. But when Peter looked at it, he could see what we were trying to achieve, and he could feel that we had achieved it. So for him the scene was dead. I have never seen a director cut so many images and moments between actors simply because we knew what the moment was telling us.

Lester found two performances on matinee days mentally and physically taxing. 'The next day when I spoke "Oh that this too too solid flesh would melt", I was speaking my own tiredness. I served Hamlet's feelings with my own: "Oh God, how weary", and so on. I did it in a way that existed on the edge of acting; it was a very dangerous but very freeing experience.' But he was heartened by an experience after one matinee.

I was very tired, and getting ready to do the evening performance, and grabbing some food. After congratulating me on my performance this woman, probably in her seventies, said to me quietly: 'You do wonder whether it's worth continuing sometimes, don't you? With everything that's happened, why carry on? But you showed me that every breath is worth living.' And I thought, That's worth a year of running the play, to have that effect on just one person.

The production had a mixed response from the critics. Kate Bassett described Lester as 'quietly magnetic … Picking up on the remarkably modern, broken sentences of Hamlet's soliloquies, his thoughts appear to be changing tack even as we watch.' Patrick Marmion noted that 'Lester's performance describes a strong and moving journey towards personal enlightenment'. Michael Billington wrote: 'Lester is a figure of endless contradiction: snarling and considerate with Polonius, coarse and tender with Ophelia, brutal and chivalric with Laertes. It is a remarkable performance that puts emotional spontaneity before rhetoric.'

Bassett thought the production 'fascinating and exciting – often ingenious in its simplicity, intensely absorbing, and ultimately in tune with our times'. Robert Hewison described it as 'engrossing', while Benedict Nightingale thought it 'nimble and pacey'. But Charles Spencer was savage in his criticism: 'This radical reworking of *Hamlet* would surely have been shot down in flames if the sainted Brook hadn't directed it.' He criticised the cutting and re-ordering: 'Far from clarifying the play, they actually serve to diminish and confuse it.' This was, he concluded, 'a dismally diminished *Hamlet* with a deeply unappealing atmosphere of smug sanctity about it. Not so much a tragedy, in fact, as a travesty.'

Lester was intrigued by the audience responses in different countries.

At the Bouffes du Nord everyone was on the edge of their seat, because they knew what to expect from Peter, they were used to watching his work. In America people were louder, they laughed a lot, they shuffled about, the attention span was shorter. But in Japan you could hear a pin drop. Students sat cross-legged on cushions two metres in front of me, and didn't move for two and a half hours. No shuffling, no mobile phones, nothing. It was incredible.

He praises Brook for the effect he had on his playing, but admitted to one regret.

Working with Peter changed me as an actor, for the better. He made me feelingly understand so many things about the art of acting, and of playing Shakespeare. But I wish I had had an extra level of confidence to do a little less physicality, so the purity of what Peter had created, and the way he created this version, could be more clearly seen.

Samuel West

Steven Pimlott

In 2001 Samuel West, directed by Steven Pimlott, played Hamlet for the Royal Shakespeare Company at Stratford, and then at the Barbican in London.

Cast: Claudius: Larry Lamb, Gertrude: Marty Cruickshank, Horatio: John Dougall, Polonius: Alan David, Ophelia: Kerry Condon, Laertes: Ben Meyjes.

During rehearsals Samuel West suggested he might be too analytical to be an actor. Many of the most gifted actors, he said, are not interested in talking about the play in general, but only the character they are playing. 'I admire that, but I am not like that. I think doing your homework can't do any harm. I want to know everything about the world of the play.'

In the opinion of his friend and director Steven Pimlott, who had recently directed him as an acclaimed Richard II, this was one of West's strengths. 'The key to his personality is his analytic intelligence and missionary zeal. There's a direct link between his art and his politics. He's a very passionate human being, who cares deeply about what's happening in the world. That gives him a vehemence and energy that comes through his work.'

West had seen 20 productions of *Hamlet* and the previous year had directed an RSC fringe production. So he was conscious of the Hamlets that had gone before:

You have only got one year of your life to play this role. Twenty thousand actors across the years have had the same problems that you are having. You have inherited this crown from them and you are staggering along under it for a few performances and then passing it on. The play has an amazing ability to fit itself around the person who is playing it.

Not surprisingly given his partnership with Pimlott, the political dimension in *Hamlet*, which had been cut from many recent productions, was largely restored in this four-hour, modern-dress production. Claudius was a presidential figure in a corporate world, surrounded by yes-men with name-tags, dressed in grey suits like City traders. In designer Alison Chitty's stark and windowless, white-box Elsinore, everyone spied on everyone else, with security guards, searchlights and swivelling surveillance cameras much in evidence.

The action included many violent modern moments. The guards tried to get rid of the Ghost with machine-gun fire. Hamlet, in black T-shirt, leather jacket and jeans, put a pistol to his head during 'To be or not to be', and used it to kill Polonius. Other touches included Horatio videoing Claudius and Gertrude's reactions to the play-within-a-play, which were shown in close-up, and Hamlet sharing a joint with Rosencrantz and Guildenstern.

West used the soliloquies as conversations with the audience: 'When Hamlet walks out to the front of the stage for the first soliloquy, he is saying, "My dad is dead. My mum has remarried my uncle. Can we talk?"' In the case of 'To be or not to be' he observed:

I didn't realise until I started studying it that it doesn't include the words 'I' or 'me'. In terms of the plot it has no purpose. What it talks about is us and dying. The reason why it is so often anthologised, and the most famous piece of literature in world history, is that it applies to each and every one of us.

Lyn Gardner felt that 'from the moment he appears as a troubled young man in sweatshirt and jeans, West's Hamlet, the believer turned sceptic, is mesmerising', while Michael Billington suggested 'the keynote of West's fine Hamlet is a mordant intelligence and sense of political impotence ... He is sardonic, clever, and cruelly aware of his own powerlessness.' Charles Spencer noted West's 'charm, wit and natural authority, and the verse delivered with exemplary clarity; I have never heard "To be or not to be" more freshly minted'. But he thought West 'laid on Hamlet's irony with a trowel', and failed to put over any sense of spiritual progress. 'There is a weary, fearful fatalism to his "Let be", not the moving sense of a man who has finally made peace with himself and God.'

After the run, West reflected: 'I find it moving that I've spent a year in a company of young actors speaking a 400-year-old language with no apology and an almost revolutionary zeal. The zeitgeist is so much about not caring, about it being cool to mumble and be back-footed. But you can't do that when you are speaking verse.' Like others, he stressed the impossibility of fully mastering a role that explores the full human emotional range.

You can never fulfil the demands of every piece of it. There will be bits that come right at different times, and some things that will never quite succeed. It's a very difficult part, but also a very easy one. It's very forgiving of things you can't do. But it brings you up against them very quickly; it brings you up quite fast against your limitations as an actor and a person ... There are no dark corners of yourself that this play won't hold your hands in, if you want to explore them.

Michael Maloney
Yukio Ninagawa

After a UK tour, Yukio Ninagawa's production, under the aegis of Thelma Holt and the Theatre Royal Plymouth, with Michael Maloney as Hamlet, was staged at the Barbican in London in 2004.

Cast: Gertrude: Frances Tomelty, Claudius: Peter Egan, Ophelia: Laura Rees, Polonius: Robert Demeger, Horatio: Bob Barrett, Laertes: Adam Dodd.

In this production staged by the legendary Japanese director Yukio Ninagawa, Michael Maloney joined that select band of actors who have played Hamlet twice. His first had been in 1996, in a modern-dress production by Philip Franks.

Looking back, he was critical of that first attempt: 'All the bits I thought were important were just dragging the play down. It was just making it about me. And the bits I thought were funny weren't necessarily.' This time he felt able to build on what he called a bedrock. 'It removes a great deal of neurosis about how you're going to come across. It is able to flow through me better. What I'm saying seems able to occur to me more.' He was now very familiar with the play, having seen ten productions in the interim. He had worked before with Ninagawa, as Edgar in a much-criticised production of *King Lear*. Now 47, he was said to be the oldest Hamlet in living memory.

Ninagawa, presenting his sixth *Hamlet*, viewed the age question as irrelevant. 'I have learnt for the first time that the age of Hamlet doesn't matter. In Michael's acting you see he has the essence of Hamlet in him, and that's all you need. One of the attractions of the character is his very rational thinking, and his very fierce emotions. I was looking for somebody who can have both elements in one.' The play, he suggested, 'is about the radical questioning of human behaviour, the profundity and scale of it'.

He pointed out the difference between Japanese and English actors in Shakespeare: 'My sort of Shakespeare is the kind that Japanese academics hate,' he said. 'There is not much of an element in Japanese culture of rationalising thoughts and turning them into actions, so Japanese actors are not very switched on to that part of playing *Hamlet*. Because English actors are good I don't have to explain unnecessary things. I just try to explain them in a simplified way.' Maloney observed: 'The notes he's given me are a series of simple statements, which if you are not awake to them would appear just that. In fact, they are absolutely loaded. The more you tune into them, the more chance you have.'

The Japanese aspect was only minimally visible in the choice of costumes: the Ghost looked like a samurai warrior, and Maloney wore a long, Japanese-style cloak that forced him to walk slightly crouched, but otherwise there was a mixture of periods and of East and West. The set consisted of a series of tall, rectangular doors leading on to the box-shaped stage, with eight vertical strands of barbed wire stretching from floor to ceiling at various points, and a dozen naked lights swinging above the actors' heads. Ninagawa explained:

> I wanted to place the actors in the centre of a symbol to portray the essence of the play. I used the barbed wire to express something very psychological, like a prison, or guarding against outside. And I wanted to place something onstage that interrupts their movements, and makes it necessary for them to have a cool head when they make very fierce movements.

The production provoked a hostile reception from the critics, most of whom had admired his previous Shakespeare productions. Nicholas de Jongh wrote: 'Ninagawa's *Macbeth*, *The Tempest*, *A Midsummer Night's Dream* and *Pericles* were remarkable for beautiful settings, each capturing the play's literal or symbolic essence. This time the design serves as a cosmetic gloss to conceal a lack of interpretative depth.' Michael Billington called the production 'a rather dry, risk-free affair', while Charles Spencer criticised it as 'one of the most punishingly dreary *Hamlets* I have ever endured, a production in which this greatest and most inexhaustible of plays has been reduced to a sterile quintessence of dust'; he likened it to 'the work of some second-rate director in a regional English rep, with a small budget and an even smaller artistic imagination'.

Maloney's Hamlet also came under fire. According to Ian Shuttleworth: 'We clearly see what he is feeling from moment to moment, but seldom grasp why, especially as he generally delivers his lines in a rapid mutter.' Spencer was again severe: 'Maloney, wearing the anxious expression of a man who has just mislaid his railway ticket, whispers, whimpers and occasionally bellows his way through the great soliloquies in such a rushed, fretful manner that their significance, both verbal and emotional, almost always gets lost.' But Billington thought his performance 'supremely watchable ... a pensive intellectual with a gift for cutting through the pretence that surrounds him ... Maloney also brings out Hamlet's peculiar mixture of spiritual grace and calculating cruelty.' Critical of the production, he concluded: 'We've all heard of *Hamlet* without the Prince. This is a case of the Prince without much of *Hamlet*.'

Ben Whishaw

Trevor Nunn

In 2004 at the Old Vic, Trevor Nunn directed his second professional
Hamlet, *with Ben Whishaw as the Prince.*

Cast: Gertrude: Imogen Stubbs, Ophelia: Samantha Whittaker, Claudius:
Tom Mannion, Polonius: Nicholas Jones, Laertes: Rory Kinnear, Horatio:
Jotham Annan.

> It seems to me that one could probably do a production of *Hamlet* every
> year, a totally different production, the play is that tolerant.

So Trevor Nunn suggested in 1989. Fifteen years later he admitted
Hamlet was for him 'unfinished business'. It was the first play he had ever
directed; at the age of 17 he had staged an amateur production in Ipswich
lasting five hours. He had been unhappy about his 1970 production
starring Alan Howard at Stratford, in which he felt 'paralysed by trying to
solve all the contradictions of the play'. In preparing his 2004 production
at the Old Vic he was struck by the many references to 'youth' in the text,
and was determined to make this a feature, starting with the company.
Hamlet, he observed, was about the generation gap, 'which changes from
era to era'.

His choice for Hamlet was 23-year-old Ben Whishaw, who had left
RADA only the year before. 'I assumed I'd be auditioning for Rosencrantz
or Guildenstern, or a smallish part, Osric or something,' he recalled.

> But I had chosen Hamlet's first soliloquy, so I did some work on that with
> Trevor. He asked me to do it again as if I was just five, which I did. Then
> he sent me away to prepare two other soliloquies. I came back a week
> later, and we worked on them. Then he called me back; he wanted me
> to do something funny that wasn't Hamlet. So I prepared a speech from
> *The Two Gentlemen of Verona*. We did nothing about the language, or
> the iambic pentameter; it was just about what was going on in Hamlet's
> head. I found the auditions gruelling and emotionally tough. I felt quite
> exposed. I told a friend I didn't think I could do the part if I were offered
> it. He told me to shut up.

Nunn was struck by the young actor's fragile physique and striking looks,
his 'face of great sensitivity and astonishing youthfulness'. But he had feared
that going for youth might prove problematic:

> I embarked on the auditions expecting I might draw a blank, that I might
> discover there was nobody sufficiently ready or interesting to take it on.

But it was absolutely the opposite: I discovered a host of young actors, many of whom I felt were ready to do it and whom I would have cast. It was so encouraging to discover there was that level of passion and commitment to Shakespeare.

He cast all the younger parts with unknown actors in their twenties; his Ophelia, 19-year-old Samantha Whittaker, was still at university. Whishaw and the company found this liberating: 'In rehearsal there was no talk of how previous actors did it, no reference to past productions. We didn't have that baggage.' But after three weeks he was on the edge of nervous exhaustion, rehearsing all day and performing his first professional part in *His Dark Materials* at the National at night. He told Nunn he couldn't cope. 'Trevor was understanding, but he didn't indulge me,' he recalled. 'He forced me to use that feeling, because it fits incredibly well with what Hamlet is going through.'

Before the opening he was pessimistic: 'I'm not anybody, I'm not a name,' he said. 'No one's coming to see Ben Whishaw do Hamlet.' Then came the reviews, and suddenly he *was* a name. Charles Spencer was effusive: 'His is the kind of evening of which legends are made, one of those rare first nights that those who were present are never likely to forget ... Whishaw, with his light, tremulous voice and painfully thin body ... presents the most raw and vulnerable Hamlet I have ever seen.' Nicholas de Jongh praised his 'raw passion', stating that 'no Hamlet has made a more powerful or emotional impact'; Alastair Macaulay relished 'an electrifying performance'; while Alan Bird observed: 'Ben Whishaw is compelling to watch, enigmatic, intense, vulnerable, as well as engaging and charming.'

But some critics were less than enthusiastic. 'What this Hamlet lacks is irony, reflectiveness, and any sense that he poses a real physical danger to Claudius' was Michael Billington's view. Matt Wolf noted 'a very twenty-first-century, barely post-adolescent Hamlet, prone to indrawn, pouty sorrow and sudden bursts of rage', but felt that 'Whishaw is so busy exhibiting every possible emotional response that he pre-empts the possibility that the audience might have one of its own. And as if to prove the theatrical dictum that stage crying leaves the audience dry-eyed, this Hamlet, for all his exhibitionism, isn't remotely moving.'

Nunn's modern-dress production, with its champagne and tennis, Versace and rock'n'roll, secret-service agents and machine-guns, gained a mixed response. Philip Fisher found it 'gripping', while others praised Nunn's characteristic intelligence, assurance and attention to detail. However, Billington felt it had 'bags of energy, but lacks the polyphonic richness of his *Macbeth* and *Othello*', while Ian Johns wrote: 'This production is like Whishaw's performance, bursting with familial grief, but lacking the essential nobility to make it truly tragic.'

Jamie Ballard
Jonathan Miller

For Jonathan Miller's fourth production of the play, Jamie Ballard played Hamlet in 2008 at the Tobacco Factory in Bristol.

Cast: Claudius: Jay Villiers, Gertrude: Francesca Ryan, Polonius: Roland Oliver, Horatio: Philip Buck, Laertes: Oliver Lesueur, Ophelia: Annabel Scholey.

Jonathan Miller once said he'd love to assemble a Shakespeare ensemble in a cockpit, and do high-definition productions with virtually nothing but the actors and the words. His listener was Andrew Hilton, founder of the Tobacco Factory, where Miller staged the play in his almost ideal conditions.

In this 250-seat theatre-in-the-round, he mounted a production that contrasted strikingly with the more lavish, concept-driven *Hamlets* of recent years, and indeed with his own three earlier productions. The scenery was minimal, consisting of just three church pews; the grey, gold and black costumes were unfashionably Elizabethan; and the barely cut text ran to nearly four hours. The play, and the actors, were very much the thing, and won golden critical opinions.

John Peter declared it 'the best and most thrilling production of this great play I've seen in years ... Miller's production is based on a rigorous respect for the text, a masterful command of the narrative, and a profound understanding of character that is ruthlessly accurate, deeply moving, and entirely unsentimental.' It was, he added, 'a master at work'. Susannah Clapp described the production as 'robust, dynamic and bitingly clear: in the best tradition of the exemplary Tobacco Factory, it is intellectually high-vaulting and materially austere'.

Other critics agreed: Georgina Brown thought 'Shakespeare's play has rarely felt so urgent, so devastating', while Benedict Nightingale called it 'grippingly alive ... Miller proves happy to let Shakespeare's language and the audience's proximity to the actors do much of the work in engaging hearts and minds.' Dominic Cavendish was relieved that 'a strong directorial personality is never apparent ... Miller's *Hamlet* is modest, wise, reverential and studiously unflashy.' Only Rhoda Koenig dissented, arguing the production felt like 'an exemplary lesson in stagecraft rather than a vision of life unfolding. Caution is the keynote, rather than passion or ease.'

Miller's Hamlet, Jamie Ballard, was virtually unknown before assuming the role, though he had played Mercutio at Stratford. His youthful Prince, quick-witted, mercurial, a sardonic joker who even greeted his death with a smile, was the opposite of sweet. His notices were outstanding. 'He's an exceptional talent: the most moving, sexy and sensitive young Hamlet I've seen since Jonathan Pryce at the Royal Court in 1980,' was Brown's verdict.

Nightingale thought him 'intelligent, incisive, sentient and humorous, using parody gestures and comic voices when he's disorienting others with what here is a mocking and self-mocking pretence of madness'. Lyn Gardner found him 'often mesmerising', while Clapp admired 'his almost revolutionary sane Hamlet ... who debated with the adroitness and avidity of the philosophy student that he was'.

His Hamlet seemed genuinely in love with Annabel Scholey's Ophelia, whose performance several critics found particularly harrowing and affecting. 'Her mad scene is one of the most convincing ever staged,' Clapp wrote. 'It has no decorative daftness – the herbs she dispenses are twigs – but nor is it all grunts and grovels: she paws Claudius, rages, bursts into laughter, shies away alarmed when her brother approaches.' Gardner noted that 'she goes mad far less prettily than most Ophelias. Her sexual repression from being constantly under the watchful eye of her father turns to sexual hysteria as she repeatedly jabs a doll in a suggestive and disturbing way.'

Speaking before the play opened, Miller argued that Shakespearean language should always be delivered conversationally, not in affected, stentorian tones. The actors abided by his advice, Peter observing that 'the verse-speaking has a loving and intelligent precision, a true fusion of form and content'. Ballard's vocal work was praised, by Peter Kirwan among others: 'His wonderful delivery of "To be or not to be", making it sound like a genuine part of the character's mental process rather than a set-piece, epitomised the skill and dexterity with language that Ballard brought to the role.'

David Tennant

Greg Doran

In 2008 David Tennant played Hamlet in the Courtyard theatre in Stratford, directed by the Royal Shakespeare Company's chief associate director Greg Doran. The production later transferred to the Ivor Novello in London.

Cast: Claudius: Patrick Stewart, Gertrude: Penny Downie, Horatio: Peter de Jersey, Polonius: Oliver Ford Davies, Ophelia: Mariah Gale, Laertes: Edward Bennett.

Greg Doran recalls the moment he first talked to David Tennant about playing Hamlet. Tennant was appearing on the TV programme *Who Do You Think You Are?*, tracing his grandparents' roots. The trail led to an old church in Scotland, where he picked up a skull. Greg Doran was watching, and rang him the next morning. 'I told him I had seen his audition for Hamlet the previous night.'

This was the first time Doran had directed *Hamlet*. 'It's a play I had always admired but not necessarily enjoyed,' he says. 'Maybe it was because it was too familiar, and sometimes became "tick-box" Shakespeare, so you're checking that's how they're doing the Ghost, and so on.' He had seen Tennant on stage many times, and worked with him on a double-bill of *Black Comedy* and *The Real Inspector Hound*. 'He was very funny in that,' he recalled. 'Then at Stratford he played Touchstone, a character that's difficult to make funny from the lines, and he did so with fantastic dexterity. The following season he played Romeo. If you can play those two parts, you've got a Hamlet there.'

Tennant was aware of the immensity of his task.

It's a part I've always been fascinated by, as I think most actors are. It exists as a mountain to climb, as one of those Olympic events. For me it became particularly vivid when as a student I saw Mark Rylance's Hamlet in 1988 at the Glasgow Theatre Royal. I'd never seen Shakespeare played like that, I'd never seen Hamlet so modern and accessible, so vivid, so clear, so anarchic, the way he moved into that language. That was when I fell in love with the notion of playing the part.

When the time came he was prey to contrasting emotions: 'You're being asked to stand in a line of Hamlets, which is flattering and seductive and absolutely terrifying in equal measure. There is no greater baggage to come with a part, or a play. So clearing your mind of past productions is part of the journey, part of the process.' He had seen plenty of Hamlets, and read about the play. 'But I didn't specifically open up any of the great texts like Hazlitt or Granville Barker. I didn't want to be continually setting myself against what had gone before. But I read the play to make sure I understood every word; even a word you think you know might not have the meaning you thought it had.'

Unusually for such a lengthy part, he didn't learn his lines before rehearsals started.

In retrospect that was an act of cavalier lunacy. We had a six-week rehearsal period, so I thought I'll learn an act a week, leaving me a week at the end when I'd know it. It was pretty intensive. Now I look at it objectively I think it was partly fear: I was in denial about the whole process until it started, I thought, I'll deal with that when I get there. But it was also partly about nerves. It was really stupid not to learn the lines beforehand, but it did make it quite immediate. We'd rehearse a bit and then I'd learn it. And I was massively disciplined during rehearsals, with enormous chunks of text to learn every night. So I learnt an act a week, and by week 6 I was off the book. But I don't think I'd do it that way again.

Doran's rehearsal method was unconventional:

I started at the RSC as an actor, in productions where I didn't feel deeply invested in or committed to them; I felt I was just third spear-carrier on the left. So now I never do a read-through, because you either get people who know exactly what they are doing and show off, or people who mumble, or a lot of the company realise how small their parts are, and get depressed. So we share the play around the table. We do it scene by scene, and I ask each actor to put each line into their own words. Nobody is allowed to read their own part or comment on their character. So David couldn't speak his own lines for quite a long time. Sometimes there were intense disagreements. But if you welcome creative ideas, people will contribute when they've got something precise to say, rather than just suck up to the director.

Tennant liked this method, which continued for the first two weeks.

Rehearsals were about trying to discover the play anew, to shed your preconceptions and expectations. Greg's scheme works on many levels. It gets you involved in every corner of the play, because everyone is in the room the whole time. It can verge on the tedious, because there's a fastidiousness that you have to be loyal to, but it's hugely beneficial, it bonds the company, and everybody understands the play. Because you're denied your own part, being forced to listen to other opinions is useful, especially at that early stage, because it can help you avoid making pat choices. There is no hierarchy: the Third Player has the same right to debate as Hamlet. We did a final read-through in our own parts at the end of the second week, so by the time we stood on our feet we knew what we were talking about.

At Stratford Doran had access to the prompt copies from past productions there. 'I always do my own cut first, then look at what others have done. It's like having Terry Hands, Peter Hall and John Barton in the room, seeing their cuts, how they have re-located scenes or re-distributed characters.' One potentially controversial decision was to remove seven lines from 'To be or not to be', from 'Th' oppressor's wrong ...' to 'under a weary life', lines which he thought something of a parenthesis. 'It's much more direct if he doesn't go off on that particular tangent. And not a single critic or academic noticed!' He also moved the soliloquy from Act 3 to shortly after Hamlet has seen the Ghost, where he felt it flowed better.

Yorick's skull was a real one, bequeathed to the RSC in the 1980s by a fan of the company, the composer André Tchaikowsky. Doran recalled its impact in the rehearsal room:

On the first day I introduced everybody, then put on a purple pair of gloves, opened the box, took out the skull, and said: 'This is André, and he will be playing Yorick.' Amazingly, most people in the room hadn't seen a real skull. I passed it round and allowed them to hold it if they wanted to. Some people were repulsed by it, others stared at it for ages. When I asked our voice coach Cicely Berry, then aged 82, whether she wanted to hold it, she said: 'No darling, I'm much too close to that already!' We had it throughout rehearsals, but when it came to the dress-rehearsal it had disappeared. Fortunately the RSC Collection had a skull that Edmund Kean had used when he played Hamlet. So that night theatre history ricocheted throughout the building. By the opening the next night André's skull had returned.

A novel piece of research took Doran and Mariah Gale, playing Ophelia, to Tiddington, just upstream from Stratford, where according to court records in 1579 a girl called Katharine Hamlet was drowned, Shakespeare being 15 at the time. There they found trees and plants mentioned in Gertrude's description of Ophelia's death. Doran wrote at the time: 'It occurs to us that if Mariah were to try gathering the long purples, nettles, daisies, crow flowers, the rosemary, fennel, pansies and rue which she collects in her imagined funerary tribute for her dead father, then her skin would become muddy, scratched and red-raw with stings. Perhaps this is how to play the mad scene.' He also noted: 'We have agreed that each time we rehearse the mad scene, the other actors will not know what route to Ophelia's madness we are taking, what instigates it. What is sense to her must seem lunacy to them.'
Tennant speaks warmly of his relationship with Doran.

Greg just creates an atmosphere of openness, gentleness, play. He's also fantastically learned, clever and creative. Shakespeare is his *raison d'être*, and his knowledge of the texts and how those plays work is bottomless. And yet he wears that incredible knowledge so lightly. He's not straitjacketed by it, he really enjoys re-discovering the plays, being disrespectful to them, tinkering with them, moving things around. Nothing is sacrosanct, nothing is holy, but his respect and love for the works is wonderful. You just trust him instinctively, and that trust is endlessly re-paid.

Tennant relished this openness and Doran's desire to new-mint the play.

The thing about Hamlet is that he's so multi-faceted, it's unlike any other part. There is something magical about him, something alchemical about what Shakespeare discovered in writing the part. It's endlessly revealing and surprising. I tried to be as receptive to that as possible, as unburdened as I could be, and just let each scene happen. That's when it worked best for me. You're also trying to take off the layers of wallpaper and trying to find its connection to you, which is when you hope it will interest the audience.

Inevitably he found 'To be or not to be' a particular challenge:

It's impossible to ignore the Greatest Hits element. The first time you step out on to the stage to deliver it in front of an audience for the Royal Shakespeare Company at Stratford, you can't help but watch yourself from above. But it works well when you manage to banish that gremlin and just experience the argument. You have to just stare the devil in the eye, and get beyond the singalong nature of the speech, and towards something meaningful to Hamlet at that moment.

He approved of the bold seven-line cut: 'We were saying we don't care about the sacred nature of the text. And, sacrilegiously, I think it helps the sense.'

During a preview for the West End transfer he suffered a serious back injury which required surgery on a prolapsed disc; he was off for three-and-a-half weeks. 'I was in so much pain I eventually couldn't stand up. When I was told I was not going to be able to go on, it was devastating; and yet there was another part of me that said, Oh thank the fuck!' His understudy Edward Bennett, playing Laertes, took over, and was warmly praised. 'He did remarkably well. Hamlet is not a part where you want to go on with scant rehearsals for it. I have endless respect that he could do it at all, but also do it so well.'

He recalls vividly his return to the production during the final week at the Novello:

> The night I came back I was very emotional, because having been under the surgeon's knife, you suddenly become aware of mortality, in a way I don't think I had quite dealt with in the process of trying to get better as quickly as possible. Then you suddenly hit Hamlet, and the sense of what you've just been through. It wasn't a life or death situation, but it makes you feel a fallible human being.

He freely admits to ambivalence about playing Hamlet.

> I did find it extraordinarily stressful: the fact that you had to come back to it every night was kind of awful. I didn't enjoy myself during the run, I wanted it to be over. And yet I don't think there's anything I'm more glad that I've done, or been proud to have done. There's no other part that has been as ultimately satisfying. It was utterly compelling, but it was tough. You do find yourself going, I would like another go at it, and I have to remind myself that it was a kind of torture. Maybe it's a bit like childbirth: as soon as it's over you want to go back there.

With some qualifications, the critics praised his Hamlet. Michael Coveney wrote: 'He moves and speaks with the speed of light, a chameleon, a prankster, a misunderstood maverick. This is easily the most complete Hamlet of recent years, and one of the most enjoyable.' Benedict Nightingale observed: 'I've seen bolder Hamlets and more moving Hamlets, but few who kept me so riveted throughout.' For Michael Billington he was 'a Hamlet of quicksilver intelligence, mimetic vigour and wild humour ... an active, athletic, immensely engaging Hamlet. If there is any quality I miss, it is the character's philosophical nature.' Caroline McGinn also made this point: 'Some of the emotional depth and breadth of existential inquiry the role can sustain does get thinned out by Tennant's quicksilver performance. But this is a play-acting Prince whose critique of the world lives most vividly in his eyeball-swivelling, lanky-limbed parodies of the parasites around him.'

Doran's work was also admired. Billington saw 'a production that bursts with inventive detail ... a rich realisation of the greatest of poetic tragedies'; Coveney argued that '*Hamlet* should be exciting, and Gregory Doran's full-value production is exactly that ... A humdinger of a hit for the RSC.' But there was criticism of what Charles Spencer called 'a brutally cut production', with Billington stating: 'Unforgivably, Doran cuts the lines where Hamlet says to Horatio, "Since no man knows of aught he leaves, what is't to leave betimes? Let be." Thus Tennant loses some of the most beautiful lines in all literature about accepting one's fate.'

For Doran,

David was the funniest Hamlet I have seen. When Hamlet says he has of late lost all his mirth, David mined into that mirth. He was mercurial, sardonic, moving and angry, and he kept it all very fresh. It had that improvisatory quality – he spoke the lines as if he was thinking of them at that moment. He had the ability to think in the line, and yet keep Shakespeare's structure, and all the clues in the text. I thought it was a great performance.

Jude Law

Michael Grandage

In 2009, directed by Michael Grandage, Jude Law took on Hamlet, first at Wyndhams as part of the Donmar theatre's West End season, then at the Broadhurst on Broadway, with a visit to Elsinore in between.

Cast: Claudius: Kevin R. McNally, Gertrude: Penelope Wilton/Geraldine James, Ophelia: Gugu Mbatha-Raw, Polonius/First Gravedigger: Ron Cook, Horatio: Matt Ryan, Laertes: Alex Waldmann, Ghost/Player King: Peter Eyre.

Hamlet is a character who asks you to unearth yourself into him. He becomes an expression of who you are, forcing you to mine your sense of self in extreme emotional circumstances, and then to apply it. The part is so broad it draws on many qualities of the actor playing him.

Unlike many actors, the young Jude Law had no burning ambition to play Hamlet. Before 2009 he had never taken a Shakespearean role on the professional stage, and at 36, and an international star on screen, he had been away from the theatre for seven years. But then Kenneth Branagh asked him to play the Prince under his direction. 'It felt like the right time,' he says. 'I didn't want to be a Hamlet who was too old to be a student. I also thought you should be young enough to have a mother still sexually active. So I was ready. Of course there were moments of fear, but that can be a good thing: it propels you to work harder.'

Because of a film commitment, Branagh asked Michael Grandage, then running the Donmar, to take over as director, before other actors were cast. Experienced and much-admired for his work, Grandage had not previously directed *Hamlet*. 'Although I had once talked briefly about it to Michael Sheen, I didn't have a *Hamlet* planned, although I had seen lots of productions. But I was thrown at it at such speed, I didn't want to do too much looking over my shoulder at past Hamlets.'

Law's preparation for the role was impressive.

I examined different theories, and gained a sense of Hamlet's place in theatrical history. I read memoirs of great actors who had played the part, Gielgud's in particular. Certain works raised useful questions in my mind. I found out what was going on in England when Shakespeare wrote the play, what was inspiring him to write such a revolutionary work. I read *1599* by James Shapiro, and Arthur McGee's *The Elizabethan Hamlet*, which looked at the effects of the play on an Elizabethan audience. I examined texts which Shakespeare might have been reading, such as Montaigne's *Essays*, which are incredibly similar to the soliloquies. All this planted interesting seeds in my mind.

He undertook a great deal of practical work before rehearsals began. He benefitted from training with voice coach Barbara Houseman, and took singing lessons 'to get my vocal equipment up to scratch'. On Branagh's advice he marked out in advance the fight with Laertes. He also learned all the soliloquies, and spent a week alone with Grandage examining them in detail. The director recalls: 'Rather than telling Jude what I thought about the soliloquies, I just asked him to read them, and then we worked out the meaning together, word by word, line by line, checking that we were in agreement.' Law found this extremely helpful:

The soliloquies are like pillars that hold the piece up, wonderful touchstones of Hamlet's psychological journey, and where he's got to at each moment. These sessions were precious. Michael is fantastically skilled at approaching a Shakespeare text afresh, rather than muddying it with theory and concept, or filling it with his personal take on it; he lets the language and the great drama speak for itself.

Grandage had seen Law's previous theatre work – as the foundling son of Apollo in Euripides' *Ion*, and in the title-role in Marlowe's *Doctor Faustus* – and was convinced he had the skills to succeed as Hamlet. 'It became very evident straight away in rehearsals that he was very physical, which was key. He wasn't going to be the standard Prince, romantic, introspective and melancholic. He uses his body to tell the story, so he inhabited the soliloquies physically as well as verbally, finding Hamlet's inner life through his exterior life.'

Law was happy with this physical approach:

It just came very naturally, the language was so expressive and powerful. Putting on the antic disposition enables Hamlet to express physically his inner frustrations, turmoil and fury at being emasculated and disempowered because the role of king was in his uncle's hands. It gives him an opportunity to speak the truth, just as often in a court the only person who can do so is the fool, as in *King Lear*. In my opinion Hamlet is never actually mad; the closest he comes to madness is hysteria. Shakespeare had Ophelia to show what real madness was. Hamlet assumes it and is able to snap out of it, whereas Ophelia is lost and takes her own life.

In Grandage's view, 'the closet scene was where Jude was at his most extreme in anxiety and fury. We pushed him being driven to distraction, but he never went mad. Once you present madness you're inviting the audience not to consider his actions, because he's mad.'

Law saw the closet scene as challenging, but no more so than the other famous ones.

I was fortunate enough to play opposite two brilliant Gertrudes in Penelope Wilton and, in America, Geraldine James. Once you've unpicked and unearthed an Elsinore that makes sense to you as a company, you're given wonderful dialogue to play with. How Hamlet handles finding a Gertrude who was having a very happy marriage with this new guy was for me a great way in to that scene. But there's no indication in the text that he wanted to sleep with Gertrude.

One question that often comes up when actors are investigating their back story is the nature of Hamlet's past feelings for Ophelia, and whether they had slept together. On the latter point there was no consensus. When Grandage asked Law and Gugu Mbatha-Raw their views, one said no and the other yes, 'but no one can remember who said which. But that didn't matter: the text supports the fact that they had feelings for each other, and that was easy to explore. Jude expressed beautifully Hamlet's feeling of rejection.'

Law acknowledged the value of past performances.

Of course you're being inspired by the people you've seen in the part. When I was growing up it was Daniel Day-Lewis, Mark Rylance, Stephen Dillane, Adrian Lester. But you hope to bring yourself to it, that's what you're there to do, especially in a part like Hamlet, where you have to be present and honest and rooted in your own emotional network. To fall back and rely on another performance would be foolhardy.

This was Grandage's only modern-dress Shakespeare production to date.

I knew straight away I wouldn't be going for ruffs or a piece of history to look at, but a dynamic and modern production. I wanted to use Jude's extraordinary ability to communicate with a young audience. I asked my designer Christopher Oram to come up with a palette of greys and blacks and silvers, which was echoed in the colours of the costumes. It was a set full of dark corners, where there was nothing standing in the way of the actors and the audience. I wanted it to be a neutral, monumental space, because Hamlet seems to be permanently lost within the walls of this world.

On one of the evenings, the sponsors United House paid for the theatre to be filled with young people from schools in disadvantaged areas, most of whom had not been to the theatre before. 'They were the best house we ever played,' Grandage recalls. 'They were silent and rapt for the most part, laughing at the jokes, and standing and cheering at the end.' Law remembers that performance vividly: 'It was like a thriller to them. They were shouting out in shock towards the end, as Gertrude drank the wine, and Hamlet was nicked by the blade. It was as if it was the first night of *Hamlet* in Elizabethan London, where the audience was vocal and emotional and shocked. It was unforgettable.'

In between playing London and New York the company performed the play in the open-air courtyard in Elsinore castle, with the current Prince of Denmark sitting in the front row on the first night. According to Grandage: 'The audience knew every single beat backwards, so it was a very still and beautifully focused occasion.' Law remembers: 'We had very little set, but that was compensated for by the turrets and rooftops, and rooms overlooking the courtyard referenced in the play. The wind whipping off the water and round the courtyard added a chill to the night. It was magical, a very moving, even spiritual experience.'

In New York Law felt no need to adapt his performance for an American audience. 'With Hamlet you're relating to the audience in an intense and prolonged way, you are nightly feeling the shifts and changes, whether they are listening, whether they warm to you, whether they are picking up on the humour, your agitation or whatever it might be. That didn't noticeably change whether it was a Broadway, Elsinore or London audience.' In

Grandage's opinion, 'Jude is so finely tuned to the nuance of an audience, he can play and riff with them as he goes.'

Law gave 150 performances over a six-month period, without missing one. The production was a sell-out on both sides of the Atlantic; the reviews were mixed, though mostly very positive. In the UK Charles Spencer wrote: 'Law joins the modern pantheon of spellbinding sweet princes with a performance of rare vulnerability and emotional openness ... There is no mistaking the intelligence of his mind or the nobility of his heart as he confides in the audience in soliloquies that allow us to follow every fleeting thought, every quicksilver change of mood.' Benedict Nightingale decided 'his verse-speaking is immaculate and his charisma comes powering out'; Henry Hitchings thought his performance 'detailed and powerful ... He brings a rumpled charisma to the role.' Ben Dowell observed 'a raw, urgent power that most of his acting contemporaries would find hard to match'. But Maxwell Cooter complained that 'there's little of the philosopher prince contemplating life's bigger questions, or of the hesitancy of a man weighing up a host of options'. Michael Billington also had reservations, confessing: 'I missed the quicksilver humour that is part of Hamlet's character'; but he thought 'Law's Hamlet has the right inwardness and self-awareness'.

In America the influential critic Ben Brantley suggested: 'Mr Law's undeniable charisma and gender-crossing sex appeal may captivate Broadway theatergoers who wouldn't normally attend productions of Shakespeare', but thought him over-robust: 'He approaches his role with the focus, determination and adrenalin level of an Olympic track competitor staring down an endless line of hurdles.' John Lahr saw a Hamlet 'swift of foot and speech, with a sharp critical intelligence', but argued that it was 'impossible to conceive of him as "pigeon-liver'd" or lacking in "gall". He has a solidity that Hamlet does not.'

Law has recently been discussing the possibility of returning to Hamlet. 'If you have an affinity with a part, why not go and re-investigate it?' he says.

I am very tempted to try it again; I would certainly be open to it. Who wouldn't be? You get to speak possibly the most beautiful lines about humankind ever given to an actor, and ask the biggest philosophical questions. Every night is an introspection and journey into your heart, your soul, your spirit, and you leave feeling inspired by it.

Jude Law was nominated for Best Actor at the Olivier awards in London and the Tony awards in New York.

8

The 2010s

Rory Kinnear
Nicholas Hytner

Rory Kinnear's 2010 performance as Hamlet at the National Theatre was staged by the theatre's director, Nicholas Hytner, first in the Olivier then the Lyttelton. The production also toured the UK, and visited Luxembourg.

Cast: Claudius: Patrick Malahide, Gertrude: Clare Higgins, Ophelia: Ruth Negga, Laertes: Alex Lanipekun, Polonius: David Calder, Horatio: Giles Terera.

Rory Kinnear was already familiar with *Hamlet*. He had studied it for A level and for an English degree at Oxford. In 2004 he had played Laertes opposite Ben Whishaw's Hamlet and had gained excellent reviews. 'But it hadn't actually been my ambition to play Hamlet,' he said. 'I hadn't necessarily seen myself as that kind of actor, whatever Hamlet is supposed to be. It was Nick Hytner whose imagination led to it.'

Hytner, then running the National Theatre, admired Kinnear's 'considerable, quirky intellect'. Having directed him as Sir Fopling Flutter in George Etherege's Restoration comedy *The Man of Mode*, he had noticed how, beneath the character's preening comic absurdity, Kinnear had suggested his insecurity and loneliness. 'I realised I'd found an actor whose intellect measured up to Hamlet's, without whom I would never have dreamed of doing the play.'

It was another three years before Kinnear played the Prince. Initially he worked on the character by himself. Later, still a year before rehearsals, he discussed Gertrude and Hamlet's relationship with Clare Higgins, already cast as his mother. Then he, Higgins and Hytner, together with the designer Vicki Mortimer and the academic Peter Holland, spent an intensive week in the National's Studio. 'We read an act a day,' Kinnear remembered. 'We made preliminary cuts – cutting anything we thought wouldn't be understandable – and discussed ideas.' Hytner, directing his first *Hamlet*, recalled: 'It was tremendous, but we committed to nothing. A play only comes into focus when the actors are on their feet, doing it.'

This reflected a basic tenet of his philosophy, that

> plays are only dimly detectable until they are performed. The actor reveals the play, for which the text is only the starting point. The experience of the play in the theatre is not by definition superior to the experience of the play in the study, but it is very different, and the element that is brought to it by the embodiment of the actors totally changes the experience.

This chimed in with Kinnear's thoughts about studying Hamlet as a student and working on the part as an actor. 'Acting requires a different skill set from academia. It was refreshing to be free from considering the various themes, and the refractions of those themes. Rather, you just think about how a certain character reacts to certain situations, then focus on what that character says at any particular time.'

As rehearsals began he confessed he had avoided seeing David Tennant's and Jude Law's recent Hamlets, 'because if they'd had a good idea that I'd had as well, it sort of halves it. You'd be playing the moment hand-in-hand with another actor.' Soon afterwards he observed: 'I find there are two ghosts that haunt the rehearsal room: of performances one has seen, and of imagined productions. There seems to be a received sense of how any particular scene goes in *Hamlet*.' His sense was that 'a certain degree of train track lies ahead of you, and sometimes unthinkingly you can follow that path. When I feel myself echoing other things, I've thought: Do you actually mean that, or are you just doing it because that's what you think Hamlet does? It's through such self-scrutiny that you find yourself shaping the part into a way of your own choosing.' He had tried during rehearsals 'to recognise when I'm hurtling down those tracks, and to make sure what I'm doing correlates with what this Hamlet is, in this world'.

Hytner had provided him with a very modern, post-Soviet world:

> I wanted to create one that would be immediately and viscerally recognisable as a world where you put your life in danger by saying the wrong thing. At Elsinore you can't unfold yourself without risking your life. Everything is observed, everything is suspect, no social gesture is trustworthy ... Hamlet is paralysed as much by the barrier the state puts in the way of anyone knowing anyone else, as he is by his desperate search to know what's going on inside himself.

His production strongly reflected this concept. The palace was awash with CCTV cameras and dark-suited, armed security guards sporting ear-pieces, with microphones concealed by their cuffs. Polonius showed Ophelia CCTV images of her and Hamlet together. Ophelia carried a bugged Bible to allow Claudius and Polonius to eavesdrop on her and Hamlet. Hamlet was never alone, and yet he was completely isolated. Hytner argued that such an invasive atmosphere reflected both today's society and Shakespeare's, a mirror of both then and now: '*Hamlet* was certainly conceived as a contemporary state-of-the-nation play about Elizabethan England: a surveillance state, a totalitarian monarchy with a highly developed spy network. That's how Elizabeth exerted power. Shakespeare's audience knew exactly what the play was talking about.'

In rehearsal one concern was to bring out aspects of Hamlet's character before the play began, for which Shakespeare provides little evidence. Kinnear explained: 'I tried to hold on to the Hamlet whom everybody thought was so commendable, as in Ophelia's description of him. We don't get many opportunities to show that "noble mind" before it has been overthrown. Audiences don't get to see the Hamlet people have loved before. So we tried to get in the happy Hamlet, the lighter relationship.'

In his discussions with Higgins they had rejected a Freudian interpretation of their relationship in the closet scene. Partly this arose from his private study of the text. 'I noticed how dense the language is; it's quite often played in a flurry of pushing and pulling, but you never get the language. Freud gets in the way of the language.' Despite this realisation, their first attempt in rehearsal ended up in just 'a noisy blur of diffuse emotion … The scene went for nothing. It will be much more powerful when he's really trying to talk to his mother.'

They also explored an idea which Higgins had raised in the Studio, whether Gertrude really did not see the Ghost in the closet scene, when others – Horatio, the sentries – had seen him quite clearly. It was eventually decided she *did* see him, but pretended not to, probably because of her guilt in knowing of Claudius' murder of her husband, if not having been complicit in it. But then was she also lying when she described Ophelia's suicide? Was she really there by the river, and yet never tried to save her? Or was this simply a cover story for Claudius having her removed and murdered because of the threat to the state she could pose in her madness? (This idea carried through to the performance.) Discovering later that the lie about seeing the Ghost was not a totally original idea, Hytner commented: 'There are few ideas about Shakespeare that someone hasn't already had. Nothing is new, the plays have been done for four centuries. But it's always worth having the ideas again, as there is nothing more vivid on stage than a scene played with the conviction that comes from its participants' own sense of discovery.'

He pointed out that his

most mind-expanding thoughts into Shakespeare have come from actors in the rehearsal room, without the long preamble with which directors usually preface even the most banal of suggestions. As a tribe, we can barely ask an actor to move to the left without writing an essay about it. And what you don't want to do is stop a rehearsal and pick to pieces an instinctive discovery.

An unusual, actor-inspired touch came during one rehearsal when, in Polonius' speech offering advice to Laertes, David Calder flinched, then seemed to dry before speaking the line, 'This above all: to thine own self be true'. Hytner was electrified by this pause, and noted: 'Suddenly we knew that Polonius had helped Claudius assassinate the old king, and was tortured by his own treachery.'

Rehearsals also involved an examination of Hamlet's relationship with the Ghost. Tradition has it that he adored his father, but as Hytner pointed out, 'the Ghost utters not one affectionate word towards his son'. There seems to be no recognisable bond between the old brutal warrior king and the graduate student from Wittenberg. 'They have little in common: it is the gulf between them that consumes Hamlet, and one of the things that makes it impossible for him to take immediate action in response to the Ghost's demands for revenge.' As it happened Kinnear's father, the actor Roy Kinnear, had died when he was ten, prompting the question whether this added depth to his exploration of the part. 'It does seem an obvious leap to make,' Kinnear said. 'But I can honestly say it didn't really ever come into my mind in rehearsal.'

On handling the soliloquies, Kinnear explained:

> They are known as poetry. But in playing them you notice how much they are part of the drama. I try to make them come out of what has gone before ... If you approach them as though you know what's about to be said, and you present them as though Hamlet had just had a thought and now he's going to explain it, then it's just not as dramatically interesting as having those thoughts in the moment ... If you work out your thoughts as you go along they cease to seem like set pieces, and retain their original impromptu quality.

After several weeks of speaking them to a white wall, seven feet away in the rehearsal room, he discovered to his surprise that it was only when he played them in the theatre that Hamlet truly discovered himself. 'To actually lead an audience of eleven hundred people through them and be open-hearted about how you share them is incredibly moving ... Hamlet's openness to the audience provides an important contrast to the artifice he uses with those around him. The soliloquies are supposed to be one-person events, but in my experience they can be the most collaborative moments in the play.'

Although aged 32, Kinnear was very much a student-style Hamlet, appearing in a hoodie and trainers, posting graffiti on the palace walls, smoking a cigarette during 'To be or not to be', taking refuge in a messy bedsit full of scattered clothes and empty wine-glasses, and squatting in a trunk reading Montaigne's *Essays*. Yet though he was bursting with energy and quick movement, he was no adolescent, but a penetratingly intelligent Hamlet, giving a performance that attracted uniformly fine reviews.

Susannah Clapp saw 'a caustic, exact, gimlet-sharp Prince', concluding 'Rory Kinnear has confirmed his place in the front rank of British actors'. Henry Hitchings thought him 'stunning ... a captivating presence', and Michael Billington wrote: 'What Kinnear portrays marvellously is a deeply rational intellectual seeking to cope with a world that makes increasingly less sense.' Charles Spencer observed: 'You can follow every shade of thought and flicker of emotion in the soliloquies, which are delivered with a beautiful mixture of intellect and feeling ... I would put him right up there with David Tennant when it comes to capturing the humanity, humour, pain and multi-layered complexity of the role.'

Hytner's production received many plaudits. Libby Purves admired its 'clarity, relevance, courage, detail'; Kate Bassett described it as 'cleverly innovative ... gripping and full of sharp insights'; Billington praised its 'revelatory detail ... Kinnear's fine Hamlet gains enormously from Elsinore itself having such a hugely living presence'. Susannah Clapp's opinion was more mixed: 'The production has so much tumbling through it that it goes in and out of focus, combining the ingenious with the idiotic, the thrilling with the flashy.'

Later Kinnear spoke of the isolation felt by actors paying Hamlet.

I was sceptical of the National's 'brotherhood of Hamlets' beforehand. But it only took one preview to show me what was meant. It is an unbelievably lonely role to perform. Onstage you are pathologically wary of everyone; offstage you are too knackered to socialise. So the togetherness of those that have played the role is obvious. It's like a supportive cuddle: 'I know it feels like no one's noticed, but I know what you went through'.

When questioned about his Hamlet's apparent lack of nobility, Hytner responded eloquently:

There is magnificence in Hamlet, but it is less in his position in court as in his mind. There is heroism in the way he thinks about himself and his place in the world. There is elation in his experience of his brutal honesty with himself, grandeur in his direct communion with the audience, and nobility in his determination never to say 'Love me', but 'Understand me'.

Of Kinnear, he concluded: 'No actor is more open to contradiction than Rory, or more capable of the wild mood-swings that are a function of Hamlet's infirmity. Like the best Shakespeareans, he subsumed himself into the role, and allowed himself to be surprised by what happened to him. I thought he was absolutely wonderful; I couldn't imagine Hamlet being played better.'

Rory Kinnear was voted Best Actor at the Evening Standard *Awards.*

Michael Sheen

Ian Rickson

Directed by Ian Rickson, Michael Sheen played Hamlet at the Young Vic in 2011.

Cast: Claudius: James Clyde, Gertrude: Sally Dexter, Horatio: Hayley Carmichael, Ophelia: Vinette Robinson, Polonius: Michael Gould, Laertes: Benedict Wong.

'I wanted to make *Hamlet* difficult and jagged again, unsettling and uncomfortable and disorientating.' This was Michael Sheen's aim, after having approached Ian Rickson to direct him as the Prince. The result fulfilled his desire, but while his Hamlet was much praised, the controversial production divided the critics.

Sheen had chalked up an impressive range of stage performances in the 1990s, including Romeo and Henry V, the latter, for the Royal Shakespeare Company, bringing him an Ian Charleson Award. He had also played Hamlet in a BBC radio version. Now 42, he stated: 'The opportunity to tell this story has come up from time to time, but it never felt right. Working with someone as inspiring and supportive as Ian, in a space full of possibility like the Young Vic, on a play that speaks to me now more than ever, made me feel this was the right time.' Rickson, making his Shakespearean debut, underlined why he accepted Sheen's suggestion. 'I had worked with him a little, and I adored his intensity, his intelligence, and his extraordinary emotional mobility. He's such a rebarbative, powerful presence. And he runs with the ball: if you give him an idea, he comes back with four.'

Rickson set the play in what appeared to be a secure psychiatric hospital. Or was it a prison? Or all a dream of Hamlet's, a disturbed mental patient? He felt the audience should make up their own minds about this question, which he deliberately left ambiguous. 'I didn't want to make it easy for them; they could take it or leave it,' he said. 'I wanted to create a world which was somehow a metaphor for Hamlet's internal state, a kind of purgatorial place where something is trapped.' To firmly engage the audience with his idea, they were encouraged to enter the theatre through dingy, backstage institutional corridors, past rooms with signs marked Secure Rooms, Chapel and Therapy. Once in the auditorium they found the stage full of chairs arranged in encounter-group style.

Rickson saw the centre of *Hamlet* as being 'the madness of blocked grief, and a really deep examination of what can happen when that grief and loss cannot be processed'. He and the actors had explored this notion in rehearsals: 'We worked on the text in all sorts of ways. We had psychoanalysts come in, and the actors role-played their characters. I enrolled as Doctor Arden, and made them do psychological exercises, including painting their life.' His influences were Jung, the critic Harold Bloom, the psychiatrist R.D. Laing, *One Flew Over the Cuckoo's Nest*, and the science-fiction writer Philip K. Dick, a favourite of Sheen.

In this hospital-style Elsinore there was a glassed observation room at the back of the stage, large security gates that keep clanging shut, and flashing red alarm-lights punctuating the action. The characters were seemingly transformed into doctors and patients. So an unusually genial Claudius was not just the king of Denmark, but the head doctor overseeing the hospital and taking charge of a group-therapy session; his second-in-command Polonius, armed with a dictaphone, became a fussy, note-taking clinician; while Ophelia was portrayed as a deeply damaged woman, distributing pills instead of flowers.

This bold, subversive concept was dismissed by some of the more established critics. Charles Spencer called it 'mindlessly modish', attacking Rickson for being 'so implacably and egotistically intent on twisting the play to his own dubious ends' with a production 'that seems determined to obfuscate rather than illuminate this demanding drama'. Quentin Letts wrote that the concept 'clumsily upstages both his star actor and that man who wrote the play', while for Michael Billington, 'the acid test of any concept is whether it liberates the play, and for me this doesn't. It may be intellectually ingenious, but its practical effect is to present the action through the prism of Hamlet's personal anxiety'.

Libby Purves disagreed: 'It could all be a tiresome directorial conceit, but the brilliant and horrible thing is that it fits. You realise how much this text oozes disturbance: timings out of joint, weariness of life, unbeing, delusion, paranoia, remorse.' Sam Marlowe thought it a 'thrilling' production: 'Electrifyingly, Rickson approaches the text without careful reverence, but with the energy and inventive flair he has habitually brought to new plays. It is a distinctly personal, rather than a political, reading, its focus sharply upon the psychological. The result is ... an arresting immediacy.'

In Sheen's view, '*Hamlet* is one of the most dangerous things ever set down on paper. All the big, unknowable questions like what it is to be a human being; the difference between sanity and insanity; the meaning of life and death; what's real and not real. All these subjects can literally drive you mad.' Yet one problem with his suggested madness as a disturbed mental patient was that his lucid soliloquies demonstrated quite clearly a mind not 'o'erthrown'.

His performance was widely praised. According to Henry Hitchings: 'Sheen magnetises attention. Whenever he is on stage he is a vortex of soulfulness. Dynamic in the soliloquies, he is adept at switching between elfin charm, puzzled remoteness, energetic derangement and blistering rage.' Paul Taylor thought his qualities suited the role: 'Nervily ruffling his mop of corkscrew curls, spasms of ecstatic elation and stricken self-doubt chasing each other over those big-eyed elfin features, Sheen has just the right electrically dangerous, mocking intelligence for the part.' Spencer also approved: 'Though often wild and edgy, this charismatic actor delivers the soliloquies with clarity and depth of feeling. He also reveals a winning wit, and sudden aching moments of tenderness.' But Matt Trueman was unhappy with his delivery of the text: 'The cast – and Sheen is the worst offender – mostly speak the text as if it was written in size 14 font ... It bloats the text and, in aiming for absolute clarity, it becomes almost unfollowable.'

Michael Sheen was nominated for Best Actor in the Evening Standard *Awards.*

Jonathan Slinger
David Farr

David Farr directed Jonathan Slinger as Hamlet at Stratford in 2013.

Cast: Claudius/Ghost: Greg Hicks, Gertrude: Charlotte Cornwell, Horatio: Alex Waldmann, Polonius: Robin Soans, Laertes: Luke Norris, Ophelia: Pippa Nixon.

On his first entrance, dressed in a suit and tie and wearing glasses, Jonathan Slinger wandered on to the stage, sobbing as he mourned the death of his father. To get inside Hamlet's state of mind at this moment he deliberately put himself in a dark space. 'I stand for ten minutes backstage, thinking the most awful things to get into the mindset of somebody who is grieving – imagining my parents dying, imagining being by my parents' bedside and things I would say to them to get me into that space. Once I'm there, it's true what they say, the part does play you. Which of course raises the question, Who am I?'

Before the opening his ambitious aim was to create a Hamlet that embraced all the character's many, often contradictory qualities.

> I'm going to try to achieve what people say is impossible. I want to make him a psychologically understandable Hamlet. I honestly think that's what Shakespeare wrote: a very complex person ... It is human nature to be contradictory: we are one thing and the opposite at the same time. Shakespeare understood that better than anybody. If you're only ever showing one side to a character, you're not doing the part justice.

Less known to the wider public than some recent Hamlets, Slinger was much admired within the profession. An experienced member of the Royal Shakespeare Company, he had already played many leading Shakespearean parts that demonstrated his versatility, including a drag-queen Richard II, Richard III, Macbeth, a malicious Puck, Prospero,

Malvolio, and Parolles in *All's Well That Ends Well*, which was playing in repertory with *Hamlet*.

Despite having to learn more than 1,500 lines as Hamlet, he found the task one of the easiest.

> The hardest part is learning and developing and trying to understand all the things to do with your character – what he is thinking, how he speaks, how he moves, what his relationship is with the other characters – all the forensic minutiae and detail of making up your character. With good writing, of which Shakespeare is, of course, the best – he writes thoughts so beautifully, there isn't a thought out of place – the lines are relatively easy to go in, once you know *why* you're saying what you're saying.

He had firm ideas about Hamlet's relationship with Ophelia, believing he truly loved her once. As Pippa Nixon, playing Ophelia, remembered: 'Jonathan thought Ophelia and Hamlet had had the most passionate love affair. So that's where we started from, two people completely in love with each other who, if the circumstances of the play didn't divide them, would have wanted to run away and spend the rest of their lives together.'

Director David Farr set his production in a fencing hall, with a stage at one end. 'As a director, I start with the visual,' he explained. 'I read the play and then a world comes into my head. That world must honour the play, enhance it, and maybe shine some new light on it ... I originally thought about doing it in the Renaissance period, and then this old fencing hall suddenly came to mind.'

Farr believed that Slinger 'brought wonderful emotional honesty to the part'. His Hamlet pleased several critics. 'He finds humour in the least expected places and is immensely touching in others,' Neil Norman wrote. Natasha Tripney thought him 'a joy to watch, his performance as unpredictable and strangely shaped and textured as it is emotionally engaging', while Fiona Mountford admired 'a constantly intelligent reading; his performance gains in depth as the action progresses'. Michael Billington described him as 'a riveting protagonist ... As always, Slinger is compelling to watch: he mines every phrase, utters heart-wrenching cries of desolate grief.'

Paul Taylor on the other hand found his performance initially 'grating to a degree', criticising especially his 'oh-so-slow delivery of the earlier soliloquies, where you could drive a bus through the pauses'. Charles Spencer thought 'the defining notes of Jonathan Slinger's Hamlet are relentless anger and withering sarcasm, a reductive view of the character that becomes decidedly wearing ... There is too much fury (despite his own advice to the Players, this Hamlet constantly "tears a passion to tatters"), too many ironic funny voices, and too much business.'

Halfway through the run Slinger reflected on his progress as an actor. 'I'm nowhere near as good as I want to be,' he said. 'I think acting is like any kind of craft, like painting or making pottery ... I don't think there's ever an end point where you go, right, I know how to do it now. You keep adding to it, you keep refining it, you keep stripping away to something pure.' Anticipating the end of the run, he admitted that 'the fact that there's going to come a point when I can't do this any more makes me very sad ... I've never experienced that in my life.'

Maxine Peake

Sarah Frankcom

In 2014 Maxine Peake played Hamlet at the Royal Exchange Theatre in Manchester, in a production staged by the theatre's artistic director Sarah Frankcom.

Cast: Claudius: John Shrapnel, Gertrude: Barbara Marten, Polonia: Gillian Bevan, Ophelia: Katie West, Laertes: Asheley Zhangazha, Horatio: Thomas Arnold.

> We didn't go in to it with some feminist agenda. It wasn't a question of putting two fingers up to everybody. It was just what we felt creatively was the next step.

Taking on Hamlet was not a sudden whim on the part of Maxine Peake. 'I've often wanted to play a male part,' she says. 'I read things and I think, Why couldn't I play that? I'm a woman, but I think I understand the male psyche. And there's something about the athleticism of male parts: you don't get that very much in female parts, which I find really annoying.'

Despite the strong tradition in the past of actresses playing Hamlet – Sarah Siddons took it on in Manchester in 1777 – Peake's Hamlet was the first for a British actress since Frances de la Tour's in 1979 (see page 43). Director Sarah Frankcom observed: 'Where is the female equivalent of Hamlet? It doesn't exist, there's nothing of similar size or challenge in Shakespeare, which is why we decided to tackle it ourselves.' The announcement created great excitement in Manchester and beyond: the run almost sold out before rehearsals began, with queues around the block to see the much-loved local actress take up the challenge.

Peake recalls:

> I never had a huge desire to play Hamlet. I played Ophelia when Christopher Eccleston played him in 2002. I don't think I was particularly successful. I remember not feeling any envy of Chris, wishing that was me. But as time went on I thought, Why not?

She and Frankcom had originally discussed the possibility of Shaw's *Saint Joan*, but the idea was dropped when they heard Anne-Marie Duff was to play the part at the National Theatre.

I wanted to play a physical and strong part, but there aren't many female warrior roles. Then Hamlet came up. I thought he had a kind of warrior element, like Saint Joan. It was an exciting prospect. But I didn't have any particular conception of how I would play him. That's how I work: I go in and find things out in the rehearsal room.

Frankcom, making her debut as a Shakespeare director, opted for several bold and unexpected casting decisions, turning five male parts into female ones. She converted Polonius into Polonia, turned the Player King into a Player Queen, cast a female Guildenstern, and had both gravediggers played by actresses. There was even some discussion about casting a man as Ophelia, but this was soon abandoned.

She points out that Shakespeare's source material for the play was gender-complex. 'He drew the story from an old Danish legend, where Prince Hamlet was actually the tale of a girl princess dressed as a boy.' With 155 female characters compared to 826 male ones in the Shakespeare canon, she saw this as part of a push for more female roles in the theatre. 'As a female director I feel it's pretty important to have equality of the gender make-up of the world you are putting on the stage. Prescribed notions of gender – what is female, what is male – are all in flux at the moment. There is now a generation of women who are not going to put up with the situation any more.'

Having worked with Peake on several productions in the round at the Royal Exchange, Frankcom was convinced she had the necessary skills to play Hamlet. 'She is a mercurial actress, who transforms herself for every role she takes on,' she says. 'She's compassionate and very generous emotionally; audiences can access her, she has an openness and a warmth and a vulnerability that makes people want to go with her.' Peake's success in Shelley's *The Masque of Anarchy* for the 2013 Manchester International Festival reinforced her opinion about her suitability. 'I was struck by how magnetic she was, communicating with two thousand people. And I could see how she could make Hamlet's soliloquies work.'

Initially she wanted Hamlet played as a woman, but Peake became uncomfortable with the idea. Frankcom recalls:

One rehearsal was quite volcanic. It became clear that so many of the pronouns and the mother/father/son business were having a massive effect on Maxine. At the end of the rehearsal she said, I don't think I am a woman. I might have a female body, but I don't think I want to be a woman. I might want to be male, but I'm confused.

Peake remembers that feeling:

Maybe if I'd been a true feminist I'd have played it as a woman. But I kept saying, this speaks to me like a trans, a woman who feels inherently male.

So we started to do a lot of research into transsexual people – both of us have got quite a few trans friends. In the end it felt right to play him like that: a man trapped in a female body. I felt it was a way of accessing bits of me as an actress that I've not been able to access before. I don't always feel female. At RADA I was a bit of a tomboy, and they said I needed to be more feminine. That's so wrong: being boisterous doesn't mean you're not feminine.

In preparing for the part she decided at first not to examine past productions. 'But it's such a marathon of a part, I did eventually do that. I saw Branagh's film, I looked at Derek Jacobi's performance on DVD, I had a look round, just to help with the text, to see how somebody else made sense of it; from that you find your own sense. And sometimes you can watch them and think, that's how I am *not* going to do it.' She found a screened interview with Rory Kinnear especially helpful. 'He said he learnt the soliloquies before starting rehearsals, but didn't learn the whole play until he interacted with the other actors. It was the same with me. It's between you and the other characters, and you don't know how you are going to respond until you get to work with them.'

She and Frankcom spent a week discussing the soliloquies before the rest of the cast started rehearsing. 'We also did a lot of mapping out of Hamlet's back story, what his student life was like, what he was studying at Wittenberg. Sarah has a real gift for understanding the human psyche. She goes one step further than most directors I've worked with in understanding what makes people tick.' In the proper rehearsals she and the company also worked with movement director Imogen Knight. 'It short cut some of the psychological and subconscious work. It can be a very speedy way of building up an emotional journey.'

Frankcom remembers her approach in rehearsal: 'Maxine is a fearless actor. She's at her best when the brakes are off, and you never quite know what she's going to do next. She never does anything in an obvious way. She often works on contradictions, on the exact opposite to what you suggest. It makes for a very bouncy rehearsal room.' However, Peake's warrior energy could be dangerous: on one occasion she pulled a muscle in her armpit when the fight director threw her. 'But that's what's been good about it,' she said during rehearsals. 'You get to stretch all the muscles. It's a bit of a dream come true; I'm doing a sword fight and then I'm punching someone in the head! I get it why men become over-excited about playing Hamlet: every emotional base is covered. It's just the ultimate part.'

But in performance the part took its toll. 'It was very tough physically,' she admits.

It felt like I was running a marathon every night, just being on that stage all that time, and having to run round the hall to get in at another entrance. I felt quite rundown: I had physio twice a week trying to get my knees back into life, my back had gone, and I lost a lot of weight. I had to have a vitamin B shot in my backside. Some nights I went on and absolutely loved it, but on others I'd think, Oh crikey not tonight! You panic and you think you're going to be sick, and then miraculously the play just takes you through. But I was done by the end; after seven weeks my voice had died. And I then found out that I was severely anaemic: my iron level was very low, and I had to have a transfusion. On the third preview night I sat on the steps at the stage door, and had a bit of a cry. I was thinking, Why did I imagine this was a good idea? I could just get into a taxi now and go into Manchester. But I think it's quite common for actors playing Hamlet to have a bit of a wobble early on.

There were no understudies, so she had to play every performance.

You can't let people down when they've paid good money. I felt exhausted sometimes when I went on, but I thought, this is an absolute privilege. Attracting a young audience and people who had never seen Shakespeare or *Hamlet* before made it all worth it. All I cared about was people connecting, and having an emotional reaction to the play when they came out.

Frankcom remembers how tired Peake was, previewing at night and rehearsing during the day:

One night she came off and said, I thought I wasn't going to be able to do it, and then I realised the soliloquies are there because actually, after playing someone who feels they are completely alone in the world, suddenly you realise that you're not, you've got all these people there, willing you on. She also said she was really upset when she died, because she felt she wasn't just communicating with Horatio, she was saying goodbye to the audience.

Her notices were mostly positive. Dominic Maxwell, praising 'Manchester's fabulous, feminised production', wrote of 'a stunningly good performance ... Peake and company make this 400-year-old revenge tragedy come alive in a way you've never seen before.' Michael Billington described her Hamlet as 'caustic, watchful, spry and filled with a moral disgust at the corruption she sees around her'; it was 'a fine performance that confirms Peake's capacity for emotional directness and a fierce, uncensored honesty'. Susannah Clapp suggested her 'delicate ferocity, her particular mixture of concentration and lightness, ensure that you want to follow her whenever she appears'. But Dominic Cavendish had reservations, noting that 'she has a lovely crack in the voice, and can soak a phrase in sorrow, but the splenetic side to the grief-wracked Prince is curiously muted'.

Frankcom found *Hamlet* her most challenging production to date: 'It's an unbelievably punishing play to direct. With a good new play you can keep digging and finding new things. With *Hamlet* you can feel like you've only got through the first layer.' But she was full of praise for Peake's Hamlet. 'There was an honesty about it, a wit, and an understated throwaway quality. There was also something magnetic in the moment she saw her father that felt very raw and real. Maxine's achievement was that it was absolutely clear all the way through what she was thinking, what she was saying, and what she was not saying.'

Peake herself was critical of her performance: ' I was very proud to have done it, but I thought there was a lot wrong with it. You get on the train and it hurtles along, and there were times when I thought I should have got off at a few stations, but I just kept going.' She found the nunnery scene the hardest one to get right.

> Hamlet's treatment of Ophelia was difficult. I remember thinking I'm not going to play the Hamlet who is aggressive to her, I'm going to be different. But it didn't happen like that. He felt absolutely betrayed by her. And trying to work out whether he was really in love with her was problematic. He'd been abroad for so long, she'd grown up; she was probably only a little girl when he left.

'Often when I am playing difficult roles I have a problem sleeping because I can't leave the character behind. But with Hamlet I was out like a light every night because you do all the psychological processing on stage.' She was, however, unhappy with her vocal delivery:

> I felt at ease playing in the round, but doing Shakespeare in that space is very different from what I'd done there before. I didn't quite get the pitch right. You're desperate to get across what you say in a very clear, concise way, and sometimes I pushed it too much. I didn't trust the space as much as I usually do, I slightly forgot how intimate it was.

Despite her physical ordeal,

> a couple of months after finishing I had a real pining to play the part again, and do it better. I didn't give myself much of a run-up to playing Hamlet, I just dived in there. Afterwards you think, that was just the tip of the iceberg, that was just one aspect of Hamlet, there's so much more to discover. I suppose my Hamlet was witty and bright and philosophical, but he wasn't an intellectual. If I do it again I probably wouldn't be so physical, I'd be more cerebral, I'd play him a bit more thoughtful. I'd also probably explore the madness more.

Looking to the future, she said: 'I'd definitely like to play other Shakespeare parts. But I don't find the leading female ones enticing. I find them quite problematic, and their storylines difficult, so I've no burning desire to play them. But I'd love to have a go at Richard III.'

Benedict Cumberbatch
Lyndsey Turner

In 2015 Benedict Cumberbatch appeared as Hamlet at the Barbican, directed by Lyndsey Turner.

Cast: Claudius: Ciarán Hinds, Gertrude: Anastasia Hille, Horatio: Leo Bill, Polonius: Jim Norton, Ophelia: Siân Brooke, Laertes: Kobna Holdbrook-Smith, Ghost/Gravedigger: Karl Johnson.

I never set out thinking of the great roles I wanted to play. But in the back of my mind I was thinking that maybe one day I would play Hamlet. I've seen some truly extraordinary ones in my time: Stephen Dillane, Simon Russell Beale, Mark Rylance, Rory Kinnear, Samuel West. At 39 I thought, Is there a biological clock ticking?

For many people familiar with his riveting Sherlock Holmes on television, Benedict Cumberbatch seemed a surprise choice to play the Prince. Yet he already had built up a fine stage reputation in a variety of parts. He had an early taste of Shakespeare in the Open Air Theatre in Regent's Park, playing Demetrius in *A Midsummer Night's Dream* and Ferdinand, King of Navarre in *Love's Labour's Lost*. He was Tesman in *Hedda Gabler*, for which he gained an Olivier nomination as Best Actor in a Supporting Role; the non-conforming hero in Ionesco's *Rhinoceros* at the Royal Court; and both Frankenstein and the monster in *Frankenstein* at the National, a feat which gained him Olivier and *Evening Standard* awards as Best Actor.

His international fame as Sherlock and his Oscar-nominated performance in the film *The Imitation Game* resulted in *Hamlet* at the Barbican selling out in a matter of minutes a year before it opened, becoming the fastest-selling show in London theatre history, and raising expectations to an extraordinary level. Yet Cumberbatch claimed to be unaffected. 'I didn't find fame a hindrance in rehearsals,' he said. The production was

the opportunity to bring a new audience to a 400-year-old piece of brilliance, to try to make Shakespeare as relevant now as he has ever been since then. He writes about the troubles of the soul, but also visceral, real, earthy, directly relatable, sensory perceptions of what our reality is.

There's real directness, because he was utterly a man of his world. There is a universality to Hamlet that makes it a role that fits any actor. I think everybody has a Hamlet in them, and as Maxine Peake has proved, it's not trapped in a gender.

In discussing the play, he said Lyndsey Turner's production aimed to highlight the dangerous gap between old and young.

This is very much a look at the play through the ideas of trans-generational trauma. The positioning of where we are on the table in the first court scene is very much seeing the youth of the court together – you have Ophelia and Laertes and Hamlet. All the youth in the play end up dead; they suffer an incredible amount at the hands of the generation above them.

He raised questions about the nature of Hamlet's father, and the basis of his marriage to Gertrude.

Was he, as in our production, much younger than Gertrude, and it was therefore probably a courtly arranged marriage? This is not to say they didn't have a conjugal relationship, but that there was something that Claudius gives her now, which is the flaming youth I accuse her of being lost in. I wonder how much the previous marriage was one of convenience, which complicates my grief and my loyalty to my father? The beauty of it is that Gertrude never says he was an extraordinary man, so maybe in her eyes he wasn't.

Madness of course is a key element in the play, both in relation to Hamlet and Ophelia, as is Hamlet's knowledge of acting. Cumberbatch observed:

There's one very specific encounter with death in the shape of Yorick's skull. Yorick had a free pass to the foibles and idiocies of those in power. That's a very strong tradition in Shakespeare. Having experienced that as a youth, Hamlet realises he can retreat behind that mask of seeming zaniness, and slowly disrupt the court. He's au fait with acting, he knows what that is, he's au fait with the craft and the skill of it, he's also au fait with clowning, and the brilliance of how a fool can navigate those in power and needle truths into them.

As most actors are, he was fascinated by the soliloquies, and the intimate rapport it was possible to have with the audience. 'With the soliloquies you get a huge amount of empathy, of more listening, and more involvement with one man's point of view, than you do in any of the other plays of Shakespeare. I think that is the romance with him: you get to understand the man. Those confessions are so stark and naked.' As to delivering 'To be or not to be', he said 'the trick is to find the need to say those words'.

How then would this hotly anticipated production be received? Before opening night there was a row, when Kate Maltby, the critic for *The Times*, was widely criticised for reviewing a preview rather than waiting for the press night. There was also concern when members of the audience started photographing Cumberbatch with their phones, though fortunately this had stopped by opening night.

The critical consensus was that Cumberbatch was a good, if limited Hamlet, playing in a poor, gimmicky production. Es Devlin's panoramic set on the vast Barbican stage consisted of a palatial hall with turquoise panelled walls, grand staircase and enormous chandelier, which often dwarfed the actors. The production was epic in style, with symphonic music linking the scenes. Some of the scenes were played in semi-darkness, while for many of the soliloquies Cumberbatch was bathed in an eerie blue light. In one much-criticised scene, his first bout of feigned madness, he dressed up in a scarlet tunic and peaked helmet as a nineteenth-century infantryman, and then paraded around in mocking fashion and firing shots from a toy fort. In another bizarre touch, for *The Murder of Gonzago* he underlined his point by donning a jacket with 'KING' blazoned on the back, and took over the role of Lucianus to administer the poison. Meanwhile Claudius, whose reaction is crucial, has his back to the audience.

Turner was widely criticised for using too many such odd or distracting ideas, including the use of slow motion, freeze framing and strobe lighting, and making seemingly arbitrary cuts or senseless textual changes. Of these, the most controversial and obvious was her decision to move the 'To be or not to be' soliloquy to the start of the play. Responding to the subsequent bewildered criticism, she soon moved it back, though not to its normal position early in Act 3, but to follow Hamlet's sardonic exchange with Polonius in a heavily re-jigged Act 2.

Cumberbatch received plenty of praise, for example from Michael Coveney: 'He's not a "young" Hamlet, but he's a compelling and charismatic one … He delivers the great soliloquies superbly, urgently, intelligently and full of concentration, right to the top of the Barbican.' Dominic Cavendish 'feared he might be too icy, too remote, but he displays a warmth of feeling that puts you on his side … His words are stamped with expressive force, of a piece with his unshowy physical confidence.' For the visiting American critic Ben Brantley: 'In the monologues he is superb, meticulously tracing lines of thought into revelations that stun, elate, exasperate and sadden him. There's not a single soliloquy that doesn't shed fresh insight into how Hamlet thinks.'

Other critics mingled approval with criticism. Paul Taylor wrote that 'he commands the stage with a whirling energy but we rarely feel soul-to-soul with this Hamlet … We don't sense that he is laying himself bare, as is the case with the greatest exponents of the role such as Mark Rylance and Simon Russell Beale.' Susannah Clapp found him 'arresting but not disturbing.

The mightiest Hamlets are on the edge of a chasm, in danger of being engulfed. I don't think I have seen a more rational Hamlet.' Michael Arditti agreed, suggesting: 'His performance is too controlled; it lacks the danger and darkness found in the great Hamlets.' Michael Billington thought him 'a good, personable Hamlet with a strong line in self-deflating irony, but trapped inside an intellectual ragbag of a production ... that elevates visual effects above narrative coherence and exploration of character'.

Arditti thought Turner's design choices were as misguided as her textual rearrangements, which he felt 'showed a disrespect for Shakespeare. Es Devlin's Ruritanian hunting lodge set is more suited to Sigmund Romberg's operetta *The Student Prince* than Shakespeare's tragedy of a student prince. While visually impressive, it swamps the actors; the closet scene in particular is hampered by the lack of intimacy.'

Cumberbatch appeared unruffled during the unusual events that preceded the opening. 'If my fame was seen as a negative because of the early review or the over-zealous fans filming the play, I really didn't let that bother me.' The calmness continued during the run.

> I'm not nervous waiting in the wings to go on. But I have a form of nerves: some nights it's a matter of, oh gosh this is going to be different, and I'm not quite sure what it's going to be. But I never have a seizure of terror that other people have talked about. I definitely have moments, but you need a bit of that to pump up the adrenalin.

In the face of such a hugely complex and lengthy role, he stressed the need to keep your focus on the moment. 'You can't afford to look back or worry forward. If you do that you become very unstable.'

He also appeared to find no difficulty in shedding the part once he left the stage and returned home.

> As an actor, a technician who has to do it again the next night, you have to immediately stop self-critiquing. Of course there's relief, an outbreath and, to put it very simply, that's it for tonight. I drop it all very quickly, because I have to eat and sleep. But it's really thrilling to think we are reaching a new audience, and that does stay with me.

Benedict Cumberbatch's performance gained him an Olivier Award nomination for Best Actor.

Paapa Essiedu
Simon Godwin

The next Stratford Hamlet was Paapa Essiedu, in a 2016 production directed by Simon Godwin. Early in 2018 it embarked on a UK tour, finishing at the Hackney Empire in London.

Cast: Claudius: Clarence Smith, Horatio: Hiran Abeysekera, Laertes: Marcus Griffiths, Gertrude: Tanya Moodie, Polonius: Cyril Nri, Ophelia: Natalie Simpson.

I remember my school taking me to see *Othello* with Chiwetel Ejiofor at the Donmar when I was 16. I'd never seen a black man playing a leading role in Shakespeare. It wasn't in my consciousness to see that, and see it done so well.

Paapa Essiedu wasn't the first black Hamlet to appear in Stratford: in 2006 Janet Suzman's South African production in the Swan Theatre had Vaneshran Arumugam in the leading role. But during the 55-year history of the Royal Shakespeare Company he was the first black actor to play the part in one of their own productions.

'If I'm the first black one, that tells its own story,' he said.

The RSC is a great bastion for classical work, and has a responsibility to do that in as diverse a manner as it can. It's part of its manifesto to inspire the next generation of theatregoers, and of Shakespeare-lovers and performers. And that next generation, I really hope, is made up of a far wider variety of people. The work we create on our stages needs to be representative of the world we live in. I think Hamlet is one of the deepest, richest, most detailed human characters ever written. So I think you can transpose him to almost any culture, any time, any society, and gender.

Born and grown up in Britain, Essiedu had travelled a lot to Ghana where his heritage lay, to visit his family. 'There was something very different there about the energy and the air and the culture,' he reflected. 'While I love it and feel very at home and rooted there, to begin with it felt quite alien. That was useful for Hamlet, because you are talking about a guy who is in a world that he feels isolated and alienated from.' He was also able to empathise with the bereaved Hamlet, because his father had died when he was 14, and his mother while he was at drama school. 'A lot of people talk about Hamlet as mad, but to me you are looking at a man going through deep, deep grief. It was certainly a huge trauma that he experienced, which I think pushed him to a frenzied mania rather than madness. I can relate to that feeling of grief and trauma at a young age.'

Aged 25, he first came to prominence when Sam Troughton lost his voice in the middle of a performance of *King Lear*, and he took over as Edmund, to widespread acclaim. But he also made an impression when he played Romeo at Bristol's Tobacco Factory. Director Simon Godwin, who had himself played Hamlet at school and directed the play at university, had seen this performance, and admired its passion and physicality. Once he and the RSC's director Greg Doran had settled on a black Hamlet, he asked himself:

What would a Hamlet be like who was very physical, sexual and very emotional, very hot, who was depressed yes, but rebellious and at war with his surroundings, rather than a Hamlet who was steeped in the intellectual equipment of his country? An estranged Hamlet, a Hamlet who was living in two worlds, who was out of joint? Paapa brought these things naturally to the part, but also a tenderness and an intelligence. I was drawn to his clarity of verse-speaking and his charisma, but also his personal narrative.

Their production was based not on colour-blind casting, but what Godwin called colour-conscious casting. 'We were saying, If I'm consciously going to create a world in West Africa, it will be appropriate for me to find actors who can carry that and realise that world most accurately. In this situation I would want to work with as many black actors as I can.' The result was a mostly black ensemble.

Before rehearsals Godwin visited Ghana with his designer Paul Wells. 'I had a very striking encounter with a country that is still extremely Christian,' he said. 'It also has a very rich relationship with the supernatural. So the notion of ghosts is very present and welcome. The traditions in West Africa, which are to do with forms of story-telling, music and movement, began to create a much more coherent world for the play than I could find in my own country. It's a cliché, but one that has come to be true, that in Ghana there's a very relaxed relationship to the body, to dance and to music, an access to body and movement as being much more a part of everyday life. West Africa had gone through certain versions of the *coup d'état*, the violent use of power, so the political turbulence of that area was very interesting for Claudius.'

He was aware of the potential danger of a white man creating a West African *Hamlet*, of being accused of indulging in cultural tourism. 'What empowered me was that I was collaborating with my Hamlet. Paapa was somebody who had the technical expertise and the emotional access to play the role, but also a history which could feed and nourish our version. He could offer a new take on that, which I hoped didn't obscure the play, but illuminated it.'

Before rehearsals began he spent time exploring the text with Essiedu alone. 'We worked particularly on the soliloquies, which are such a gift, because they are such a self-contained inner life of Hamlet. It was valuable to consider such questions as, how does one relate to the audience? Are they a reflection of you? Are they your thoughts? All those things can be explored in a one-to-one relationship.' They had further discussions during the previews: 'Paapa and I would have an hour or an hour and a half every day, to reflect together on what we had learned, and how we could go further. Hamlet is such a huge part, and one is making so many choices every night, that this felt essential, especially as he was still a young actor.'

Godwin explained his rehearsal method:

I often do an exercise where we read the play all together for the first
week or two, putting the play into our own words as well, very closely
paraphrasing, so that the actors start to embed the language in their
imaginations. Then I invite everybody to write a biography of their
character, where they were born, how old they are, where they went to
university, what they studied; what for example was Claudius' relationship
with his brother before he came to power, what was his job in the cabinet.
So everybody is feeling they are not slaves or mules carrying the author's
baggage, but are writing with the author.

He also used improvisation exercises, two of which led to the creation of a
prologue involving Hamlet receiving his graduation certificate at Wittenberg,
emphasising the very different world he is forced to leave, and a glimpse of
Old Hamlet's funeral as a cortege processes across the stage, with Hamlet
walking at the rear, and Claudius and Gertrude observing the ceremony
from a balcony.

In considering Hamlet's antic disposition, Godwin was looking for
something that would cause maximum trauma to his parents. The result
was startling. Starting out in a sombre black suit and tie, after encountering
his father's Ghost – dressed in traditional African robes – Essiedu exchanged
them for a paint-daubed, skull-emblazoned white suit; armed with a spray
can, he went round creating subversive graffiti, including one on the royal
portrait of Claudius and Gertrude, and generally trashing Elsinore. His
'madness' was also expressed in huge paintings that hung from the roof,
echoing the vibrant canvases and spectral faces of the very political punk-
style New York artist Jean-Michel Basquiat. The final production had a
vaguely militaristic West African setting, featuring pounding drums between
scenes, whirring fans, vivid colours and lighting, limbo-dancing by the
Players, and a final duel fought with wooden sticks rather than swords.

The critics relished Essiedu's young, quick-witted, cocky and intensely
vital Hamlet. Paul Taylor found him 'in thrillingly unforced command of
the role, radiating the impudent charisma, energy and wounded idealism of
youth'. Sarah Hemming felt 'he lets us see his character's wit and cockiness,
but also conveys his pain and vulnerability', while Dominic Cavendish
admired 'his lucid, intelligent handling of the verse and his baby-faced
vulnerability'. Natasha Tripney wrote: 'He has a clarity of voice, a musicality
of delivery and a precision of gesture that's incredibly engaging.'

Essiedu worked well with his director. 'Simon was brilliantly collaborative,'
he says. 'From day one he was asking me what I thought about Hamlet, what
resonated with me, what we should pull out from him, and I was talking
about my history, my culture and my heritage. He has a real bravery in
giving himself to collaboration. I've never been in a more joyful rehearsal.'
He spoke eloquently about Shakespeare's skill.

He's got this real talent to distil intangible feelings and emotions. For
mere mortals language is often a barrier. There's only a certain level of
specificity I'm able to get when I'm trying to describe how much I love
someone. But Shakespeare's got this incredible ability to crystallise, really
get the physical feel of an emotion, and translate it into language. It's
beautiful, and I love it.

Andrew Scott
Robert Icke

*In 2017 Andrew Scott played Hamlet in Robert Icke's production at the
Almeida, which transferred to the Harold Pinter in the West End.*

Cast: Claudius: Angus Wight, Gertrude: Juliet Stevenson, Polonius: Peter
Wight, Ophelia: Jessica Brown Findlay, Laertes: Luke Thompson, Horatio:
Elliot Barnes-Worrell, Ghost/Player King: David Rintoul, Player Queen:
Marty Cruickshank.

It's a play about family and love, it's a thriller, and it's the best play ever
written. But at the beginning I thought I had to speak in some way I don't
normally speak. So part of the process was having the confidence to say
no, and just speak in my own voice.

Surprisingly, although not out of choice, until he took on Hamlet,
Andrew Scott had never performed in Shakespeare during his professional
career. But he has a vivid memory of a teenage moment, when he took part
in a local drama festival in his native Dublin. 'It's in a community hall in
May. There's sunlight streaming in and maybe four people in the audience,
and it's kids doing Shakespeare. You could do an extract from *Richard II*
in your Mum's coat. I did Lancelot Gobbo from *The Merchant of Venice*. I
remember thinking, Oh my God, this is brilliant.'
    Coming late to the part at the age of 40 after his enormous success in
the television series *Sherlock*, and feeling the weight of past productions
on his shoulders, he was filled with self-doubt about his ability to succeed.
'My fear about playing Hamlet was, am I in possession of the attributes
to do Shakespeare? I'd never done a Shakespeare on stage before, and I
wondered if there was a thing I was not in possession of.' He was reassured
by director Robert Icke. 'He said you have to deliver your own Hamlet. He
was absolutely insistent on it.'
    Icke, who had recently directed highly original and acclaimed versions of
Oresteia, Uncle Vanya and *Mary Stuart*, holds very firm views about staging
Shakespeare. 'I never need to see people in Elizabethan costumes again,' he
insists. 'The play opening with dry ice and people carrying spears, and pacing

back and forth – I've seen it a thousand times. It's dead. It's completely boring.' He is especially critical about the way Shakespeare is spoken.

The water is completely poisoned by reverence, and bizarre, operatic methods of delivery. Actors will take lines that are completely colloquial and naturalistic and will say them like it's the Bible. They are often intimidated by this false and absolutely insidious sense that there are certain ways it has to be spoken. All this nonsense about 'pause at the end of every line' that Peter Hall perpetuated in the 1960s. Hamlet gives you the rules: he says, just speak it, speak it like I am speaking to you, quickly, don't mouth it, don't overdo it, try and make it as natural as possible.

Such opinions influenced Scott's performance, which was notable for his naturalistic delivery, reinforced by traces of Irish lilt. His speaking drew critical approval: 'This is one of the least declamatory of *Hamlet* stagings,' Susannah Clapp observed. 'It has extraordinary conversational ease.' David Benedict shared her opinion: 'His handling of the verse is so adroit that it sounds at all times conversational. He's talking *to* the audience, not *at* them.' For Michael Billington his performance fitted 'the quiet, non-declamatory tone of the production. He is, for the most part, softly spoken and gently ironic.'

Icke's modern-dress production was less subversive than his previous treatment of the classics, but it was definitely contemporary. Elsinore was a place of maximum surveillance, with CCTV and news cameras and video screens much in evidence. There was a screening of news footage of Hamlet's father's funeral; the Ghost was first caught on the Danish guards' CCTV cameras before appearing in person; most strikingly, to watch *The Murder of Gonzago* Claudius sat with Gertrude in the theatre's front row, where every shade of his growing unease was captured by a news camera, and shown in close-up on screen.

There were other innovative touches, including the use of Bob Dylan songs as a soundtrack to the action, which some criticised as incongruous. But the most controversial decision involved the scene with Claudius at prayer, with Hamlet uncertain whether to kill him there and then ('Now might I do it, pat'). Instead of Claudius being unaware of Hamlet's presence, they made eye contact and their words were addressed to each other, so that Claudius made his confession of murder directly to Hamlet, who was standing in front of him with a pistol.

Both Icke and Scott wanted to create a *Hamlet* for younger audiences, and those who hadn't seen the play before. There were free tickets for young people at the Almeida, and it was a condition of the West End transfer that 300 tickets for under £30 were made available. It's an issue Scott feels passionately about:

I hate the idea that there are a lot of big Mercedes cars with drivers outside waiting to pick people up because that's who theatres are for, because they're not. The whole purpose of art is to help us live a better life. And a better life is not just for people who can afford it. But I don't believe in forcing people to see Shakespeare. It's something you experience, and if you experience something you love, you will love it enough to go again. If you don't, you won't. It's as simple as that.

His sell-out performance at the Almeida prompted critical praise. Paul Taylor admired his range: 'I've never heard a Hamlet that takes us from quiet despair to the tantrum-throwing of sardonic scorn and self-mockery.' Natasha Tripney saw 'a moving and human Hamlet' and 'a performance of wit, delicacy and clarity', while Henry Hitchings wrote: 'Scott finds new paths through Hamlet's soliloquies, dwelling on certain words as if caressing their edges.'

At the end of the Almeida run Scott confessed: '*Hamlet* is exhausting, but it feeds you a lot of energy. It's a real play about love and life, and there's an awful lot of stuff in there, a lot more heart than I ever realised.'

9

Hamlet Observed

The National Theatre at Work

Simon Russell Beale

John Caird

John Caird's production, with Simon Russell Beale as Hamlet, was staged in the Lyttelton at the National Theatre, toured the UK and Europe, visited Elsinore, and played at the Brooklyn Academy in New York.

Cast: Claudius: Peter McEnery, Gertrude: Sara Kestelman, Polonius/Gravedigger: Denis Quilley/Peter Blythe, Horatio: Simon Day, Ophelia: Cathryn Bradshaw, Laertes: Guy Lankester, Ghost/Player King: Sylvester Morand.

1. The Beginnings

The idea of staging a new production of *Hamlet* emerged in the early summer of 1999. Trevor Nunn, who had become director of the National in 1997, had broken with recent tradition by creating an ensemble of actors, who were to perform six works in repertory during that year. One of the plays chosen was *Money*, a rarely performed Victorian 'serious comedy' by Edward Bulwer-Lytton, to be directed by John Caird and starring Simon Russell Beale.

John Caird
Lytton's hero, Alfred Evelyn, is a kind of cross between Hamlet and himself. In the play he frequently breaks into soliloquy mode, and muses on the relationship between man and money. One of his speeches was so Hamlet-like that within days of starting rehearsals I thought, this is

ridiculous, why has Simon never played Hamlet? Here he was working on a part he could do in his sleep; we had been using a Rolls-Royce to get to the corner shop. By the time we got to the technicals it was clear to me that he was going to be a triumph as Evelyn. So I said to him, this is clearly a sketch for our production of *Hamlet*: why don't we do the real thing? He bit immediately.

Now 39, Simon had been wanting to play Hamlet for many years, and had got near to doing so more than once. Tentative plans for Sam Mendes to direct him in the part had been recently revived, with the production to be staged at the Donmar Warehouse. However, when it became clear that the film *American Beauty* was going to send Mendes' career into orbit, he agreed Simon should go ahead without him. John Caird therefore approached Trevor Nunn, who immediately offered to stage his production of *Hamlet* with Simon at the National. It was also decided that the play should tour in the UK and Europe, and possibly in America.

Simon Russell Beale

I seriously think this is my last chance of playing Hamlet. It seemed to me a wonderful idea, because John is one of the most collaborative directors I know, if not the most. As I was aware from working with him on *Money* and *Candide*, he's incredibly open and generous to other people's ideas, which is a very great strength. I think we worked well together because we complemented each other: I'm obsessed with the logic of story-telling. He is too, but much freer, and much more aware of what's beautiful to look at. Intellectually he's very impressive, yet not too heavy. He's also very funny: I thought there would probably be more laughs than usual in a *Hamlet* that he was directing.

Although both Olivier and Hall had done the longest possible version, which normally runs for around four-and-a-half hours, John followed more recent directors in deciding to cut the play substantially. In doing so he knew he wanted to lose the political background, much of which he felt Shakespeare may have added at a later stage. As well as making many major cuts in advance, he chose to do the detailed cutting in collaboration with the actors at the beginning of rehearsals.

One of his early intentions was to emphasise the play's religious elements. This idea informed his initial discussions with the designer Tim Hatley, who had worked with him at the National on his production of Pam Gems' *Stanley*.

Tim Hatley

Having talked at length with John about the play, my aim was to create a design that made Elsinore both a prison and a religious place, but also flexible for the actors. My original design was a big ruined cathedral, with corridors and tunnels and levels, a banqueting table, lots of icons, and chandeliers inspired by the reference to 'this majestical roof fretted with golden fire'. But this proved too expensive, and not very practical for touring. So we started again, and stripped everything down to the minimum.

Left with just a floor and three walls, John wanted a design that would reflect a more metaphorical look at the play, something that would get away from architecture and focus on the idea of journeys, of which there are so many in *Hamlet*. He was also playing with the idea of the company becoming a group of strolling players, or maybe ghosts, re-enacting the tragedy of *Hamlet*. This notion inspired the final design, a set consisting solely of the chandeliers, and a collection of trunks that the actors would bring on, rearrange or take off the stage as required.

Because of the delay caused by the need to re-design the set, the lighting designer Paul Pyant was not able to see it until the first production meeting. By then John was already working with the composer and orchestrator John Cameron, whose brief was not only to find suitable existing music, but also to create new material.

John Cameron

Several months before rehearsals began we started to talk about a suitable musical language for the play. We tried to think of the music as being like a lighting cue, as part of the flavour of the piece rather than an add-on feature. John gave me pointers to where it might be needed, and I eventually came back with a load of unaccompanied motets, which seemed to convey the right spiritual feeling we were looking for.

Finding the right actors for the main parts was straightforward in some cases, less so in others. John preferred not to cast according to physical type, as was evident in his decision to work with Simon, whose short, stocky physique flew in the face of the received wisdom about Hamlet's looks. For John this was irrelevant. 'Simon is wonderfully equipped for the part. He's a man of extreme intelligence, of great complexity emotionally, and fantastic humour. That's what his Hamlet is going to be like.'

In casting Claudius he wanted to get away from the conventional notion of the hard-drinking, swaggering, big 'bloat' king, and to create a more subtle character. To this end he chose Peter McEnery, who had played both Laertes and Hamlet in earlier productions.

I felt Peter would be perfect as a plausible, complicated machiavellian villain, who was also a sexy and attractive younger brother, someone who could have turned Gertrude's head at a time of great grief. He's an intelligent man with great feeling, capable as an actor of combining a glamorous exterior with a steely interior. I loved the thought of the wry and ironic delivery he would bring to Claudius.

As Gertrude he cast Sara Kestelman, an experienced Shakespearean actress who had previously played Goneril and Lady Macbeth for the RSC.

I've so often seen Gertrude played as the once-beautiful flibberty-gibbet who regrets her looks are going. I felt it was essential to have a Gertrude who was mighty, someone who was capable of Greek-tragedy size of feeling, because I knew Simon would be doing that. Sara is an emotional and vulnerable woman, who as an actress has instant access to the complexities of her own character, and can turn them on brilliantly. Gertrude is a small part when measured by the number of her lines, but a large part for the amount of time she's on the stage. You need an actress who can bring an awful lot to it that isn't in the text. Sara has an ability to fill a silence with a look or a gesture, the great gift of making an unspoken moment eloquent.

The choice of Polonius was made for him. Denis Quilley, who had doubled as Claudius and the Ghost in Peter Hall's 1975 production, was a member of the ensemble at the National, with a leading part in *Money*.

As Denis was leaving the first-night party he said to me, 'I'll do a Polonius for you if you like.' I said, 'You're on.' It was that simple. I wanted a Polonius who was neither a doddery old fool nor simply a nasty, evil politician, but a complex human being. I knew that Denis, one of the finest Shakespearean actors of his generation, would give me that. He's also one of the great comedians, capable of being brilliantly and effortlessly funny without ever being crude or cheap. This made him a perfect choice for the Gravedigger once I'd decided to double up parts in a smaller ensemble.

In casting Ophelia he settled on Cathryn Bradshaw, who had played the part ten years before in a Cheek by Jowl production.

The central thing about the relationship between Hamlet and Ophelia is that they understand each other. She's not as emotionally complicated as him, but she has the same sense of morality and goodness. Cathryn is an instinctive actress, and emotionally accessible and vulnerable in all the right ways for the part. You've got to have someone who understands the importance of spirituality in Ophelia, and she has that kind of imagination. I thought she would make a suitable emotional twin for Simon. One has to be able to believe that when Hamlet returns from Wittenberg for his father's funeral, she will be the first person he will turn to in his grief, and that from that moment until his first line in the play there's been a close relationship between them of friendship and love.

Having taken on Sylvester Morand for the Ghost and Simon Day for Laertes, John still had no Horatio.

'Angels and ministers of grace defend us!'
1. Simon Russell Beale, National Theatre, 2000. © Catherine Ashmore.

'Here hung those lips that I have kissed I know not how oft.'
2. *Mark Rylance, Globe Theatre, 2000. Photo John Tramper, © Shakespeare's Globe.*

'Look here upon this picture.'

3. *Adrian Lester and Natasha Parry, Young Vic, 2000. © Jean-Pierre Muller/ AFP/Getty Images.*

'Do you think I am easier to be played on than a pipe?'

4. *David Tennant, Courtyard Theatre, Stratford-upon-Avon, 2008. Photo Ellie Kurttz, © RSC.*

'And now I'll do't.'
5. *Jude Law, Wyndhams Theatre, 2009. Photo Johan Persson.*

'I am but mad north-north-west.'

6. Benedict Cumberbatch, Barbican Theatre, 2015. © Johan Persson/ ArenaPAL.

'I'll be your foil, Laertes.'

7. *Maxine Peake, Royal Exchange Theatre, Manchester, 2014. © Jonathan Keenan.*

'The time is out of joint.'

*8. Paapa Essiedu, Royal Shakespeare Theatre, 2016. Photo Manuel Harlan,
© RSC.*

The part is rather mysterious and without clear character or age delineations. The only important stipulation is that he should be a genuine friend of Hamlet. At the same time, as I began to see Horatio as the storyteller of the play, he was becoming increasingly important. It became apparent that we needed someone who was completely au fait with Simon, who enjoyed working with me, and who would have an instinctive sympathy for the ideas I was proposing. Simon Day had been a member of the National's ensemble, and worked with me in both *Money* and *Candide*. The minute I had the idea of moving him from Laertes to Horatio, I knew I had the right answer.

Once this was done, he could bring in Guy Lankester, an actor he considered a perfect Laertes.

John consulted Simon about all the main casting decisions.

With major parts it's always wise to check that there isn't a history of difficulties that might cause a problem. Simon is an extremely generous actor who finds it very difficult not to have something nice to say about somebody, whatever his experience of them. Very occasionally he will voice a negative opinion about an actor, but that's usually because they've behaved extremely badly or cruelly to another actor. But having given his opinion he'd say, it's up to you.

Contrary to his normal way of approaching a part, Simon began to learn Hamlet's lines well in advance. Two months before rehearsals began he and John started to meet once a week. At each session they read an act together, discussed the set and John's concept for the production. They agreed that the play was essentially about a group of people who all loved or wanted to love each other, but whose love was destroyed by circumstances. It was here that other important ideas used in the production emerged, including the central one of having Horatio act as the storyteller, and the character who starts and ends the play.

These fruitful preliminary sessions had an extra dimension because, by a sad coincidence, both John's and Simon's mothers had died shortly before they started to meet. Before rehearsals began Simon was asked to give a lecture on *Hamlet* at Stratford.

My first response was that I wouldn't have anything to say until we'd started to work on the play. But writing it actually sorted out a lot of my ideas. The most important personal one was the death of my mother. She was an extraordinary woman, and my relationship with her was a very close and loving one. I felt it would be a privilege to be able, with her, to explore the greatest meditations on grief and death ever written, and that my performance would be a kind of tribute to her.

2. The Rehearsals

Monday 22 May

Rehearsal Room 2, in the National Theatre. Morning. The company has assembled for the first day of rehearsals. After being greeted by Trevor Nunn and introduced to the National's heads of department, the actors settle round a makeshift square of tables, armed with their Arden editions of the play. John Caird sets out his ideas.

'The most significant and tricky thing about directing *Hamlet* is that it's both an intensely naturalistic drama and an extraordinary piece of metaphysical poetry and philosophy. Sometimes the two run in parallel, and sometimes they defeat each other if you're not taking into account the difference between them. A good production needs to supply both of these elements to an audience.'

Of all Shakespeare's plays, *Hamlet* is the one which most profoundly examines the nature of mankind, in a world where people reflect deeply about themselves. It's the portrait of the life and death of an unbelievably complex man: all Shakespeare's most fascinating thoughts are here in Hamlet's mind. It seems to me a deeply autobiographical play; you can almost hear him as he is writing, not caring where he takes the play, being driven by his thoughts rather than by the plot.

He outlined a few problems and questions, and some tentative solutions:

- *Hamlet* is textually the most complex of all Shakespeare's works. It went through more changes than any of his other plays, and is a curious mixture of styles. To play a full version, using all the available material, is to shirk the responsibility to make the evening coherent.

- Part of it is a history play, but a rotten one: the history is boring, it doesn't work dramatically. Fortinbras seems not to be part of the original version. The Danish politics could be dropped.

- The play is ostensibly set in medieval Denmark, but actually it's an Elizabethan Denmark. So it's really a mythological place. The time is now, when ever now is.

- The story is about real people and real relationships. But it also has a ghost with a personality, who is not a figment of Hamlet's imagination. How do you deal with the supernatural element?

- The society is one that believes in God; Hamlet's thoughts are pre-enlightenment. So the production must be suffused with religious certainty. If you set it after the seventeenth century an audience loses patience with the religious arguments.

- How do you physicalise the metaphysical? The production needs a set that allows all the imagery about heaven and earth to be liberated, one that reflects the extraordinary beauty of the form, line and imagery of the play. The solution is to have one that doesn't require conventional scenery.

Tim Hatley shows the company the set model, its floor littered with trunks, and its ceiling hung with numerous lamps that can be individually lowered to any level. The back wall of the set opens a chink to let people in from the world outside Elsinore. The actors comment approvingly on the set's beauty and simplicity.

Tim then reveals his provisional thoughts about costume. He is aiming for a mixture of period and modern, clothes that will emphasise the dark, ecclesiastical tone of the production. 'Maybe Danish Renaissance sludge, with gold for the royal characters,' he says. He has been looking at Eastern fabrics, and also Renaissance paintings for the dark, rich colours he wants to achieve.

During the lunch break news gets round of the death of one of the great Hamlets, John Gielgud. Denis Quilley, who worked with him at the National, recalls his powerful rendering of Hamlet's 'Oh what a rogue and peasant slave' soliloquy at a gala celebration on the National's last night at the Old Vic.

The actors start to read the play. This is no ordinary read-through: having accepted in principle John's idea of losing about an hour's running time from the play, they begin the collective cutting exercise. 'I think we should cut early and stick to it,' John says. 'We need to be bold, look out for scenes that overstay their welcome, or speeches that just go on too long.'

The radical intentions are clear from the start, the first scene being cut ruthlessly from 180 to 50 lines. Gone is the exchange between Marcellus and Horatio on the political background, and the conflict with Norway. Throughout the afternoon the actors seem more than willing to lose lines, and sometimes substantial speeches, for the greater good of the production.

The constant cutting meant many interruptions, during which John and the actors share some first thoughts about the characters. At moments the session seems more like a university seminar than a rehearsal: there's a learned discussion about why Hamlet is studying theology at Wittenberg. But already some of the motivation is being teased out. Why, it's asked, does Claudius want initially to keep Hamlet in Denmark? 'He didn't want to just kill his brother, he wanted to *be* him,' John suggests. 'So nothing must change, he needs Hamlet to be his son.'

The attention to detail and the skill of the cutting is impressive, as is John's breadth of knowledge. The actual reading is downbeat, almost throwaway; emotions are being kept well in check. But there is already an arresting quality about Simon's reading of Hamlet, and his speaking of the verse. His first soliloquy, 'O that this too too sullied flesh would melt', is clear, unflashy and intelligent.

At this rate the read-through seems likely to last for a couple of weeks. Surely the actors will want to be on their feet well before then?

Simon Russell Beale

Hamlet is so extraordinary, and yet there's an everyman quality about him. So he's really what you want to make of him. I haven't any game plan, because I don't think the part demands that. It's more a question of looking down into yourself, which makes it difficult.

I flatter myself that the wit will be all right, and the wryness and the self-deprecation. I know I'd quite like him to be funny, but I don't quite know how I'm going to achieve that. I know I have a weakness to be vocally over-elaborate, but the really difficult bit will be controlling the huge waves of emotion. I don't want to indulge in sobbing too often, so it's a question of finding the right moments for the distress to show, such as perhaps the Yorick speech or the closet scene.

I was worried about the madness, whether I might have to do something extraordinary like stand on my head. I'm not very good at tricks or inventing bits of business, I'm not the type. In any case, for all his intelligence there's something very innocent about Hamlet, which I think is probably best served by not trying to be too clever with him. So I suspect my interpretation will be quite simple in the end.

John Caird

I work in a way that requires people to study the play together, to say what they think. There's no hierarchy of opinion: from the most senior actor to the most junior member of stage management, if people have an idea I like them to voice it. Some ideas are excellent and ought to be used, but even if it's a bad idea, it's all the better for being voiced, because it might start a good one, or put to bed some bad ones that are fomenting in other people's minds. One should never mock a bad idea, one should always think about it, and explain why it's not going to work.

If you have everybody able to voice their opinion, they slowly become a company, they pull together well, they become equal partners in the sharing of the play's message. In this way you lose any sense of hierarchy, or of subversion or bitterness or disappointment – which is often an artist's life just under the skin.

Tuesday 30 May

Rehearsal room. Afternoon. It's Day 6, the company are up to Act 4, and still cutting. 'It's important to keep the story active, so that the only things we hear about are new things,' John says. Scene four, Hamlet's meeting with Fortinbras' army, disappears, and with it the entire soliloquy 'How all occasions do inform against me'. Simon is relaxed about this decision: 'I've got too much to say anyway.' Sometimes single lines or even half lines within a speech are dropped, though care is taken to preserve the iambic pentameter.

There's a discussion about the drowning of Ophelia, whether Gertrude actually witnessed it, and if so why she didn't try to save her. John believes there's a reason why Shakespeare gave the speech to the queen rather than have the story told by a shepherd or a waiting woman. 'There's evidence that he wanted us to be mourning two women at the same time,' he suggests.

On to Act 5, and the graveyard scene. Hamlet's musings on lawyers ('Where be his quiddities now?') has to go. Here the question of Hamlet's age comes up. Simon: 'I know he's thirty, but couldn't we make it thirty-nine?' John: 'If Denmark is a state of mind, so too is Hamlet's age.' Simon: 'And his weight?'

The more obviously tedious lines or speeches are met with groans or giggles. John greets the penultimate scene with horror: 'Another killer! The whole thing is a rewrite.' The necessary lines are cut, after which the company reads it again. 'It never makes sense in the theatre, but now it does,' John says. The session ends with a debate about Hamlet's state of mind in the 'Not a whit' speech: how reconciled is he to the idea of death?

Tomorrow will see the end of the cutting exercise. On Thursday the actors will get the resulting script, and read the play straight through.

John Caird

I've always felt that Ophelia and Gertrude are deeply connected emotionally, and that was why Shakespeare has Gertrude bringing the news of Ophelia's death. The play fools around a lot with the concept of time and generations, and in a way they are the same woman, they have a similar relationship to the men in the play. Gertrude is the present queen, and Ophelia would have been the new queen, and they would both have been married to a man called Hamlet. In many ways Hamlet is his father made young, so it's almost as if Gertrude is watching what happened to her when she was a young woman. These connections are in the text just waiting for you to discover them.

Sara Kestelman

I've thought a lot about the nature of Gertrude's relationship with Claudius. Were they having an affair or not? Was it a one-night fling that suddenly blossomed into something else? Was it something they had been nursing for years from a distance? How bad was the marriage with Old Hamlet? Was it arranged, a marriage they had to suffer?

I've asked myself some basic questions about her by examining the text just from her point of view. The more I did so, the more I saw her as enormously courageous. She's rightfully a queen, and is able to inhabit the world of the men and find her place naturally in it. Apart from the closet scene, which has a real emotional and inexorable dynamic, her part is very spare. But I don't think her lack of words weakens her.

Cathryn Bradshaw
With Ophelia you have to do a lot of detective work, as the part is
underwritten. One thing I didn't want to do was to present her as a victim
from the very first moment. Ophelia is often seen as passive throughout,
but I want to get away from that. My idea is to show a fairly happy
woman, blossoming from being in love: for a fleeting moment she has all
her hopes ahead of her, and then slowly she disintegrates.

Monday 5 June

Rehearsal room. Late afternoon. The session has ended, and most of the
actors have left. At the side of the stage area the stage manager Trish
Montemuro is sorting out the schedule for the week's rehearsals, while
her assistants Andrew Speed and Valerie Fox are busy clearing away the
trunks. Near the back wall Simon and Guy Lankester, playing Laertes, are
rehearsing the duel with the fight director Terry King. It's still early days, and
they work gingerly through the first two sequences of the fight. Simon, who
seems anxious as they parry and thrust, is surprisingly quick and light on his
feet for someone of his build.

Trish Montemuro
We try to create a conducive environment for rehearsals, but every
production is different. With this one we've had a huge input into what's
been going on onstage, because John has left all the box-changing to us.
If he wants something to be created for a scene, he says what its central
architecture is – a clifftop, Polonius' desk – and we work out how to do it.
With a really complicated change we ask him for help. For the quayside
scene, for example, he had the idea that Rosenscrantz and Guildenstern
would climb over the hilltop, so that all eyes would be drawn to them,
and away from the box-shifting.

To supplement the stage crew, we have the actors moving the trunks,
with the help of Andrew and Val, who will be in costume. It's known as
Pickfords, and the actors get paid a few pounds extra for doing it. But it
doesn't come naturally to everyone, so it will be up to us to watch every
scene change very carefully.

Simon Russell Beale
Before I started I was very worried about the question of Hamlet's
madness. But now it's all become much clearer. He's not mad, but the
pressure he's under makes him think he might be. If people around you
start saying you're losing your marbles, of course you begin to worry
about it. I think he's just slightly off-kilter, but for a perfectly normal
and understandable reason, which is his grief at discovering that his
stepfather has killed his father, and that his mother has married a
murderer.

Thursday 8 June

Rehearsal room. Morning. The cutting is over, the exercise has produced a script that, read without interruption or pause, is just over two hours long. The actors are now on their feet, and blocking the moves for the long second scene in Act 2. The room is full of trunks.

The atmosphere is relaxed and jokey, but purposeful. Simon and Denis work on Polonius' meeting with Hamlet as he reads ('Words, words, words'). In place of the usual mockery of Polonius, John wants to introduce an element of danger, even a hint that Hamlet might kill Polonius. At once the scene takes on a different edge. When it comes to Hamlet's soliloquy 'What a piece of work is a man', Simon starts to put light and shade into the speech, conveying both intelligence and world-weariness. Unlike most of the company, he's already off the book.

When they reach the entry of the Players, with Sylvester Morand doubling the Player King with the Ghost, John observes: 'This is where a crack opens in the play, and new characters come in from another dimension, from the real world. Maybe we need a touch of music here? It's a Pirandellian moment. We need to find a magical way of Hamlet meeting the Players.' The Players sit on the trunks for a few minutes, discussing Hamlet's keen interest in the theatre, and how it might be used.

The 'pastoral-comical' speech is then explored. Denis plays it as Polonius showing off to those around him, which works well; the tricky part is to choreograph the rising laughter from Hamlet, Rosencrantz and Guildenstern. Eventually they get there.

Later, for the Player King's Hecuba speech, John suggests that Hamlet, with his passion for the theatre, might decide to mime the early part, sword in hand. Mesmerised by this suggestion, Simon becomes intense, enjoying the melodrama – but then wonders if the idea isn't a bit heavy-handed. It's decided to leave it in for the moment.

At the end of the session the costumes are wheeled in on a dress rail. 'Let's do it with just a rail and a skip', says John, who minutes before has refused to be drawn into discussions about possible cuts to the design budget.

Denis Quilley

Polonius is a difficult character. You have a feeling, as Harley Granville Barker says in his *Preface*, that Shakespeare changed his mind about him halfway through: he starts with his wise advice to his son, and then you get this silly stuff. So he's often played simply as an old buffer, and for all the comic mileage that can be got out of him.

Both John and I think that's wrong, so we're taking the opposite approach, and going for the reality. If you look at his lines, for example in his scene with Ophelia, and forget how you've seen it done before, they're the words of a very intelligent man and a very loving father, who has a deep concern for his daughter. He's conceited and a bit of a bore, but extremely intelligent and powerful. He's the kind of guy who would stand up at the bar in the Garrick Club and tell long, boring stories that he thinks are funny, but which aren't.

But that doesn't make him any less formidable. He's the king's right-hand man, so he's not an idiot; in fact he's a consummate manipulator, a real diplomatic fixer who manipulates Claudius.

Peter McEnery

I think Shakespeare wrote Claudius as an out-and-out-villain, and I've often seen him played as that from his first entrance. But I'm more interested in the denial in his character, in the fact that he doesn't want to face his crime, and his guilty conscience about it. As we're emphasising the religious aspect of the play, John suggested you could see Claudius not just as the king but also as the chief priest. That's been very helpful to me, it gives him an austerity, it's made it easier to avoid the obvious, moustache-twirling villain.

Wednesday 14 June

Rehearsal room. Afternoon. The blocking has reached the graveyard scene. John has decided that the second character at the start of the scene is not another gravedigger, as he is often played, but the tiresome courtier Osric, played by Michael Wildman. This seems to fit with the officiousness of the character. Simon Day wonders if Horatio knows of Ophelia's death and imminent funeral, and has brought Hamlet there on purpose. Or does he want to stop him going into the graveyard? They experiment with alternative versions, including Horatio only meeting Hamlet by chance at the graveyard.

Denis is playing the Gravedigger as an ex-army rather than a rustic type. There's a brief debate about the kind of man he is. John sees him as uneducated but intelligent, in contrast to 'the educated Hooray Henry' that is Osric. 'When Hamlet the aristocrat arrives he has a real rapport with him,' he suggests. They look at ways of highlighting this rapport.

They come to 'Alas, poor Yorick', which Simon delivers with effective sadness. Denis wonders if the Gravedigger could belatedly realise who Hamlet is? Though there's no hint of this in the text, it's seen as a good idea, and a bit of business is inserted: a raised eyebrow to Horatio, a nod, and the Gravedigger doffs his cap.

Another inventive stroke from John is to convert Hamlet's four rhymed lines 'Imperious Caesar etc.' into a song, begun by Denis and taken up in harmony by Simon. Both actors have excellent singing voices, and allied with some inventive comic business with the skull it works a treat.

The day ends with the actors trying to choreograph the difficult moment when Laertes, played by Guy Lankester, and Hamlet both jump into Ophelia's grave, and have to be restrained.

Guy Lankester
Laertes is a difficult part to play, because you disappear for such a long time. By the time you come back a lot of the story has been told, and you then have three scenes each with a major speech, which you have to do at top pitch in response to your father's death, your sister's madness and then her death. With each of them there's very little time to build up to anything, and no real time for discovery.

Simon Day
I think you have to play Horatio straight down the line, as a very generous, unselfish man, who doesn't really have an attitude to things unless it reflects Hamlet's reaction. He's a support for Hamlet, but not a sounding board, he never offers him advice. He's just there so Hamlet can think that there's someone out there in the world who is good, that despite all the shit that's going on and people's dodgy moral frameworks, there's still Horatio.

Monday 19 June

After four weeks the company is halfway through the rehearsal period. With the cutting and blocking completed, the actors are starting to come off the book. Some of them are also beginning to have short sessions with the staff director Stephen Wrentmore, who is working on the kind of detail there's no time to go into during the main rehearsals. John is pleased with progress so far.

John Caird
I think we're very much on course. The actors are beginning to be in control of the words, they're starting to increase the tension, but still doing a great deal of refining. We've had no major problems. There have been some difficulties of interpretation, but nothing that hasn't been amicably sorted out through discussion.

One of my jobs is to persuade the actors to be compelled by the choices I've made, otherwise you get no unity. I think they've been given plenty of opportunity for their own invention, even if there's no real room for fundamental differences of interpretation or opinion. But together we've discovered things in the text that we didn't realise were there, which have surprised me as much as anyone else.

My concept has been easier to put into practice than I thought it would be. The success of a production that relies on the metaphorical use of objects is always difficult to estimate until you get started. But this one has yielded very well, because it's so adaptable. With this kind of set you're not tied to anything, it's all so easy. At any moment you can say, Let's have a completely bare stage, or, You need such and such a prop, why don't you use a box. You don't have to say, We'll bring a cupboard in, or, We haven't got a chair. The literal way is such a curb to the imagination.

I really am inventing it as I go along. I think it through with each scene, because that way you get a pure sense of what is necessary. If you work it out on paper without the actors there, often it just seems stale and intractable in practice. It's a high-risk method, but it's the only way to do it, to wait until you're in the company of all the different intelligences you're working with, and then let it come out of the imagination.

I talk to the actors quite a lot about what a line means, but I never tell them how to say it. If you take a moment where you think a character is angry or grief-struck, there are fifty ways of showing that. If you try and lead an actor into the way you would do it yourself, you're simply limiting their mode of expression. You have to give them the what and the why, but never the how. They know much better than you how to do it: that's what makes them good actors.

If you have an open relationship with the actors you'll get plenty of surprises. But you have to be receptive to atmosphere and vigilant to spot the good stuff coming from them. You can analyse a character as much as you like beforehand, but you won't get much out of it until an actor plays it. Then the magical chemistry happens, the combination of the actor's personality and the written role gives it the absolute reality that Shakespeare intended, but could never exactly prophesy because he didn't know the actors. That's the great genius of his work, it allows so many different types of actor to play the same role successfully.

Simon Russell Beale

I'm beginning to sniff the shape of the part now. The more I explore it, the more I think Hamlet is an innocent abroad. He's fantastically clever, but completely inexperienced. I'm sure that's why Shakespeare makes him a student at Wittenberg; you don't send a crown prince off to university unless you're deliberately saying something. He certainly has no experience of the real world, and he's not at all a political animal.

I still haven't decided whether it's the chip of ice in the heart, and that Hamlet's problem is that he can't breathe. You could spend so much of the time sobbing, and I don't want to do that; I think his problem is deeper and colder than that. I'm trying not to have too many moments of crisis. But I have found one where I want the distress to happen, and that's the Yorick scene. Here was someone Hamlet loved, so it must be devastating for him to be suddenly holding his skull. Talking about death in the abstract is all well and good, but this is the first time he has actually seen the physical degradation.

I don't want to force the emotion, I need to get there a little bit more slowly. The next weeks are going to be the interesting ones, because what we have been doing up to now has all been quite technical, and we've been able to do the gags. But from here on the challenge will be to get the emotional arc right.

Peter McEnery
A lot of Claudius' part has been cut, notably his long scene with Laertes, which is fine. Those two weeks spent cutting were very valuable. What often happens is that when you run the production you find that it's too long, so you start dishing out cuts. That's very disconcerting, it throws everybody, and upsets the rhythm. But going through the text with a toothcomb and getting everyone's agreement about the cuts has prevented anything like that. Of course you keep an ear open all the time in case a line needs to go back, and that's happened now and then.

Cathryn Bradshaw
John's explanation at the beginning was so scholarly it had me worried. But when it comes to his directing, all that intellectual stuff stops, and something much more organic takes over. He really lets us fly, but he'll also tell us if something isn't working. For instance he slightly toned down my exasperation with Polonius in the first scene, but I was still able to keep that feeling within me. He doesn't disturb you on the path you're on, he just shows you another way.

Stephen Wrentmore
It's been a remarkably happy production so far. The period when you're cutting the play is usually the most fraught, because people are counting the number of lines they've lost. This time they were offering to have lines cut. That spirit has continued all through.

Sara Kestelman
During rehearsals we've been able to say whatever we've wanted to say. As a result everyone feels engaged. As a director John is absolutely at the helm. But this is a huge play, and it would be easy to get a little bit lost. To create an atmosphere where there is so much laughter and so much ease, and all the inhibitions have been broken down, is quite astonishing.

Denis Quilley
Because of John's collaborative approach the atmosphere in the rehearsal room is very relaxed, with lots of jokes and suggestions from the actors. It's only when a director is very confident and on top of it like John is that he can afford to allow this. Everyone's really enjoying themselves: although the work is very serious, it's not solemn, we don't have to be po-faced about it. I've enjoyed these rehearsals more than anything I've done for a long time.

Nothing is being taken for granted, every line is being analysed for what it really means. This is difficult with a well-known play like *Hamlet*, because you think you know what the lines mean. But John has the gift of saying, Why can't it mean this, why can't we show it this way rather than that way? For my money it's paying off in spades: I think it's going to be a very fresh look at the play without being gimmicky, and without distorting its meaning and intention.

Friday 23 June

During the week Simon and Sara have been making progress with the emotional heart of the play, the closet scene.

Simon Russell Beale

Yesterday I think we knocked it on the head. We did it three times, and I went for it full throttle, as Sara did. I was always terrified of it, so there was an enormous amount of beating around the bush before we got started. The third time we did it we were cooler, and I think that was the best version. The emotion was more natural, we didn't have to force it.

With highly charged scenes like this one, the more emotionally wrapped up in it you are, the less good it is. I did desperately not want it to be maudlin or sexual. I don't necessarily buy in to the Oedipal thing, though it's a perfectly reasonable option. I don't think Hamlet wants to have sex with his mother, even subliminally; he just wants her to stop having sex with his uncle. I didn't want to be throwing her on the bed and that sort of stuff, because you don't treat your mother like that. Perhaps that's being terribly middle class, but to my mind the argument of the scene is more important than its physicality.

It's such a complex relationship he has with his mother, and there are all sorts of reasons why he puts off going to her. One of the principal ones in my head is that he's frightened of the confrontation, he really doesn't want to have it. He finds it very difficult to say, You're a whore and a murderess, as anyone would. Especially as Sara is playing it from the beginning of the play as her having absolute concern for him. And then his instructions to his mother are so feeble. Confess yourself to heaven – Don't go to Claudius' bed – what good is that going to do? It would only alert Claudius and make him suspicious. So you get a feeling of, What good was it telling her, except for one's audit from heaven?

At the end of the scene what is so devastating for me is that they're not separated. He's said what he has to say, and she still loves him. It's very sad, it would almost be better if they could wash their hands of each other and get on with their lives. But whereas Hamlet and Ophelia can determine their relationship, he and Gertrude can't, because a mother and son can't do that.

John Caird

There's nothing that worries me about Simon's progress as Hamlet, but inevitably he will become more dextrous with the text. He works from the big picture, which he gets in his head very clearly, and then develops the details. He's not one of those actors who starts with the details and then builds up slowly. That's what's wonderful with a part of such scale, he can have a clear idea of the map of the whole play because he's controlling it from the centre. But now I'm encouraging him to find more and more emotional and intellectual detail.

Monday 26 June

Rehearsal room. Afternoon. Paul Pyant is present to check on lighting possibilities. The music, which is normally put in at the tech, is being inserted into the action for the first time, so John Cameron is on hand to see how his chosen Orlando Lasso motets fit in at different points.

The stage management team are increasingly in evidence. From her desk at one side of the rehearsal room, stage manager Trish Montemuro controls the pace of the rehearsal, continually reminding John to keep it moving so they can get through the day's schedule. The music is being controlled at another desk by the deputy stage manager, Fiona Bardsley. The assistant stage managers, Andrew and Valerie, are on constant call to move the trunks and suitcases – a task variously dubbed boxology or Trunkspotting.

John Cameron

Finding the Lasso motets has helped to give the play a setting that is completely different from other concepts of *Hamlet*. John's decision to lose all the political stuff makes it a much more cerebral production, it gives it a lightness and a floatiness, a more spiritual feeling which I'm trying to match in the original music I'm creating.

In the old days directors could hold a tune in their head and talk to you about it, but they rarely had the kind of music skills that John has. His being a hands-on musician is a great advantage, he can feed off what he hears, he knows how music can be used in different ways.

Paul Pyant

With the lighting you have to think first and foremost about how best to tell the story. You try to service the production, and avoid any jiddery effects: there's nothing worse than coming out of a show humming the lighting or the set. So with each scene in *Hamlet* I need to know what time of day it is, where we are, what the weather's like, what kind of atmosphere we're trying to provide, and what that means for the set.

John's good musical ear helps me in creating atmospheres. But he's not the sort of director who briefs you on the lighting. So it's been up to me to work out in rehearsal what his intentions are and what he wants the play to look like. Having worked with him on *Candide*, I've got to know his likes and dislikes. He tends to like quite painterly pictures, quite dramatic shifts.

Wednesday 28 June

Rehearsal room. Morning. The actors are wearing different clothes, though not their own costumes. The men have put on jackets, the women have taken to long skirts, and Denis Quilley has found a cane for Polonius. Most of them are now off the book, and beginning to put more power as well as subtlety into their performances.

They work on joining Acts 2 and 3 together, then move on to the 'To be or not to be' scene. Simon speaks the soliloquy with great simplicity, sustaining its argument very clearly. John suggests that the first line is simply a repetition of what Hamlet has already concluded, and the idea emerges of Simon writing it down in his notebook before he starts the speech. John stresses that it begins casually – 'There's always the suicide option' – but then becomes more serious: 'It's not just about himself, it's not just about suicide, it's about existence.'

With Ophelia's arrival, there's a discussion about her attitude to this pre-arranged meeting. 'You need to play it knowing she's playing a scene she doesn't want to,' John suggests to Cathryn. Arising from this idea, it's decided that in response to Hamlet's question 'Where's your father?' she should let him know that Polonius is eavesdropping by shaking her head while replying 'At home, my lord'. This then makes more sense of Hamlet's subsequent fury.

Simon Russell Beale
Patsy Rodenburg has been helping me with the soliloquies. As a voice coach she's very good at seeing the whole arc of an argument. Quite often I get bogged down in the detail of a particular word, but she's very skilled at showing you how a thought may be five lines long rather than five separate thoughts, and pinning you down to that.

But I haven't got the soliloquies right yet. 'To be or not to be' is fine, it's a single arc. 'Oh that this too too sullied flesh would melt' is a repressed, hysterical brood, but I think I'm in the right area, though technically it's a nightmare. But I'm not so sure what to do about 'Oh what a rogue and peasant slave'. It's very long, with three or four sections, and half way through I think I'm boring people to death. I don't know where Hamlet's brain is, so I'm trying it in different ways. Is this a man who can't feel anything, in which case you can play it as self-mocking throughout, or does he really feel something, then pulls back and says 'Why what an ass am I'? It's a really tricky one.

Patsy Rodenburg
Simon has an incredible technique, but his brain moves so fantastically fast it's easy for him to get ahead of himself, and not connect emotionally. But he understands that, so we're working at reining him in and trying to break him of the habit. We're also looking at the meaning of the verse

– not just the intellectual meaning, but the sensoral, visceral meaning. What is brilliant about Shakespeare is that form and content match, and that means that the shape of the word often releases something physically. We're exploring the physical structure of the verse, the iambic pentameter, the breaking of the thought and the line. Fortunately Simon absolutely understands the language, it's in his bloodstream, and that's a huge advantage.

Friday 30 June

Rehearsal room. Afternoon. The company are working on the mad scene. Cathryn handles the violent shifts in Ophelia's thought-processes skilfully, her pure singing voice adding to the poignancy of the scene. John suggests that for her second entry she should wear her dead father's coat, drop it on the floor, and then re-enact his funeral using the coat as his body. 'It might be too literal, but let's try it,' he says.

The effect is moving and powerful, not least on Laertes, who is now witnessing not only his sister's madness, but a version of the burial that he missed. At the end of the scene John has the idea that Cathryn should push some of the low-hanging chandeliers, so that their swinging reflects her state of mind. It's a complicated manoeuvre to rehearse, with plastic buckets and makeshift pulleys standing in for the real thing.

Backtracking to Act 3, the actors work through its key scenes. Simon conveys a more steely Hamlet than before in the recorders speech to Rosencrantz and Guildenstern after the play; Peter works up a fine anguish in conveying Claudius' guilt in his 'O my offence is rank' soliloquy; and Sara and Simon take another emotional roller-coaster ride through the closet scene.

Afterwards John gives some general notes. 'That's a very fine chunk, we've made good progress. What we need to do now is run it, so we have a section that more or less works. The big job is going to be rhythmic, and we can't tell how that's working until we run scene for scene. So next week is going to be an education for us.'

Cathryn Bradshaw

I was frightened of the mad scene, because if you don't hit it properly it can be very embarrassing. But I got a lot from seeing a mad woman on a train the other day. I've been using gestures she used – for instance she did a lot of stamping. She was so vehement, and I've been trying to catch the intensity of her contact with people. It really helped me, seeing someone who was on her own track, yet saying quite profound things. You couldn't make any sense of it, but she obviously had a theme.

One of the problems with Ophelia is to decide whether she has a theme, whether in the mad scene she's gone in there to tell people specific things, or whether they're just coming out of her inner life. I think it's the latter, even though they say she's importunate, that she needs to see the queen. I don't think she has any rationale for it. I want to give the impression of someone who is 'home alone' – no parental control any more, no brother, no one to turn to. I imagine her up in the middle of the night, not eating, and losing track of life.

Sara Kestelman
When we did the mad scene this morning it was the first time for a week. Cathy is astonishing in it, and we got very, very upset. I couldn't stop crying, but John rightly said, You have to stop, you have to find a way of feeling it when it's appropriate and not falling apart, of finding the steel in the character. Ophelia is in her own bubble, you're not in it with her, and you have to fight not to be. It was a brilliant note to give, because it means you have to investigate those areas of your character that will steel you against crying.

Like a lot of observing roles Gertrude is a slow burn for the actor. Last week I thought, I hope everyone doesn't think I'm trailing here, because I am, I'm way behind. But I can only catch up by listening and watching and absorbing, and hoping that some stuff begins to happen.

Monday 3 July

In addition to working on the detail of their speeches with some of the actors, Stephen has been working with the understudies.

Stephen Wrentmore
I try to make sure that no one in the production is ignored, so for example with Chris Staines and Paul Bazely I've been sorting out the relationship between Rosencrantz and Guildenstern, because they're such a tricky pair. I've been working with Guy on Laertes' emotional journey, which is a hellish job for him because most of it happens offstage. And I've worked a little with Cathy on the mad scene, though John has been very focused on that, so I'm just picking up the end of it.

The main difficulty with working with the understudies is time. In this production essentially there are 16 people on stage all the time, and I need to be working with eight of them in another room. You just have to fit them in somehow: part of the philosophy of the National is that understudies are thoroughly rehearsed, it's not just a matter of, 'Learn the part and on you go'.

In the case of Simon Day, who's understudying Hamlet, it's especially important to fit him in with the choreography of the production, while helping him to invest independently in the part, and we've been exploring that together.

Simon Day

I'm meant to be off the book by the first preview, and I think I'll just about be there. I've been working quite a lot with Stephen on certain speeches, but once the previews are out of the way we'll be able to have proper sessions and run whole scenes.

It's difficult rehearsing Hamlet while I'm also rehearsing Horatio, as they're on stage together so much. A lot of the time the motto is, Keep your lips together. I've gone back to something I used to do in drama school, which is highlighting the text – blue for Horatio, pink for Hamlet. Unless I can see the two parts in separate colours, there are bound to be scenes I'll mess up.

I have to play the part in a way that won't throw any of the other actors. But to attempt a slavish imitation of Simon's Hamlet would be wrong, and also impossible. Of course I haven't been thinking, Should I play it on crutches or as a Martian? I'm just trying to fit my personality into the situation, and see what I would do under those circumstances.

I think the soliloquies are the key, because they're Hamlet stripped bare, talking through his thoughts and feelings. They provide stepping stones, and if you can get them right, then everything else falls into place.

Wednesday 5 July

Rehearsal rooom. Afternoon. The company are re-visiting Act 1. With just a fortnight until the technical Trish pushes the rehearsal on at a swifter pace. 'Play it for the full emotional value', John tells the actors, who proceed to do so. The work is more intense, there are fewer gags now. Simon is much more contained, more submerged in Hamlet's world: his fear seems palpable as he listens to the Ghost tell his story.

Laertes' farewell has been set on a quayside, demanding an immensely complex scene change. But the trunk-shifting, planned in minute detail by the stage management, is beginning to work more smoothly, and the energy the actors use to move the set gives extra pace to the story. John Cameron is in attendance again, to see where the music might need cutting or extending. Three musicians are also present, with recorders to provide live music for the play scene. As the company works through the cues it becomes clear that more music is required in at least two places, in one instance because lines originally cut have been restored.

John Cameron

The challenge with the original music has been to find a style that reflects the Lasso, but which also has a contemporary feeling. I've always been a great fan of late medieval and renaissance music, but I didn't want to go just into the renaissance, I wanted to use its sonorities in a twentieth-century way.

It's not like writing a movie score, you don't want to overstate it. In the theatre you have to be more detached and subtle, to try to gauge the music so it sits very lightly with the production, and enhances it without ever being obtrusive.

John Caird
In a part the size of Hamlet you can rehearse each scene until the cows come home, but it only starts to make total sense and reveal itself fully after you've run it several times. Then you can start making adjustments in how you pace it, and see what it's telling you at different moments in the story. For as well as performing *it*, it starts to perform *you*. The character starts telling the actor what it wants, and begins to have a life. Provided an actor is receptive and responsive to those demands, the relationship between character and actor becomes increasingly productive.

Simon is becoming more and more impressive. The way he holds the whole play together in his imagination is quite extraordinary. His fascination for the development of the character, his appetite for experiment, and his daring as an actor are constantly astonishing. He lives on the experience of driving the play through with his will and passion and fire. He's like a racehorse at the start of the Grand National: every time we go into a single scene or a run of part of the play, he can't wait to get at it.

Denis Quilley
Simon is not most people's idea of how Hamlet should look. But although he's not tall and willowy and conventionally pretty, he's very attractive. His intelligence and wit and emotional directness are among the things that make him attractive, as well as his nice face.

The great thing is that he always comes to a part with a clean slate, with no preconceptions based on what other actors have done with a part – his Iago was a good example of that. Here he's said, Let's forget Gielgud and Olivier and John Neville, and just see what the character means. I think he's going to be an exceptional Hamlet – and I don't often say that kind of thing at this stage in rehearsals.

Tuesday 11 July

Rehearsal room. Afternoon. The first complete run-through. John explains that the lights won't be sorted out until the technical, but that today the music will be integrated as fully as possible. He warns the actors that it will be louder than in the theatre, but also that it's still negotiable, that their opinions will affect decisions still to be made.

Meanwhile he's looking for pace and concentration: 'Keep it buzzy, but not racing, keep it performance size,' he says. 'Don't get lost in your own problems: you must be in the moment for yourself in your character, but the minute you stop the scene, watch the rest of the play, get a sense of its atmosphere, so that you know what its true nature is when you next walk on the stage as your character.'

The run-through is impressive, both technically and emotionally. There are few dries or missed cues, the scenes are knitting well together, and the music lifts the performance to another plane. Suddenly there is a true ensemble feeling, and the thematic logic of the play seems beautifully clear. Simon is now in control of his soliloquies: the difficulties of 'Oh what a rogue and peasant slave' have vanished, and he gives it a subtle, assured rendering.

John is delighted. 'That was very impressive, a real quantum leap,' he says. 'Where we got to today is where we have to get to in performance. The move to the theatre will tend to knock us off our perch, but this is what we have to hang on to, this is sacrosanct.'

He offers the actors advice about the technical rehearsal.

The tech will tune the house to your voices and your spirits. But part of your job is to sit and watch your peers at work, to get a sense of how they look on stage. So go up to the circle, or come and sit with us in the stalls: don't let the proscenium arch and the pass door get in the way.

Trish asks the actors to make a list of any problems they have, and reminds them of the schedule for the rest of the week: three days of technicals, tomorrow, Thursday and Friday; dress rehearsals Friday night and Saturday afternoon; and the first preview Saturday evening. It sounds an exhausting schedule, and John is sceptical: 'I don't ever remember having one dress rehearsal at the National, never mind two.'

John Caird

The first complete run-through is always a very important moment. It's the time when the actors start to feel how their journey through the play fits together and makes sense for them, and so will ultimately make sense and be satisfying for an audience.

You find that things that seemed all right when you were rehearsing scenes on their own now feel less appropriate. A run-through also gives you a chance to add elements of story-telling and character that you'd perhaps missed, and make thematic connections between the actions of characters and ideas shared between different plots.

Simon Russell Beale

I was pleased with the run-through. In the gap when Hamlet goes to England, I'd been going off and having a fag and a glass of water, and losing my concentration. I suddenly became aware of that, and today I got it back.

I also began to get the feel of him being a changed man when he returns. Before, he's reacting to things a lot, he has very firm stimuli like the Ghost and the Players to react to. But after England he shuts off, he stops soliloquising, and you've got to find a reason for him doing that. Does he not want to communicate with his friends the audience, or does he feel no need to communicate with them? I believe it's the latter. And at what point does he resign himself to death? I think that comes early in the fifth act, soon after his return. If he discovers it too late, the fight becomes less irrelevant.

The tech days can be an incredibly useful period. The most important thing is that you keep working on your performance, and don't just sit back and work on technical things. I'm still honing ideas that I've had, some of which are very fresh and new, so they've not yet been thought through properly.

Patsy Rodenburg
To help the company with the move into the theatre from the rehearsal room I've been working with them on their voices, getting strength in them, extending their capacity and range, so they have a big landscape to play on vocally, and can handle the text as it becomes more heightened.

The trouble with most British theatre is that we rehearse in a room with a wall where the energy is very limited, and the actors then go into a big space and think they've lost their performance. And of course the rehearsal room is acoustically alive, so when they go into a dead theatre they panic, and start pushing or over-emoting. My priority is to do warm-ups for the first few shows, so they begin to understand the different energy the theatre requires. That's why the previews are so important.

Thursday 13 July

The Lyttelton theatre auditorium. Evening. The last session of the second day of the technical rehearsals. Trish and John are directing operations. John is sitting at a desk placed in the middle of the stalls, with lighting designer Paul Pyant and sound designer Christopher Shutt at computerised monitors beside him. Tim Hatley and John Cameron are also on hand nearby.

Trish moves constantly between the stalls and the stage as problems arise, in touch via her headphones with her team backstage, as well as with Fiona in the control box at the back of the stalls. On stage the actors seem suddenly distant, and briefly unrecognisable in their full-blown costumes. While they work through the scenes, a running conversation about the sound, lighting and music takes place in the stalls between John and his team.

'The chandeliers are beautiful, but do they dominate the action?'
'Could we make the jig about 50 per cent faster?'
'Let's have a green up on the white.'
'I think we should move the trunk about six inches upstage.'
'Backlight the cross, it looks too neony.'

'Don't start the iron [safety curtain] until the music reaches the tonic.'
'The colour is still work-in-progress, it looks too equatorial.'

The play scene is worked on in great detail. Ophelia needs more light downstage left. The height of certain chandeliers needs adjusting. The recorder music needs to be speeded up. But the changes are not purely technical. John is worried that the visual device used to suggest Claudius' guilt is not working: 'We're losing the mirror image with the hands,' he says. 'Let's do something really tricky, and have Gertrude rising and the Player Queen moving forward at the same time.'

Despite the long day, the actors patiently accept the constant interruptions and endless adjustments. Trish maintains a balance between problem-solving and keeping the rehearsal moving.

Trish Montemuro
For the technical I knew we would have to do a lot with the flying of the chandeliers, and it has been quite difficult. We have about 19 flying cues, and we've needed a lot of time to decide what configuration they should be in for each scene, which involved discussion with Tim, John and Paul. So beforehand we made sure we'd done all the box changes in detail, and had a list made of each actor's movements with them.

Simon's performance has grown enormously: you see little grains happening, and then they build into something very powerful, such as the end of the closet scene. Usually I get bored with Hamlet's angst, but he makes it such a human journey, everyone can relate to it. It also lacks vanity, which you often see with Hamlet. I think it's going to be a very special performance.

3. The Previews

Saturday 15 July

The actors now face the first of six previews. It is, John stresses, a critical moment.

The longer you rehearse a play, the more involved the actors become in the detail of their own performances and of their relationship on stage with the other actors. Those relationships become more and more exclusive of outside enjoyment, so the first previews are something of a shock to them, because they've gone deeper and deeper, and so further and further away from their own first reactions to the play.

Before the performance he offers the actors a word of caution. 'I know you're never going to give any less than 100 per cent, but for the moment try to keep 5–10 per cent of your minds out of your performance, so you can spend time observing what you're doing. Part of your responsibility during this preview period is to talk to me and each other about how it's going, and you can't do that if you're completely bound up in your performance.'

The evening's performance before a full house in the Lyttelton goes extremely well. There are no serious technical problems, the scene changes go like clockwork, and the actors respond to the rapt stillness of the audience with an assured and confident performance. Simon's Hamlet is clear, witty, swift and poignant; in the soliloquies he has the audience in the palm of his hand. At the end there is sustained applause and loud cheers. Afterwards in the green room the main feeling is one of relief, that this first difficult hurdle has been successfully cleared. But Simon, though pleased, is cautious: 'You have to be careful, preview audiences are always on your side, and the first one is not typical.'

Thursday 20 July

The morning after the first preview. The actors are gathered in the front row of the Lyttelton stalls for John's notes. Last night's running time was 3 hours 15 minutes, five minutes longer than Monday's. John is not happy, and delivers a stern lecture.

Those extra five minutes are serious, and need our attention. Last night you were falling into patterns of speech, putting inflections on lines and phrases without thinking about it. It's the kind of thing that doesn't normally happen until you're in a long run. There was also a lot of emotional generalisation: In this speech I'll be sad, and so on. When this happens you start singing, your vowels get longer, and you buy yourself a little more time. It's as if you'd rather be in an opera.

There were quite a few fluffs, and spoonerisms, and lines being thrown. The reason was that you were not connecting with each other. You were listening to yourself, and not enough to others. You were digging away in your own character, so you were less infected by the language. You were doing things to the words, rather than letting them do things to you.

I know there is tiredness, which is understandable. But I'm going to be brutal, I'm not going to let you do this patterning, because it's catching, and it can become competitive. The solution lies in the power of thought. Take care of the thoughts, and the emotions will look after themselves. If you're truly thinking, you'll never find the same pattern, except by chance. So police it, be merciless with yourselves. It's essential that your thoughts stay fresh, that you keep them sizzling away beneath you. Get your pulses racing from the half, don't go on with cotton wool in your mouth.

We must avoid long-run-itis, we have to be intellectually excited every night. This is a remarkable and wonderful play that we're going to be carting round the world. You've got to wake up in the morning and think, It's *Hamlet* today! Otherwise what are we here for?

He then gives individual notes, adjusting a move here, pinpointing a loss of concentration there. The actors spend the rest of the morning refining these details on stage. Afterwards there's praise for John's forthright talk. 'It was really helpful,' Cathryn says. 'You try to police yourself and be a third eye, but if you do it too much you're outside of what you're doing, and then it all goes wrong anyway. So you need someone like John to be that honest. Not everyone would bother to tell you.'

Friday 21 July

The lecture has had an effect: last night two minutes were taken off the previous night's running time. John is clearly pleased that the actors have responded to his criticisms:

> The performance last night was extraordinarily alive and fresh, and underivative of anything they'd ever done before. Of course new patterns may emerge, and they too will have to be got rid of. The great difficulty actors have with the first few previews is their own comfort. After the arduous business of rehearsal and the technicals they're emotionally exhausted, and the repetitiveness of the work is enervating. In that state their choices can sometimes become motivated by safety and comfort, rather than by the daring and risk they should be involved in.
>
> It actually happens when an entire cast feels comfortable with the work. In a troubled company that's at odds with itself, where some people have fared much better than others, it won't be so apparent, because people are still trying to experiment themselves out of their own unhappiness. But in a company like this one, where everyone is more or less at the same level of performance and understanding of the play, the patterns can be set up much earlier. In fact it's quite a good thing that they have been, because now they can get them out of their system.

The previews have given the technical team a chance to consider whether any scenes or moments need re-thinking. Seeing the lighting or hearing the music in continuous action for only the second or third time, they're able to tighten up or change aspects of the production at several points.

Saturday 22 July

The final preview. After today there's to be a week's break, then the start of the tour at Malvern, followed by the trip to Elsinore. As the press night is not until early September, when the company returns to the Lyttelton, John suggests they treat tonight's performance as the opening, and use it for all the normal first-night rituals, exchanging good-luck cards and so on. In this way he hopes they will feel the show has already opened when they get to Malvern, and that the London press night will then be more of an ordinary night, when the press just happen to be there.

The audience reaction to the evening's performance is as enthusiastic as it has been throughout the week. Afterwards Simon reflects on the value of the previews.

Their main use is to just get you through the play. The first one was pretty good, I thought we were rather well prepared, but there's been a lot of fine tuning since then. For instance, tonight we changed the blocking for the closet scene. It had seemed all right in the rehearsal room, but on stage it seemed too static. There's more movement now, and that's released us emotionally. I've also begun to get more of a sense of the shape of the play, the rising graph that goes up to the point when Hamlet goes to England, and then this extraordinary last act, which is almost like a separate play.

Someone told me I was a very cerebral Hamlet. I think what he meant was that there wasn't a lot of hysteria in my performance. Hysteria has its place, and wonderful Hamlets have been much more emotionally expressive than me. But every Hamlet is different. My response to him is not what I expected it to be. I thought it would be more savage, more grotesque and less self-assured. But I seem to have found a great calm in him.

John is also very satisfied with the week's work.

Previews are always deeply instructive. There's a well-known theatre axiom that the audience is the missing character in any play you're doing. In a Shakespeare play that's probably more true than in others, because the story is so full of soliloquy. So many characters have a relationship with the missing character, that when you get an audience for the first time you complete the circle of communication, and find what the play needs in order to have a meaning. Consciously or otherwise, actors learn a tremendous amount from a live audience, about attention, about timing, about tension.

He feels Simon has benefitted a great deal from these first six performances.

In a positive and creative way he's fallen in love with the audience. I think it's a necessary part of his journey. To arrive in front of an audience and have them so manifestly and audibly appreciative must have been music to his ears. He's bound to be seduced by their response, but as he's an honest player he won't be corrupted by it. Over the next few weeks he'll continue to play with the audience, but he'll become more rigorous in the way he does so. The great risk in the first few previews in a big, romantic part is self-indulgence. But Simon is an extremely self-denying actor, so I don't think he'll ever be guilty of that.

4. The Tour Begins

Wednesday 2 August

Malvern, Worcestershire. The actors have arrived in this small, attractive spa town, strung out along the hills overlooking the Severn Valley. Tonight the *Hamlet* tour begins with the first of ten performances in the Festival theatre.

Jenny Mann, the National's tour publicist, is mounting the production's photographs in the theatre foyer. Her role in publicising these first performances, and those soon to come in Brighton and Glasgow, is complicated by the fact that the press night is not until next month. 'Without review quotes, I'm lacking part of the weaponry I usually have to sell a show,' she says.

There's a brief comment today in a preview paragraph in the *Guardian*, describing Simon as 101 per cent brilliant. But that's a bit unofficial, so I can't use it as an ad, though I could perhaps in a mailing letter. But protocol is a difficult matter. We've asked the press to come in to the Lyttelton in September, but these performances in Malvern are not previews, nothing about them is embargoed, so there's nothing to stop a critic coming along. Fortunately they usually respect what is asked of them.

During the morning Stephen holds a word-run in the modern Forum theatre, across the foyer from the Festival theatre. The actors have had a ten-day break from the play, and need to re-acquaint themselves with the text, and each other. With no lights, music or sound, and chairs standing in for boxes on the bare stage, there's no attempt to give a proper performance: the aim for the actors is simply to get the lines right, pick up their cues promptly, and get back under the skin of their characters. The run also serves as a re-bonding session, and the playing is light and casual. More than a hint of camp is allowed to creep in, and in the last scene, played up to the melodramatic hilt, the gags begin to come. Hamlet's dying words 'Let be' provoke a collective hum of the Lennon/McCartney song. The mood at the end is merry and relaxed, as was the intention.

In the afternoon it's back to reality, and the technical rehearsal. The small, late-Victorian theatre poses an immense challenge after the larger space of the Lyttelton. Since Sunday the production and stage management team have been in the theatre, where lighting has been one of the major problems. 'It's been a pretty tense few days, and a lot of midnight oil has been burnt getting the new plan right,' Paul Pyant says.

The stage is a quarter of the size, and we've brought less than a third of the set. Only some of the back wall has come, and the side walls have been cut completely. We haven't got room for all the boxes, and we've only got 18 chandeliers out of 30. So it's all very scaled down. But we've tried to keep the principal lighting elements of each scene.

The tech throws up problems for the actors. With no side walls, fewer entrances, and no space to cross behind the cyclorama, the feeling is slightly claustrophobic. The stage gets very crowded in some of the scene changes, which need careful re-rehearsing. ('It's ages since I did pub theatre,' one actor remarks.) Because of the rake everyone has to be careful with their movement, especially Simon and Guy in the fight scene. Sometimes they mask each other in the smaller space, so Stephen darts around the stage, suggesting new positions. Occasionally they are unable to hear their cues because the music is too loud. A huge amount of adjustment is needed.

In the evening the Malvern audience becomes totally absorbed in the performance. At the end they stand, applauding and cheering loudly. Afterwards the actors receive many enthusiastic comments as they mingle with members of the audience at a buffet reception in the theatre's restaurant.

Friday 4 August

The first reviews appear, in the local and regional press. They are extremely positive. John's production is applauded for its care and inspiration, while Simon's Hamlet attracts widespread praise for its intelligence and clarity. But one paper headlines its review 'Tubby or not tubby, fat is the question', a witticism which Simon finds a little hurtful. 'It wouldn't be so bad if it was just slipped in during the article,' he says ruefully.

John is not happy with the decision to bring the production to such a small theatre.

While everything is smaller or closer together, the actors are still the same size, so the effect is a Brobdignagian version of *Hamlet*. It looks muddled, like a rehearsal-room fit-up production with an unnecessarily elaborate back-wall device. Or it looks like a nice design that hasn't been quite completed, as if we couldn't afford the sides. I feel the show should either be done with its three walls and fifteen openings and clear delineation of a prison-like interior space that could be a church, all the evocative things that the set in the Lyttelton expresses – or we shouldn't have the walls at all, we should just use the metaphor of the trunks and lamps, and get on with it. Luckily in Trish we've got the most organised and persuasive stage manager in the history of stage management, so things have gone very smoothly here.

Saturday 12 August

The last night at Malvern. Overall, despite the problems with the set, the ten days here have been a success. Simon is delighted with the audience reaction. 'It was good, very friendly, and much more vocal than I had imagined.' But his feelings are less positive about the move from the Lyttelton to the smaller theatre: 'I didn't particularly like the mix and match feeling of it. The stage was a bit crowded, and the production lost something with half the chandeliers gone. On the other hand the smaller space made the play more intimate, which was useful: you could take your foot off the pedal.'

After the performance ends, Trish and her team supervise the striking of the set, and along with Stephen prepare to fly out tomorrow to Denmark.

Sunday 13 August

Kronborg Castle, Elsinore. Here, exactly four hundred years after its first performance, the actors are to perform *Hamlet* in the very castle in which Shakespeare set the play. The building is quite unlike the Gothic, gloomy place high above the sea that everyone had been expecting. Built in the Dutch Renaissance style in warm, Cotswold-coloured stone, with a lighthouse beacon shining at night from one of its towers, the castle stands at sea level on the edge of the Sound, the strip of water that separates Denmark from Sweden. There is in fact no direct evidence that Shakespeare ever visited Elsinore, although members of his company, the Chamberlain's Men, certainly did so. Scholars and critics remain divided over whether the many local references in the text are based on direct observation by Shakespeare, or on reports from his fellow-actors.

There has not been a production of *Hamlet* here for ten years. Recent ones, including those starring Kenneth Branagh and David Threlfall, have been staged on the battlements rather than in the courtyard where the National company will be performing. The stage being set up in one corner of the yard is nearer in size and shape to the Olivier than the Lyttelton, with its 680 seats spread round three sides on a steeply banked, purpose-built scaffolding construction.

The control box is behind the back row, under a tarpaulin cover, alongside two spotlights: otherwise the stage is lit by a series of tall rigs placed around the courtyard. The set is minimal: there is no back wall, and so no cross, and no crack for characters to step through from the real world. The task of adapting the production for these very different conditions is complicated by the absence of both director and designer. It had always been intended that Stephen should supervise this part of the tour on John's behalf. But it had also been assumed that Tim, who had already come out on a reconnoitring trip, would be on hand to supervise the re-design. His enforced absence has put considerable extra pressure on Stephen, who now has to make crucial design as well as directing decisions. One of these has involved a disagreement with the festival organiser, who didn't like the flats that had been put up, and wanted the production to be played against the castle walls. 'That's a different production of *Hamlet*,' Stephen explains. 'This isn't a play about Denmark; this is a play about a man. Elsinore is just a device.'

Tuesday 15 August

The actors and musicians arrive in Elsinore in the late afternoon, and are driven almost immediately from their accommodation to the castle, to start the technical rehearsal in the new venue in preparation for tomorrow night's opening. Also in the party are Jenny Mann, Roger Chapman, the National's Head of Touring, and Head of Press Lucinda Morrison, who's here to look after two British journalists writing features on the production.

The tech begins in daylight, and continues as darkness falls. One immediate problem is communication within the stage management team, whose headphones only work poorly in the open air because of interference. Another is the actors' visibility to the audience as they leave the stage and walk the few yards to the dressing-room in the castle. Originally their movements were covered by screens, but the local fire officer has insisted on a five-metre gap between the castle and the stage, and they have had to come down. As a compromise, two side flats have been erected to mask the movements of the actors standing backstage.

With no time to recuperate after travelling for most of the day, the actors are cold, exhausted and obviously stressed. Then, as they rehearse the closet scene, Sylvester enters in the guise of the Ghost, gliding on to the stage in unexpectedly smooth style on a micro-scooter hidden beneath his cloak. The actors collapse with laughter, and the tension is broken.

Afterwards Simon ponders the challenges that face him and the company in this historic venue.

> My main worry is the sheer size of the stage, which means you lose many of the subtleties. Although it was calm this evening, I'm told the wind can take your voice right away. I've never played outside before, and I'm worried about the physical effort, the need to be much more rhetorical. Even tonight I got bored with the sound of my own voice, because you have to do it at such a pitch. But it's a thrilling place to be playing in. I found it very exciting as the light was dying, and you got all the different colours of the sky. At one point I went to the loo and came back through the dark and I thought, I'm Hamlet, and I'm walking through Elsinore!

Wednesday 16 August

A brief press call at Lo-Skolen, the conference centre where the company is staying. The mayor, Per Taersbol, dressed casually in jeans, turns out to be a former actor who once played Hamlet. He explains that after a break of several years in the tradition of companies doing *Hamlet* at Elsinore, the town now plans to stage a production every year.

The actors field questions from local journalists: Simon emphasises the domestic nature of the National's production, while Denis suggests that cutting out the politics has improved the play. After lunch they return to the castle, where the crew are uncovering the stage after this morning's rain and, in the face of a strong wind, Jenny is setting up the publicity boards at the entrance to the courtyard.

Trish and Roger Chapman have had a difficult meeting with the festival producer Terence Davies. Without insurance, which was too costly, he's nervous about any interruption that might lead to postponement or cancellation, and wants to be able to sit backstage in order to be party to any such decision. Trish and Roger, however, feel the actors' safety is paramount, and that she should be the one to halt or postpone the action if need be. 'You can't have a committee meeting about stopping a show,' she explains. Their view has prevailed.

One necessity during the tech is to get the new box moves right. But the greatest problem is audibility. The castle is still open to visitors, so that as well as seagulls and the occasional plane, the actors have to contend with the noise of groups of Japanese tourists and Danish schoolchildren, who walk through the courtyard and behind the stage area on their tour of the building. Stephen, running up to the back row from time to time, warns the actors if and when their words are lost.

Unlike in the Lyttelton or at Malvern, the actors have to negotiate steps on to the raised stage. This means careful re-rehearsing of certain entries, such as the carrying of Ophelia's bier into the graveyard. There are a couple of minor injuries: Denis cuts his hand while he's inside the grave, and Janet Spencer-Turner, the Player Queen, is stung on the foot by a bee, causing her to walk with a visible limp.

Just as Simon comes to 'The readiness is all' it begins to rain, the tech is abandoned, and the stage hastily covered again. The actors huddle in the dressing rooms, a series of bare, dank vaulted rooms within the castle directly behind the stage. Though spacious enough, they have no running water, which means a kettle has to be boiled in order to be able to get the Ghost's make-up off.

Here Trish offers the actors some last-minute advice. She warns them they may have problems in seeing their floor markings in the darker scenes, and to be careful with their footing once the dew descends towards the end of the evening. She also explains the scenario if, as now seems likely, rain should interrupt the performance: 'I might let a bit of drizzle go, but I won't let it get dangerous,' she says.

Miraculously, the heavy rain stops an hour before the scheduled start, and the show begins on time under a clear, pale-blue sky. The audience, laced with local dignitaries, is at first slow to react, and there's noticeably no response to the line 'Denmark is a prison'. As the play proceeds the open air

gives a special resonance to references to the elements, though not always at
the right moment: Hamlet's allusion to the 'brave o'erhanging firmament'
is made in broad daylight. As Simon reaches 'Oh what a rogue and peasant
slave' the handful of clouds in the sky are turning to pink, and by the time
he arrives at 'To be or not to be' it is dusk. A rare jet plane drowns Hamlet
and Ophelia's 'country matters' exchange, but otherwise only the occasional
shrieking of a gull and the chiming of the clock tower disturb the action.

During the interval members of the audience wrap themselves up in
blankets lent by the local fire brigade. Night thickens, and thus protected
from the biting cold they become increasingly enthralled by the action
unfolding under the starlit Danish sky. Their response at the end is full of
warmth and enthusiasm.

Afterwards the actors attend a candlelit buffet reception in the castle's
magnificent banqueting hall. Later, walking through the castle grounds
alongside the moat lit every few yards with flares, with a full moon shining
above the silhouetted walls and towers, they talk about the magic of acting
in the famous courtyard. Paul Bazely says: 'It's wonderful not to have to
think a scene in your head, but to be actually playing it here.' Cathryn adds:
'It took me a while to settle down, but when I was waiting to go on for the
mad scene it came upon me how thrilling it was.'

Simon is equally enthusiastic:

> It was a fantastic occasion, and wonderful to see the sky and relate it
> to the play. Because you were in the open air you felt you were talking
> about the whole world, about God, about everything. There were noises,
> but unless it was very loud, like the planes, I was unaware of it. The bells
> didn't worry me, or the birds or the wind or the sea; they were all part of
> the soundscape.

But he was less certain about his performance.

> I honestly didn't know whether it was good or bad, I just aimed to get
> through it. Until the interval I was scared of the audience; I prefer them to
> be well out of sight. Also I was oddly outside myself, I was feeling slightly
> remote, and thinking it was a bit of a weird thing to be doing, standing
> and shouting on a stage.

Stephen is generally satisfied with the Elsinore opening.

> The actors were a bit scared at the start, it's an enormous stage which
> involves a lot of walking. With a new venue there's always a sense
> of tiptoeing back into the play. I think tonight Simon was slightly on
> the back foot for the first few speeches. But overall it went very well.
> The elements that didn't quite work were because we were outside.
> The opening, for instance, where the actors are seen to be ghosts, only

really makes sense in the dark; here it just looked like a line-up of the cast. The other thing we've lost because of the open auditorium is John and Tim's concept of the enclosure, that end-on view where you look into the box, and the only knowledge of the outside world is the small chink at the back, where there's life rather than death. Only when it became dark did we begin to get that back.

Thursday 17 August

Over breakfast, in the cold light of day, the actors reflect on last night's performance. Most of them disliked playing the first part in daylight: 'It produces rather unsubtle acting,' Janet says. 'I don't like seeing people's wig lines and their make-up. When I first came on there was a clash of colours in the audience which put the actors out of focus. It was also rather distracting seeing a woman breastfeeding her baby.' Simon Day enjoyed speaking his line 'Flights of angels sing thee to thy rest' to the elements, but found the conditions difficult. 'The stage was very damp with dew, and you felt a bit hammy hitting every consonant really hard, like an RSC actor.' Sara found it physically very demanding and hard to project: 'If someone told me I'd never have to play in Elsinore again, I'd be secretly very pleased,' she admits.

There's also some concern about the actors' visibility between the flats, which seems especially awkward when the 'dead' Polonius is seen returning to the dressing-room. Denis suggests it might have been better to have had no flats, and have the actors sitting on chairs at the side of the stage, 'so at least you were making a statement'.

At noon, in bright sunshine, the company arrives at the Marienlyst Hotel near the castle for a reception given by members of the National's development department. On the terrace looking across to Sweden they mingle with a group of the theatre's financial supporters who have been brought over from London for 24 hours to see the production, then join them for an excellent lunch inside.

Six-thirty in the evening. The castle courtyard. During the afternoon there's been a thunderstorm and torrential rain, but now it's finally stopped, and right on cue the sky is clearing. The crew are sweeping the water from the stage, while others are drying the seats with towels and sponges. The actors stand around anxiously, getting individual notes from Stephen, who is again stressing the importance of being heard.

Once again, the show goes on. This time the performance is more assured and relaxed, the audience more responsive, and the rapport between them and the actors more evident. Simon plays with confidence, giving Hamlet more bite without losing his other qualities; after 'O what a rogue and peasant slave' he gets a round of applause. The heavens more obviously become another character in the play, making its spiritual qualities sharper. The reception at the end borders on the tumultuous. 'They cracked it,'

Stephen says as the audience vanishes into the night. 'They established a relationship with the audience from the beginning. I feel they're back on top of it.'

At supper afterwards the actors are clearly pleased: they know they've regained control of the play. Simon senses a significant improvement. 'In general I'm unaware of whether a performance is more or less powerful, but tonight I felt it was much better played by everybody,' he says. 'The pace was different, the audience was less formal, they got the jokes from the beginning. So we were more relaxed, and we did a proper show.'

Friday 18 August

Over breakfast Simon talks about Hamlet's faith, and how far his own tentative religious feelings have informed his performance. 'I suppose my faith is borderline really, it's been building up for years, and it's time I jumped one way or the other. But I think it affects my playing of the part enormously, and of course my personal circumstances, the death of my mother, make it especially important.'

> The play is unquestionably Hamlet's debate with his God, and where that leads him in the final act is probably to a good place. That's what it's been most nights; there's that whole sense that all will be well. Perhaps that's too sentimental, but I think it's a valid reading. I think his line 'I am dead, Horatio' is a happy line, because he's meeting his God. I'm playing around with giving it a smile, but it might change every night, depending where I've got to in his journey. I might sometimes feel more resigned, abdicating responsibility and judgement for my own life, or it might be a wonderful moment of happiness and release – or both.

Thursday 24 August

The last of the eight performances at Elsinore. This time the torrential rain comes later, and prevents a prompt start. Some of the actors don't want to go ahead, but others are keen not to cancel. Eventually the skies clear, and despite it being bitterly cold, with a high wind causing the lighting towers to sway and the tarpaulins to flap noisily, the decision is made to risk going ahead. Darkness is falling, and a deal is struck with the audience: they may want to leave at the interval, but if they stay on they must do so until the end, and transport will be arranged back to hotels.

For once, the actors have that cocoon of darkness they have missed in the opening scenes, and Hamlet's meeting with the Ghost strikes an appropriate note of terror. By the interval they're playing under a calm, starlit sky, and in the second half they achieve a thrilling and magical intensity. At the end Simon leads the company in applauding the audience. 'Normally I hate actors doing that, it looks so self-congratulatory,' he says afterwards. 'But this time I wanted to do it. I thought, poor sods, it's half-past twelve, they deserve a medal for sticking in there.'

Friday 25 August

The actors leave Elsinore for Copenhagen, from where they will fly back to London. The trip is considered a success. The Danish notices have been excellent, calling Simon the finest Hamlet of his generation; the Swedish critics who have crossed the water to Elsinore have also been very approving. Despite the atrocious conditions there have been no cancellations, and the eight performances have been a sell-out.

'The trickier the weather, the more responsive the audiences have been,' Stephen says.

> Because they've invested so much, they've got an enormous payoff. The whole experience here has helped everyone bond together, so that we're now a very strong and happy company. Part of that is due to Simon, who insists that the production is about sixteen actors, and not just one. He doesn't play the star offstage, he's friendly with the crew and talks to everybody, and that engenders in the company a desire to do well.

5. The London Opening

Wednesday 30 August

The rehearsal room at the National. The actors have reassembled to prepare for this evening's performance, the first of five before next Tuesday's press night. It's been six weeks since the previews were held in the Lyttelton, so this afternoon Trish and Stephen will top and tail the production technically, re-rehearse exits and entrances, and go through the lighting cues now that the full complement of chandeliers is restored to the set.

The morning is spent working in detail on several scenes or parts of scenes. A few of them clearly need attention after Elsinore; others have been causing concern in the previews. In some cases they have been identified by Stephen, in others by one or more of the actors. 'Today is about sorting out niggles and shaking Elsinore away,' Stephen says. 'The aim is to turn things that have been bellowed and big in the open air into something intimate and domestic again.'

One such is the opening scene, which he feels should be swifter and smaller. Another is Hamlet's cliff-top meeting with the Ghost. Stephen suggests to Sylvester that he could be less of a tormented spirit, and more of a father passing on responsibility to his son. A third is Polonius' 'pastoral-comical' speech, where Hamlet's and Rosencrantz and Guildenstern's laughter has been peaking too early.

Cathryn and Denis work on the scene in which Polonius forbids Ophelia to see Hamlet. They try to pinpoint more precisely when it turns serious; John had said earlier they were playing its outcome at the start. 'I have to try and lighten it,' Cathryn says. They play it, and she does so. 'That time I believed it,' Denis says.

In Elsinore Sara was unhappy about having to play the closet scene in an exaggerated way, so she and Simon play it again, bringing it down a few notches. They feed off each other expertly, making small adjustments to their moves to give the argument a greater coherence.

The actors also look at Laertes' departure for France. Peter wants to put over more strongly the idea of a happy and relaxed court, one which only later starts to fall apart. Meanwhile both Guy and Simon have been concerned that until Hamlet's apology just before the duel, when he calls Laertes 'brother', there is no sign that the two know each other. It's agreed that a hint of this should be given in the scene. At first Guy tries touching Simon on the shoulder as he leaves; then a handshake is suggested. 'Make it a hard handshake,' Simon says. 'I need to boost my heterosexuality all I can.'

Afterwards Simon talks about the effect the Elsinore week has had on the production.

> Our performance had to be much grander, and also much simpler, otherwise it got swallowed up by the wind. The verse had to be more muscular, more banged out, which isn't a bad thing; the bounce does provide you with a kind of confidence. Making it more economical wasn't as difficult as I thought it would be, because the audience couldn't see the minutiae. But it was an odd experience, there were so many practical things to think of: making sure you were being heard, turning your face in the right direction.
>
> I'm sure when John comes back he'll have some strict words to say about all the original intentions that we've lost. That's why it's been good to have this morning's session, just to be able to get back to the words and think about them again. In the closet scene, for instance, the emotional landscape is still there, but what we'd lost was all the detailed thought.

He is, he admits, longing to be back in the Lyttelton.

> Doing the play at Elsinore without the original set was a real trial of strength. I kept wanting to say to the audience, This is not the show you'll see in London – which of course would have been unfair. But I can't wait to get back to the original set, because it's such an integral part of the production, and it looks so ravishing and beautiful in the Lyttelton.

Saturday 2 September

Evening. The stage management box at the back of the Lyttelton. With a clear view of the stage through a glass screen, Fiona Bardsley is seated at the controls, a board full of lights and switches. In her headphone set she has three separate 'rings': one connecting her with the sound and the musicians, another with the flies, stage management and stage crew, and a third with the lighting team.

Next to her is an infra-red monitor, allowing her to see what's happening on stage during any blackout: as the eyes and ears of the production she keeps a constant watch for problems or mistakes. She also controls the complex sequence of sound, music and lighting cues, of which there are about a hundred in *Hamlet*. 'You have to be able to concentrate and keep calm, and not panic if something goes wrong,' she says.

The performance begins. 'LX cue one, fly cue one, sound cue one – stand by.' In between giving the instructions Fiona talks through the headphones with Pete Bull on lighting and Adam Rudd on sound, who sit at computerised desks in control rooms on either side of her. Together they pinpoint any technical elements needing attention: a 'birdie' light at the front of the stage needs adjusting in one scene, to catch Simon's face better; the lighting in another seems to come up too gradually; the music linked to the opening of the back wall is a fraction too early. Fiona also talks frequently to Trish, Val and Andrew backstage.

Interval. The Lyttelton flytower, high above the stage. In an early scene the actors had been disturbed by noise from the flies, and Trish has come up to check on what happened with the man in charge. He and seven others are positioned on a narrow walkway, from where they operate by hand the numerous pulleys, cradles and counterweights that control the raising and lowering of the chandeliers.

The play resumes. Backstage, Trish sits in the prompt corner 'on the book', while also keeping a wary eye on her monitor on the flying of the chandeliers. Nearby Denis, now in his Gravedigger costume, is climbing into his 'grave' ready to be pushed on stage. 'I spend nine minutes in this bloody box,' he says in mock horror. 'You see how I suffer for my art?'

As the play continues Val and Andrew move around the wide spaces behind the side walls, where the various props, labelled in white to be visible in the semi-dark, are set out on long tables. Dressed in black costumes, they make sure the actors are in position at the right moment, occasionally joining them on stage for the more complicated scene changes and box-shifting.

Trish deals with a few routine problems: an actor goes missing, but is found just in time for his cue; one of the musicians is heard practising on the recorder in a dressing-room, so Andrew is dispatched to stop the playing. Overall the performance is a smooth one technically, and her nightly report a very satisfactory one.

Tuesday 5 September

Press night. For Lucinda in the press office the unusual timetable has proved a blessing. Normally interviews with the company have to be arranged late on in the rehearsal period, when the actors and director have little time or energy to spare. 'Having the press night so late was an enormous advantage,' she says. 'Journalists have been able to come and see the show in the Lyttelton, and talk to Simon when he had some time off, or even in Malvern, before writing their pieces. Normally he gets quite nervous about interviews, but he's terribly willing. This time he'd done the previews, the show was up and running, and so he was more relaxed. The result has been four extensive interview-based features before the official first night.'

Few actors enjoy press nights, and Simon is no exception. 'I hate them, they're a real trial,' he says before the performance.

> I'm trying not to think about it too much. *Hamlet* will never get universal admiration, it's such an enormous piece. Some people won't be happy that we've cut all the Fortinbras stuff – although this far on I've forgotten that it's missing; the play as we're doing it seems to be quite coherent without all the geo-politics. Really I just want to get tonight over, and then I can sit back and enjoy the play.

Before the performance John gives the actors the advice he gives every company he works with, recommending them not to read the reviews. If they have to do so, he asks them not to assume that anyone else in the company will want to know what they say. 'If you do read them, don't take them too seriously,' he says. 'The people to take seriously are your audiences, how they respond, what they feel and what they say. What matters is the relationship between you, them and the author.'

With the benefit of six previews and five ordinary performances in the Lyttelton, the actors come up with a fine ensemble performance that holds the audience throughout, and provokes a sustained ovation at its end. Simon very quickly sheds his nerves and is on top of his form. Beforehand he had placed a framed picture of his mother on the prop table. 'It meant so much to me,' he says afterwards. 'Every time I came off she was there.'

Thursday 7 September

The critics are almost unanimous in their praise of Simon's performance. Dismissing the notion that he might be physically unsuited for the role, they write admiringly of the intelligence, wit and moral authority of his Hamlet, and the crystal-clear and unaffected way he handles the verse. Rare, remarkable, haunting, perfect are among the epithets used. In the *Daily Telegraph* Charles Spencer writes: 'Russell Beale's Prince was the finest I have seen – beautifully spoken, and blessed with a sense of grief, intelligence, warmth and humour. There was also a deeply moving sense of spiritual illumination in the last act.'

The other actors get a more mixed reception and, in many cases, totally conflicting comments on their performances. The views on the production are also mixed. As Simon anticipated, many of the critics find fault with the decision to cut Fortinbras and the politics. They argue that the play is diminished if it is treated as a domestic, personal drama within Elsinore, and that the warrior Fortinbras is useful as a foil to Hamlet the thinker. John's production is seen as original and imaginative by some, but others dislike the overtly religious emphasis, reinforced by the motets and the cathedral-like set. There is also some uncertainty about his concept of the actors as ghosts, and a general dislike of the luggage-based scene-shifting.

Monday 11 September

The Sunday critics have come up with much the same range of views as those on the daily papers. While writing warmly of Simon's lucid and heartfelt Hamlet, their comments on the production are less ecstatic, with the absence of Fortinbras and the political backdrop again being widely mourned. Meanwhile, with several critics having crossed the Atlantic, some very appreciative reviews have begun to appear in the American press

John sticks to his policy of not reading the critics. 'They have an important job to do, but their relationship should be with the audience, not the creative artists,' he says. 'I find reviews disturb me whether they're positive or negative. I'm as disturbed by feelings of pride that my work is being appreciated as I am by feelings of disappointment if it isn't. I find both feelings irrelevant to my thought-processes, so increasingly I shut them out.'

Simon had originally decided to take John's advice. 'I told my family and friends and the cast I wasn't going to read the reviews, and they were all fine about it,' he says. 'But then Sara phoned me after the opening last week and said, I know you're not reading the notices, but I'm told they're good. So then I read them almost immediately; I decided not to be a puritan after all! I'm not sure whether the other actors are reading them or not. Nowadays you assume people don't, so out of courtesy you don't talk about it.'

> My biggest relief was that my decision not to play Hamlet as mad came off. I knew that was a risk, and it was cowardice really, I didn't know where the madness would go, so I thought I'd have to take another route. But most critics seemed to get the idea of what we were trying to do. I was also pleased that the ones who liked it saw a romantic performance. That was entirely to do with John's faith, which I thought misguided, in seeing me as a romantic actor. He gave me tremendous confidence, encouraging me to be just who I am, and not worry about the way I look or move.

After the wounding Malvern headline he seems relaxed about the constant references to his physique. 'In the end they really haven't worried me. I am the shape I am, and they haven't been offensive. One critic called me overweight, which pleased me, because it was so non-judgemental. If they'd said, He's grotesquely fat and therefore he cannot play this part, I would have been very upset.'

6. The Tour Continues

Two weeks after the press night the company is due to resume the UK part of its tour. But before that a crucial event takes place in the Lyttelton: a full understudy performance, played to an audience of some 50 people scattered around the stalls, most of them friends of the actors.

Previous understudy rehearsals have been sporadic. Some work was done in Malvern, but none was possible in Denmark, and much of the time since returning to the National has been spent getting the production in as good a shape as possible. Before the performance Stephen explains:

> We had just three days last week, in effect fifteen hours, which isn't ideal for a production this size. Today will be useful for finding out which of the actors I still need to do more work with. But the performance will be especially important for Simon Day, who's put in a lot of work, and will now have the chance to play Hamlet at least once before an audience.

He proves to be an extremely impressive Hamlet. An excellent verse-speaker, he's a harsher, more intense and bitter Prince than the other Simon. The other principals provide intriguing contrasts to the actors they're standing in for: Janet Spencer-Turner is a more fragile Gertrude, Chloe Angharad an angrier Ophelia, Martin Chamberlain a more ferocious Claudius. In the few places where two characters being understudied by the same actor appear on stage together, Stephen plays one of them with a script in his hand, a situation that inevitably poses an extra challenge to the actors.

Afterwards Simon Day ponders on the experience. 'It felt like a good showing. It certainly gave me a window on what Simon goes through every night. It's like getting on this enormous thoroughbred racehorse, which is a joy to ride, but gives you no time to think, have I messed up that scene? because it just keeps going.'

> I've watched Simon a lot, and tried to be as honest as I could about the part. I loved going on the stage and seeing what would happen, opening myself up to the experience. When you play Hamlet you bare your soul and your personality comes through. I was probably an angrier Hamlet than Simon, but also a less funny one. He gets a lot of laughs, and I think that it's tremendous to be able to do that in a tragedy. But I felt I didn't know how to get them without faking it.

With the understudies firmly established in their roles, the actors take to the road again. During September they do a week each in Brighton and Glasgow, followed by a week at the Dublin Festival in early October. They then return for a further 24 performances in repertory in the Lyttelton before going abroad again in December for a week in Stockholm.

At each theatre the production is received with great enthusiasm. No audiences are more enthusiastic than those in the Stadsteater in Stockholm, where the play is listened to with intense concentration, and the actors are called back for countless curtain calls during standing ovations. But some audiences are less attentive. At one performance at the Gaiety in Dublin the rowdy behaviour of school groups attracts dozens of complaints from the audience during the interval, and the management has to make an announcement over the tannoy before the second half can begin. But equally annoying is a mobile phone, which rings throughout Hamlet's 'What a piece of work is a man' speech.

In Glasgow there's a special school matinee at the Theatre Royal, with 1,200 children booked in for the performance. Simon is terrified at the prospect, imagining that 'The last thing they want is an overweight, middle-aged Englishman talking to them about life and death.' Before the curtain rises the noise is intense, and bits of paper are flying across the auditorium. But once the play starts the children seem mesmerised, and at the end there are raucous cheers.

Like most actors, Simon has mixed feelings about an audience made up of school parties. 'I love kids coming to the theatre, because we need them, they're our future audience. But it can be very difficult playing to them, because many of them just don't want to be here. You just have to say to yourself, If there's one person who goes away inspired by what we're doing, then that makes it worthwhile.'

The critical reception on the tour is mostly very positive. The Irish press are particularly effusive, and in general more appreciative of the subtleties and visual beauty of the production than the English critics have been. In Scotland there is also enthusiasm, though one critic with a rather obvious nationalistic chip on his shoulder can't find a good word to say about this 'utterly E-N-G-L-I-S-H ... stiff upper-lipped and most frigid of *Hamlets*'.

Each venue poses a different problem for the National's technical and stage management team. In the Theatre Royal in Brighton the chandeliers have to be flown using heavy hemp ropes. With no counterweights, this means having two men for each rope, so the cues have to be simplified. In Stockholm, by contrast, the theatre is equipped with a power fly system operated by one man at a computer. This allows for a more sophisticated lighting design than has been possible even in the Lyttelton, where a shortage of manpower on the flies has ruled out some of the original ideas.

After the unhappy compromise at Malvern, it was agreed that for the smaller theatres there would be a simpler, more coherent set, with uniform black flats, just a single entrance in the back wall, and a ceiling from which some of the chandeliers could be hung permanently. There has also been a return to one of the original ideas, of using the luggage to create parts of the walls. The result has satisfied everyone.

During the tour Trish continues to keep a wary eye on the running time, which sometimes increases by three or four minutes.

> I have to tell the actors when they're slowing down, and that can drive them insane. One or two of them get so caught up and lost in the moment, they forget. I do feel a bit crass having to tick them off and get them to speed up. But they know that in watching the play every night I participate in the event and am therefore in a position to make a judgement.

Throughout the tour Simon works to improve his performance. After the Stockholm week he is still unhappy about some of his speeches. 'The first soliloquy is going through a bad patch: I think the balance should be lighter, it's become a bit aggressive. The speech after the Ghost disappears has become a one-note rant, and I need to see how far I can take it down. The recorder speech doesn't work sometimes, I seem to get the rhythm wrong. And I can't seem to get enough different colours into the chapel scene, where I consider killing Claudius while he's at prayer.'

> The one that's working quite well is 'Oh what a rogue', I think because it's broken up into clearly defined sections, and because it's the one where I most directly address the audience. As for 'To be or not to be', it's wonderful when it works, but that's quite rare. Although it's a stopping soliloquy, it musn't grind to a halt. It's a delicate balance, and I tend to slow down far too much. The sentences are oddly constructed, and you can lose the main verb. Also 'puzzles the will' comes at a very odd place, and if you slow down too much before that on 'the undiscovered country', you have a problem.
>
> On the positive side, the closet scene has become a completely moveable feast. I love it, because every night I have no idea where it's going to go. Sara and I trust each other, and if one of us makes a small decision at the start, it takes us into a completely different area. Sometimes for instance we don't touch at all, and sometimes I end up very angry. It can go in completely opposite directions. It's a lovely feeling.

Hamlet has consistently attracted full houses during the tour, as well as being a complete sell-out at the National. Before the play returns for another spell in the Lyttelton, Simon and John look back with pleasure on their work.

Beforehand Simon had been sceptical of the claims by other actors who had played Hamlet that it could be a life-changing experience. Now he is not so sure. 'The part just adapts itself to you, it's one of the most hospitable an actor can play. It says, Come and get me, I've got everything here, just pick what you want. But it does demand that you strip everything away. Hamlet takes you right through that process, until you end up with nothing – "Let be".'

As an actor the part enables you to say, I don't need to do any tricks, I don't need to show off in any way. You're able to stand on stage and allow people to have faith in you, to see that you are interesting as a human being – that of course applies to everyone on stage, but particularly to Hamlet. It's a most liberating experience, if you can get anywhere near that. You think, This is it, this is the Holy Grail of acting.

For John, directing *Hamlet* has been a deeply rewarding experience. 'I've spent a great deal of my life wondering about Shakespeare. You get closer to him, then he recedes, then you get closer again; he's a wonderful mystery. But when you encounter him in the flesh through one of his great characters, then he is most emphatically present. There's nothing mysterious about him then, just a profound talent, which you're getting straight into the vein.'

Hamlet embodies those depths of thought and analysis and observation that Shakespeare was haunted by all his life, the dreams and uncertainties and inquiries about human existence that drove him. Those hauntings were what made him write three plays a year, and return constantly to those central characters who reflected his thoughts and visions about the way the world wags, whether it was Richard II, Rosalind, Cleopatra, Lear, Macbeth – or Hamlet.

Always the greatest portrayers of those characters have been actors who have a Shakespearean imagination, which Simon certainly has. His greatness is contained within his rightness for the part. It's been an extraordinary privilege, and one that no scholar can have, however deeply they read the play: to get close to the man Shakespeare through a brilliant portrayal of his most profoundly philosophical character.

I've seen many Hamlets, and admired some of them. But my only deep relationship with the play is one that I have developed in Simon's company. I think the way he has played Hamlet has taken me closer than I've ever been to understanding what Shakespeare is all about.

Simon Russell Beale won the Evening Standard *Award for Best Actor, the Critics' Circle Award, and was nominated as Best Actor for an Olivier Award.*

7. Afterthoughts

Simon Russell Beale
No other part, not even Lear, requires you to be more just you. Let be – It's like saying to the audience, I'm sorry folks, but this is me; which is why my Hamlet will never be the same as another actor's Hamlet. At the end you are standing there in your raw humanity, going, This is what a human being

is. That's why it transfers across the sexes so wonderfully, because it's just about a human being.

If you play Hamlet, you are somehow putting yourself up to be part of a sequence.

Every Hamlet has to have an attitude to the living father. I think I slightly ducked out of that one, because I basically just loved him.

I never quite decided whether my mother knew about Claudius' murder of her husband.

I felt Hamlet and Ophelia didn't have a relationship at all. I think his knowledge of sex was probably zilch.

I rather skirted over the deaths of Rosencrantz and Guildenstern, because I wanted him to be a sweet prince in the end.

Almost my favourite image in the whole play is of Gertrude wearing the same shoes at the wedding as she was at the funeral.

My first thought about 'To be or not to be' was, this is rather pedestrian. I had no idea why it was such an important speech in our culture. That first line: is it that profound? But then it eats into your soul, and you suddenly realise it's a profound statement, and that's why it's survived so well. There's a physical flavour to it, but it's about calm. I hated it at first, but I grew to love it. It seems to me to be unlike any other speech in the play, partly because it's so steadily written. The other soliloquies are so much more dynamic, they seem to come out of the situation and then return to it, whereas this one seems to come out of thin air. It's an independent, self-contained meditation on the afterlife.

It seems to me that by the time you get to the deaths at the end there's something arbitrary or irrelevant about it – it's a mess, everyone dies. I don't know what the significance of those deaths is. Because everyone dies, including Hamlet, and he dies because of a mixed-up sword and poison, it doesn't seem to me a significant part of the last act.

Hamlet's great speech to Horatio about dying, 'If it be now … ' I think that's my motto.

I wanted to die standing up, and so I did 'The rest is silence' standing up. The life has left him before he leaves us; he's been dying for quite a long time.

I remember Paul Rhys, who had just played the part, coming up to me and saying, 'You're about to do Hamlet – it will change your life,' and me going in my head, 'No part can do that.' But I think it sort of did.

John Caird

Religion had a great deal to do with my interpretation, but not religious controversies. The main reason I set the play in a discernibly Renaissance period is that I don't think the play works if it's set in a post-Enlightenment world. The central characters are deeply concerned with the mortality of their souls. Without the religious and spiritual context in which Shakespeare was writing it's hard to make sense of the play philosophically and intellectually.

I see a lot of *Hamlets* where the actor plays the madness card in order to escape a proper investigation of the part. Of course it's exciting for an actor to walk onto the stage looking or acting completely nuts, but there's nothing in the language of the scenes to suggest madness at all. Hamlet doesn't say ´ anything mad. I came to the view, after rehearsing it and extrapolating all the sense I could from what he says in each of his scenes, that Hamlet is the only sane person in the play. Almost everyone else is to some extent mad, with the obvious exception of Horatio ... What's amazing about Hamlet is that, in the circumstances he finds himself in, he doesn't go mad. Instead he gets saner and saner as the play continues.

For the play-within-a-play I used a staging trick. It was performed at the very edge of the stage with Claudius, Gertrude and Polonius watching from upstage. The two audiences – for *The Murder of Gonzago* at Elsinore and for *Hamlet* at the National Theatre – became reflections of one another. By the device of building false prosceniums on either side of the stage, I created 'wings'. Hamlet stood in the wings, reacting as a director or an author would in the wings of an actual theatre. The National Theatre audience could thereby watch Hamlet watching the play, while he simultaneously observed the reactions of Claudius and Gertrude as they watched from their own auditorium. This solved the problem of Hamlet having to whisper things quietly enough for Claudius and Gertrude not to hear them, but loudly enough for Ophelia and the National Theatre audience to hear.

Earlier in the play other people have seen the Ghost, so you know he isn't a figment of Hamlet's imagination. But in the closet scene he isn't real to Gertrude, or doesn't appear to her. This is psychologically apt. She can't 'see' her husband any longer. If she could still see him she wouldn't have married his brother. It is Hamlet's perception of his father that brings her to her senses. He reminds her of her former happiness and her love for her husband and son. This is the beginning of Gertrude's madness. She never recovers from this scene.

The 'Let be' is not in the Folio, but Simon and I both thought it indispensable. It is the perfect spiritual punctuation for that speech and it must, surely, be by Shakespeare's hand. No other writer could have been at the same time so bold and so succinct.

10

Hamlets at Elsinore

During the last 80 years companies of English actors have travelled to Denmark to perform *Hamlet* where Shakespeare set his play. Kronborg Castle in Elsinore is quite unlike the romantic, Gothic, gloomy place high above the sea fixed in many people's imagination. Built in the Dutch Renaissance style in warm, Cotswold-coloured stone, the castle stands at sea level on the coast of Denmark on the Sound, the strip of water that separates it from Sweden. Built in the 1420s, it was given a Renaissance refurbishment, completed in 1585.

The Earl of Leicester's men visited from England as part of the inauguration; the troupe included Will Kempe, later Shakespeare's most popular clown. There is no direct evidence that Shakespeare ever visited Elsinore, although members of his company, the Chamberlain's Men, and other companies did so in the late sixteenth century, and he may have had accounts of the place from them. The idea of staging *Hamlet* in the castle began in 1816, when a Danish translation/adaptation was performed by soldiers around the castle precincts, to celebrate the bi-centenary of Shakespeare's death. In 1916, to mark the tri-centenary, the Royal Theatre in Copenhagen performed the play on the ramparts overlooking the Sound.

In 1937 Laurence Olivier and the Old Vic company became the first English company to stage the play there since the sixteenth century. The castle was open to tourists, so they could only rehearse on the platform stage in the courtyard at night. It frequently rained, but the Old Vic's manager Lillian Baylis was on hand to dispense sandwiches and lemonade to the weary actors and, on one especially wet night, a keg of rum.

But a last-minute storm made the courtyard impossible, so director Tyrone Guthrie decided to perform it in the large ballroom of the nearby Marienlyst Hotel. This had only a tiny cabaret stage, so he ordered the chairs to be rearranged so the actors would play in the middle of the room, with the audience around them. Olivier improvised exits and entrances and rearranged business; Guthrie apologised to the audience for 'the strangest performance of *Hamlet* on any stage'.

Although the term had not yet been invented, this was effectively theatre-in-the-round. As Guthrie later recalled: 'The audience thought it a gallant effort, and they were with us from the start; actors always thrive on emergency, and the company did marvels.' The critic Ivor Brown wrote: 'Triumphantly, it worked. What I saw was as good a performance of *Hamlet* as I have ever seen. The words, the story, the driving emotional pressure of the play were clear and compelling.' The occasion had a profound effect on Guthrie, who had a growing conviction the proscenium arch was unsatisfactory for Shakespeare. 'At its best moments that performance in the ballroom related the audience to a Shakespeare play in a different, and, I thought, more logical, satisfactory and effective way,' he recalled.

Two years later John Gielgud directed his Lyceum company, with himself as the Prince. Again the weather was atrocious: it rained nearly every day. He described one performance as 'extracts from the Lyceum production with wind and rain accompaniments'. The Ghost scene was performed in broad daylight, thus ruining any atmosphere. Gielgud felt vulnerable: 'I hate being able to see the audiences so clearly,' he wrote. 'We feel defenceless, with our painted faces, until halfway through the evening, when the artificial lights are turned on.'

Three of the leading Copenhagen papers headed their reviews 'World's Best Hamlet'. The critic of *Politiken* wrote: 'Never has English sounded more beautiful from the human mouth.' The *Spectator* critic wrote:

> The audience was docile and all agog. The evening was a personal triumph for Gielgud, and a moving experience for his hearers. I don't think anyone there will easily forget Mr Gielgud's speaking of 'this brave o'erhanging firmament, this majestical roof fretted with golden fire', while the setting sun caught the pale-green copper rooftops and the swallows flew about high overhead.

The third English Hamlet to play there was Michael Redgrave, in 1950, heading the Old Vic company directed by Hugh Hunt. Comparing his performance to the one he gave in London, *The Times* remarked on 'the wonderful difference between an art which had been carefully thought out but not completely felt, and a part with which the actor's self has been securely identified'. In 1953 came Richard Burton, directed by Michael Benthall for the Old Vic. *The Times* noted: 'In Edinburgh he appeared to have selected from Hamlet's character all the most unsympathetic traits he could find. His playing had power, but it was curiously without charm. He has since come by a charm which sits extremely well on youthful melancholy, and in gaining charm, the performance has lost none of its original power.'

There was a gap of 25 years before Derek Jacobi came with his Hamlet. Toby Robertson, directing for Prospect, decided to restore the 'How all occasions' soliloquy, leaving Jacobi only three hours to re-learn it. The actor recalled his battle with the weather: 'The wind howled, the rain poured down so mightily I had to shout all the way through that soliloquy: possibly appropriate for the weather, but hardly for the more ruminative

"To be or not to be".' Michael Billington wrote: 'It didn't just rain, it pelted down, with the audience sitting wrapped in protective polythene sheets like giant contraceptives. Yet Jacobi and the Old Vic company bravely battled on; and, although he nearly slipped up on "Get thee to a nunnery", Jacobi managed to give us all of Hamlet's confusion, rage and sweetness of soul.'

In 1986 David Threlfall headed an Oxford Playhouse company, who played on a new covered stage outside the castle. This was a cut version, which omitted Hamlet's instructions to the Players. Two years later Kenneth Branagh, under Jacobi's direction, also played outside the castle for his Renaissance Theatre Company. Ten years on Bill Alexander staged a Birmingham Rep production back inside the courtyard. His Hamlet was Richard McCabe, who bravely played four acts barefoot on the freezing flagstones.

In 2009 Jude Law gave five performances, the audience being assisted by Danish surtitles. Robert McCrum observed: 'The British cast seems to get a buzz from performing in the shadow of the historical site, with the wind coming in over the ramparts, and those memorable lines echoing round the turrets and battlements. Jude Law wins a big ovation. He gives a film star's account of the part that's highly intelligent, but possibly misses the depth and range of a truly great performance.'

The Globe's 2011 production, directed by Dominic Dromgoole and Bill Buckhurst, with Joshua McGuire as Hamlet, fittingly ended its tour at Elsinore, as did the same theatre's worldwide Globe to Globe tour five years later, when Ladi Emeruwa and Naeem Hayat shared the lead role. The play was staged in the castle's long ballroom. Jasper Rees reported: 'You shiver when the Ghost appears; it's almost as cold in here as it is on the ramparts, so pretty much everyone makes use of the blankets provided.' He also noted that 'there are titters at "Something is rotten in the state of Denmark" and "Denmark's a prison" – perhaps because of no other country does either statement seem less apposite.'

MAIN SOURCES

Full publication details of books cited are in the Bibliography on page 188.

The 1950s

Michael Redgrave 1950 – Hugh Hunt, *Old Vic Prefaces*; Michael Redgrave, *In My Mind's Eye*; Richard Findlater, *Michael Redgrave*; Joan Plowright, *And That's Not All*; Kenneth Tynan, *He That Plays the King*; J.C.Trewin, *Five and Eighty Hamlets*; Audrey Williamson, *Theatre of Two Decades*; T.C.Worsley, *The Fugitive Art*.

Alec Guinness 1951 – Elaine Dundy, *Life Itself!*; Diana Rigg, *No Turn Unstoned*; Kathleen Tynan, *The Life of Kenneth Tynan*; John Russell Taylor, *Alec Guinness: A Celebration*; Kenneth Tynan, *Alec Guinness*; Alec Guinness, article in the *Spectator*, 5 July 1951. (Alec Guinness 1938 – Alec Guinness, *Blessings in Disguise*; James Forsyth, *Tyrone Guthrie*; Tyrone Guthrie, *A Life in the Theatre*; Ronald Harwood (ed.), *Dear Alec: Guinness at 75*; J.C.Trewin, *Five and Eighty Hamlets*; Audrey Williamson, *Old Vic Drama*; Garry O'Connor, *Alec Guinness the Unknown*; Piers Paul Read, *Alec Guinness*.)

Richard Burton 1953 – Paul Ferris, *Richard Burton*; Melvyn Bragg, *Rich: The Life of Richard Burton*; J.C.Trewin, *Five and Eighty Hamlets*; John Elsom, *Post-War British Theatre Criticism*; Michael Hordern, *A World Elsewhere*.

Paul Scofield 1955 – Peter Brook, *Threads of Time: A Memoir*; Peter Brook, *The Quality of Mercy: Reflections on Shakespeare*; Garry O'Connor, *Paul Scofield*; Stanley Wells, *Great Shakespeare Actors*; J.C.Trewin, *Five and Eighty Hamlets*; Ronald Hayman, *Playback: Essays and Interviews*; Richard Findlater, *The Player Kings*; Kenneth Tynan, *Tynan on Theatre*.

John Neville 1957 – J.C.Trewin, *Five and Eighty Hamlets*; John Miller, *Judi Dench*; Rose Collis, *Coral Browne*.

Michael Redgrave 1958 – Alan Strachan, *Secret Dreams*; Vanessa Redgrave, *An Autobiography*; Corin Redgrave, *Michael Redgrave My Father*; Michael Redgrave, *Mask or Face*; Brian McFarlane, *Double-Act: Googie Withers and John McCallum*; Rose Collis, *Coral Browne*; Zoe Caldwell, *I Will Be Cleopatra*; Michael Billington, *The Modern Actor*; J.C.Trewin, *Five and Eighty Hamlets*; Ralph Berry, *Changing Styles in Shakespeare*.

The 1960s

Jeremy Brett 1961 – BBC documentary, *Playing the Dane*; Jeremy Brett website, *Early Stages*; J.C.Trewin, *Five and Eighty Hamlets*.

Peter O'Toole 1963 – Daniel Rosenthal, *The National Theatre Story*; Peter Lewis, *The National*; Terry Coleman, *The Old Vic*; Nicholas Wapshott, *Peter O'Toole*; Robert Sellers, *Peter O'Toole*; Derek Jacobi, *As Luck Would Have It*; Siân Phillips, *Public Places*; Robert Stephens, *Knight Errant*; Anthony Holden, *Olivier*; Terry Coleman, *Olivier*; Philip Ziegler, *Olivier*; Lyn Haill (ed.), *Olivier at Work*.

David Warner 1965 – Stephen Fay, *Power Play: The Life and Times of Peter Hall*; Peter Hall, *Making An Exhibition of Myself*; Peter Hall, article in production programme; Tony Church, *A Stage for a Kingdom*; Sally Beauman, *The Royal Shakespeare Company*; Peter Holland, 'Peter Hall', in John Russell Brown (ed), *The Routledge Companion to Directors' Shakespeare*; *Hamlet*, the RSC edition; John Elsom, *Postwar British Theatre Criticism*; J.C.Trewin, *Five and Eighty Hamlets*; Jan Kott, *Shakespeare Our Contemporary*; Anthony B. Dawson, *Hamlet*; interview with David Warner, BBC World Service; Samuel Cowl, *Screen Adaptations*.

Nicol Williamson 1969 – Tony Richardson, *Long-Distance Runner*; Tim Adler, *The House of Redgrave*; Garry O'Connor, *Alec Guinness*; J.C.Trewin, *Five and Eighty Hamlets*; Ralph Berry, *Shakespeare in Performance*; Ralph Berry, *Changing Styles in Shakespeare*; Sheridan Morley (ed.), *Theatre '71*; Phil Davidson, obituary, *Financial Times*.

The 1970s

Alan Howard 1970 – Sally Beauman, *The Royal Shakespeare Company*; Peter Holland, 'Peter Hall', in John Russell Brown (ed.), *The Routledge Companion to Directors' Shakespeare*; Norman Cockin, 'Postwar Productions of Hamlet'; Ralph Berry, *Changing Styles in Shakespeare*; Marvin Rosenberg, *The Masks of Hamlet*; interview with Trevor Nunn, programme for his 2004 *Hamlet*; J.C.Trewin, *Five and Eighty Hamlets*; BBC Past Productions website; Helen Mirren archive.

Ian McKellen 1971 – Mark Barratt, *Ian McKellen*; Joy Leslie Gibson, *Ian McKellen*; Ian McKellen website; production programme.

Albert Finney 1975 – Quentin Falk, *Albert Finney*; John Goodwin (ed), *Peter Hall's Diaries*; Stephen Fay, *Power Play: The Life and Times of Peter Hall*; Michael Blakemore, *Stage Blood*; Daniel Rosenthal, *The National Theatre Story*; John Elsom and Nicholas Tomalin, *The History of the National Theatre*; Peter Lewis, *The National*; Samuel Crowl, *Screen Adaptations*.

Ben Kingsley 1975 – John Goodwin (ed.), *Peter Hall's Diaries*; Ben Kingsley, 'The Architecture of Ideas', in Susannah Carson (ed.), *Shakespeare and Me*; Sally Beauman, *The Royal Shakespeare Company*; Jonathan Holmes, *Merely Players*; Elizabeth Schafer, *Ms – Directing Shakespeare*; John Elsom, *Postwar British*

Theatre Criticism; Mary Z. Maher, *Modern Hamlets and Their Soliloquies*; George Baker, *The Way to Wexford*; Marvin Rosenberg, *The Masks of Hamlet*; Jonathan Croall, *Performing King Lear*.

Derek Jacobi 1977 – Stanley Wells, *Great Shakespeare Actors*; Derek Jacobi, *As Luck Would Have It*; Timothy West, *A Moment Towards the End of the Play*; Mary Z. Maher, *Modern Hamlets and Their Soliloquies*; Interviews with Derek Jacobi, Globe Muse of Fire project, and BBC 'Talking Hamlet' archive; Sally Beauman, article in the *Dial*; *Hamlet* weblog.

Frances de la Tour 1979 – *Hamlet*, RSC edition; Stages of Half Moon project – interviews with Frances de la Tour, Maggie Steed, Robin Soans, Iona McLeish.

The 1980s

Jonathan Pryce 1980 – Richard Eyre, *Utopia and Other Places*; Richard Eyre, *National Service*; Richard Findlater (ed.), *At the Royal Court*; Harriet Walter, *Other People's Shoes*; Robert Hapgood, *Hamlet on the Stage in England and the United States*; Interview with Jonathan Pryce by Andrew Dickson, *Guardian*.

Michael Pennington 1980 – Michael Pennington, *Hamlet: A User's Guide*; Michael Pennington, *Sweet William: A User's Guide to Shakespeare*; Michael Pennington, 'Hamlet', in *Players of Shakespeare 1*; Michael Greenwald, *Directions by Indirections*; Michael Billington, *One-Night Stands*; *Hamlet*, RSC edition; *South Bank Show*, December 1979; Interview with Michael Pennington by John Higgins, *The Times*.

Anton Lesser 1982 – Jonathan Miller, *Subsequent Performances*; Kate Bassett, *In Two Minds: A Biography of Jonathan Miller*; Michael Romain, *A Profile of Jonathan Miller*; David Bevington, *Murder Most Foul*.

Roger Rees 1984 – Frances Barber, 'Ophelia in *Hamlet*', in *Players of Shakespeare 2*; Kenneth Branagh, *Beginning*; Marvin Rosenberg, *The Masks of Hamlet*; Sylvia Morris, *The Shakespeare Blog*, July 2015; *Hamlet*, the RSC edition.

Kenneth Branagh 1988 – Derek Jacobi, *As Luck Would Have It*; Kenneth Branagh, *Beginning*; Anthony B. Dawson, *Hamlet*.

Mark Rylance 1988 – *Hamlet*, RSC edition; *Hamlet*, New Cambridge edition; Robert Hapgood, *Hamlet on the Stage in England and the United States*; Murray Cox (ed.), *Shakespeare Comes to Broadmoor*; Michael Billington, *One-Night Stands*.

Daniel Day-Lewis 1989 – Richard Eyre, *National Service*; Daniel Rosenthal, *The National Theatre Story*; Peter Lewis, *The National*; John Miller, *Judi Dench*; Michael Billington, *One-Night Stands*; Richard Allan Davison, 'The Readiness Was All', in Lois Potter and Arthur F. Kinney (eds), *Shakespeare, Text and Theatre*; Marvin Rosenberg, *The Masks of Hamlet*; Interviews with Richard Eyre and Judi Dench, NT website.

The 1990s

Kenneth Branagh 1992 – Anthony B. Dawson, *Hamlet*; Peter Holland, *English Shakespeares*; Samuel Crowl, *Screen Adaptations*; Interview with Kenneth Branagh by Michael Billington, *TheatreVoice*.

Stephen Dillane 1994 – Peter Hall, production programme; Peter Holland, *English Shakespeares*; Robert Hapgood, *Hamlet on the Stage in England and the United States*; Michael Pennington, *Sweet William*; Michael Pennington, *Hamlet: A User's Guide*.

Ralph Fiennes 1995 – Peter Holland, *English Shakespeares*; John Lahr, *Joy Ride*; Interview with Ralph Fiennes by Andrew Billen, *Guardian*.

Alex Jennings 1997 – *Hamlet*, RSC edition; *Hamlet*, Evans edition; Robert Smallwood in Stanley Wells (ed.), *Shakespeare Survey 51*; Interview with Alex Jennings by Lyn Gardner, *Guardian*; Diary article by Alex Jennings, *Independent*.

Paul Rhys 1999 – John Russell Brown, *Hamlet*; Robert Smallwood, *Shakespeare Survey 53*; Interviews with Paul Rhys by Matt Trueman, *Stage*, Walter Roberts, *Japan Times*.

The 2000s

Mark Rylance 2000 – Interview with Giles Block by Heather Neill, production programme; Interviews with the company, *Globe Research Bulletin*, March 2001; Bridget Escolme, 'Mark Rylance', in John Russell Brown (ed.), *The Routledge Companion to Directors' Shakespeare*; David Bevington, *Murder Most Foul*; Arthur F. Kinney, *Hamlet: New Critical Essays*.

Adrian Lester 2001 – Author interview with Adrian Lester; Jonathan Holmes, 'Adrian Lester', in John Russell Brown (ed.), *The Routledge Companion to Actors' Shakespeare*; Maria Shevtsova, 'Peter Brook', in John Russell Brown (ed.), *The Routledge Companion to Directors' Shakespeare*; Young Vic programme.

Samuel West 2001 – Profile by Lyn Gardner, *Guardian*; Chris Hastings, 'Three Hamlets', *Daily Telegraph*; David Bevington, *Murder Most Foul*; Bridget Escolme in Michael Neill and David Schalkwyk (eds), *The Oxford Handbook of Shakespearean Tragedy*; production programme.

Michael Maloney 2004 – Interview with Yukio Ninagawa and Michael Maloney by Jasper Rees, *Daily Telegraph*. (Michael Maloney 1996 – Interview for Macmillan Readers.)

Jamie Ballard 2008 – Tobacco Factory website; Kate Bassett, *In Two Minds: A Biography of Jonathan Miller*; Susannah Clapp, 'Ten Best Hamlets', *Observer*.

David Tennant 2008 – Author interviews with David Tennant and Greg Doran; Interview with David Tennant by Abigail Rokison-Woodall, *Shakespeare*, September 2009; David Tennant news website; production programme; DVD film.

Jude Law 2009 – Author interviews with Jude Law and Michael Grandage; Interviews with Jude Law by Julian Curry, *Shakespeare on Stage*, and Charlie Rose, US television; Michael Grandage, *A Decade at the Donmar*.

The 2010s

Rory Kinnear 2010 – Author interview with Nicholas Hytner; Nicholas Hytner, *Balancing Acts: Behind the Scenes at the National Theatre*; Abigail Rokison-Woodall, *Shakespeare in the Theatre: Nicholas Hytner*; Rory Kinnear, 'Character and Conundrum', in Susannah Carson (ed.), *Shakespeare and Me*; Paul Prescott, 'Rory Kinnear', in John Russell Brown (ed.), *The Routledge Companion to Actors' Shakespeare*; Daniel Rosenthal, *The National Theatre Story*; Michael Pennington, *Sweet William*; production programme.

Michael Sheen 2011 – Interview with Michael Sheen, Caroline McGinn, *Time Out*; Interview with Ian Rickson, Heather Neill, *TheatreVoice*.

Maxine Peake 2014 – Author interviews with Maxine Peake and Sarah Frankcom; Interviews with Maxine Peake by Bernadette McNulty, *Daily Telegraph*, Sarah Walters, *Manchester Evening News*; Conversation between Maxine Peake and Sarah Frankcom, Royal Exchange Platform; Interviews with Sarah Frankcom by Lyn Gardner, *Guardian*, Mark Shenton, *Stage*, Judith Hawkins, *Mancunian Matters*; DVD film.

Benedict Cumberbatch 2015 – *South Bank Show*, interview with Melvyn Bragg.

Paapa Essiedu 2016 – Author interview with Simon Godwin; Interviews with Paapa Essiedu at the Hay Festival, on the RSC DVD, by Heather Neill, *TheatreVoice*, Kate Kellaway, *Guardian*, Daisy Bowie-Sell, *whatsonstage*, Nick Curtis, *Evening Standard*.

Andrew Scott 2017 – Interview with Andrew Scott and Robert Icke, Louis Wise, *Sunday Times*; Interviews with Andrew Scott by Andrzej Lukowski, *Time Out*, Kaleem Aftab, *Independent*, Marcus Field, *Evening Standard*.

Hamlet Observed

Afterthoughts: Simon Russell Beale, Conversation with Adrian Lester, Danish Embassy, London, 2016; John Caird, *Hamlet*, RSC edition.

Hamlets at Elsinore

BBC Shakespeare Lives, 'Elsinore, a Castle Fit for a Prince'.

Laurence Olivier – Tyrone Guthrie, *A Life in the Theatre*; Ivor Brown, *Shakespeare*; Hugh Hunt, *Old Vic Prefaces*; J.C. Trewin, *Five and Eighty Hamlets*.

John Gielgud – Jonathan Croall, *John Gielgud*; review in the *Spectator*.

Michael Redgrave – Alan Strachan, *Sweet Dreams*; Richard Findlater, *Michael Redgrave, Actor*.

Richard Burton – Review in *The Times*.

Derek Jacobi – Michael Billington, 'Top Ten Hamlets', *Guardian*; Derek Jacobi, *As Luck Would Have It*.

Jude Law – Robert McCrum, review in the *Observer*.

Globe to Globe tour – Jasper Rees, article in the *Economist*.

BIBLIOGRAPHY

Editions of *Hamlet*

Arden fourth edition – ed. Harold Jenkins, Bloomsbury, 1982
Cambridge edition – ed. John Dover Wilson, Cambridge University Press, 1934
New Cambridge edition – ed. Philip Edwards, Cambridge University Press, 1985
RSC edition – eds Jonathan Bate and Eric Rasmussen, Macmillan, 2008
Penguin edition – ed. T.J.B. Spencer, Penguin 1980
Signet Classic edition – ed. Edward Hubler, New American Library, 1963
Evans Shakespeare edition – ed. John Tobin, 2012

Books on *Hamlet*

David Bevington, *Murder Most Foul: Hamlet through the Ages*, Oxford University Press, 2011
John Russell Brown, *Hamlet*, Palgrave, 2006
Norman Cockin, 'Postwar Productions of Hamlet 1948–1970', MA thesis, Birmingham, 1980
Jonathan Croall, *Hamlet Observed*, NT Publications, 2001
Samuel Crowl, *Screen Adaptations: Shakespeare's Hamlet: The Relationship Between Text and Film*, Bloomsbury, 2014
Anthony B. Dawson, *Shakespeare in Performance: Hamlet*, Manchester University Press, 1995
Barbara Everett, *Young Hamlet*, Oxford University Press, 1989
Miriam Gilbert, *Jonathan Pryce* (unpublished account of his Hamlet)
Miriam Gilbert, *Mark Rylance* (unpublished account of his Hamlet)
Robert Hapgood, *Hamlet on the Stage in England and the United States*, a reworking of *Shakespeare in Production: Hamlet*, Cambridge University Press, 1999
Tony Howard, *Women as Hamlet: Performance and Interpretation in Theatre, Film and Fiction*, Cambridge University Press, 2007
Arthur F. Kinney, *Hamlet: New Critical Essays*, Routledge, 2001
Andy Lavender, *Hamlet in Pieces: Shakespeare Revisited by Peter Brook, Robert Lepage, Robert Wilson*, Bloomsbury, 2001
Mary Z. Maher, *Modern Hamlets and Their Soliloquies*, Iowa State University Press, 1992
Raymond Mander and Joe Mitchenson, *Hamlet through the Ages: A Pictorial Record from 1709*, Rockcliff, 1952
Kenneth Muir and Stanley Wells, *Aspects of Hamlet*, Cambridge University Press, 1979

Michael Pennington, *Hamlet: A User's Guide*, Nick Hern Books, 1996

Marvin Rosenberg, *The Masks of Hamlet*, Associated Universities Presses, 1997

J.C. Trewin, *Five and Eighty Hamlets*, Hutchinson, 1987

Books on Shakespeare

Sally Beauman, *The Royal Shakespeare Company: A History of Ten Decades*, Oxford University Press, 1982

Ralph Berry, *Changing Styles in Shakespeare*, Routledge, 2005

Ralph Berry, *On Directing Shakespeare: Interviews with Contemporary Directors*, Hamish Hamilton, 1989

Ralph Berry, *Shakespeare in Performance: Castings and Metamorphoses*, Palgrave, 1993

Philip Brockbank (ed.), *Players of Shakespeare 1: Essays in Shakespearean Performance by Twelve Players with the Royal Shakespeare Company*, Cambridge University Press, 1988

Peter Brook, *The Quality of Mercy: Reflections on Shakespeare*, Nick Hern Books, 2013

Ivor Brown, *Shakespeare*, Collins, 1949

John Russell Brown (ed.), *The Routledge Companion to Actors' Shakespeare*, Routledge, 2012

John Russell Brown (ed.), *The Routledge Companion to Directors' Shakespeare*, Routledge, 2008

Susannah Carson (ed.), *Shakespeare and Me: 38 Great Writers, Actors and Directors on What the Bard Means to Them – and Us*, Oneworld, 2014

Murray Cox (ed.), *Shakespeare Comes to Broadmoor*, Jessica Kingsley, 1992

Jonathan Croall, *Performing King Lear: Gielgud to Russell Beale*, Bloomsbury, 2015

Julian Curry, *Shakespeare on Stage: Thirteen Leading Actors on Thirteen Key Roles*, Nick Hern Books, 2012

Andrew Dickson, *The Globe Guide to Shakespeare: The Plays, the Productions, the Life*, Profile Books, 2016

Peter Holland, *English Shakespeares: Shakespeare on the English Stage in the 1990s*, Cambridge University Press, 1997

Jonathan Holmes, *Merely Players: Actors' Accounts of Performing Shakespeare*, Routledge, 2004

Hugh Hunt, *Old Vic Prefaces: Shakespeare and the Producer*, Routledge & Kegan Paul, 1954

Russell Jackson and Robert Smallwood (eds), *Players of Shakespeare 2: Further Essays in Shakespearean Performance by Players with the Royal Shakespeare Company*, Cambridge University Press, 1988

Russell Jackson and Robert Smallwood (eds), *Players of Shakespeare 3: Further Essays in Shakespearean Performance by Players with the Royal Shakespeare Company*, Cambridge University Press, 1993

Jan Kott, *Shakespeare Our Contemporary*, Routledge, 1990

Michael Neill and David Schalkwyk (eds), *The Oxford Handbook of Shakespearean Tragedy*, Oxford University Press, 2016

Michael Pennington, *Sweet William: A User's Guide to Shakespeare*, Nick Hern Books, 2012

Lois Potter and Arthur F. Kinney (eds), *Shakespeare Text and Theatre: Essays in Honour of Jay L. Halio*, Associated University Presses, 1999

Abigail Rokison-Woodall, *Shakespeare in the Theatre: Nicholas Hytner*, Bloomsbury, 2017

Elizabeth Schafer, *Ms – Directing Shakespeare: Women Direct Shakespeare*, St Martin's Press, 2000

Robert Speaight, *Shakespeare on the Stage: An Illustrated History of Shakespearean Performance*, Collins, 1973

Stanley Wells, *Four Major Productions at Stratford*, Manchester University Press, 1977

Stanley Wells, *Great Shakespeare Actors: Burbage to Branagh*, Oxford University Press, 2015

Stanley Wells, *Shakespeare: A Dramatic Life*, Sinclair-Stevenson, 1994

Stanley Wells and Sarah Stanton (eds), *The Cambridge Companion to Shakespeare on Stage*, Cambridge University Press, 2002

Stanley Wells, Michael Dobson et al (eds), *The Oxford Companion to Shakespeare*, Oxford University Press, 2001

David Weston, *Covering Shakespeare: An Actor's Saga of Near Misses and Dogged Endurance*, Oberon Books, 2014

Books on Theatre

Michael Billington, *One-Night Stands: A Critic's View of Modern British Theatre*, Nick Hern Books, 1993

Michael Billington, *The Modern Actor*, Hamish Hamilton, 1973

Terry Coleman, *The Old Vic: The Story of a Great Theatre from Kean to Olivier to Spacey*, Faber & Faber, 2014

John Elsom, *Post-War British Theatre Criticism*, Routledge & Kegan Paul, 1981

John Elsom and Nicholas Tomalin, *The History of the National Theatre*, Jonathan Cape, 1978

Richard Eyre, *Talking Theatre: Interviews with Theatre People*, Nick Hern Books, 2009

Richard Findlater (ed.), *At the Royal Court: 25 Years of the English Stage Company*, Amber Lane Press, 1981

Michael Grandage, *A Decade at the Donmar 2002–2012*, Constable, 2012

Ronald Hayman, *Playback: Essays and Interviews*, Davis-Poynter, 1973

Harold Hobson, *Theatre 2*, Longmans, Green, 1950

Laurence Kitchin, *Mid-Century Drama*, Faber & Faber, 1960

Peter Lewis, *The National: A Dream Made Concrete*, Methuen, 1990

Robin May, *A Companion to the Theatre: The Anglo-American Stage from 1920*, Lutterworth Press, 1973

Sheridan Morley (ed.), *Theatre '71*, Hutchinson, 1971

Michael Redgrave, *Mask or Face: Reflections in an Actor's Mirror*, Heinemann, 1959

Diana Rigg, *No Turn Unstoned: The Worst-Ever Theatrical Reviews*, Elm Tree Books, 1982

Peter Roberts, *The Old Vic Story: A Nation's Theatre 1818–1976*, W.H. Allen, 1976

Daniel Rosenthal, *The National Theatre Story*, Oberon Books, 2013

Kenneth Tynan, *He That Plays the King: A View of the Theatre*, Longmans, Green, 1950

Kenneth Tynan, *Tynan on Theatre*, Penguin Books, 1964

Audrey Williamson, *Old Vic Drama: A Twelve-Year Study of Plays and Players*, Rockcliff, 1948

Audrey Williamson, *Theatre of Two Decades*, Rockliff, 1951

T.C. Worsley, *The Fugitive Art*, John Lehmann, 1952

Biography and Autobiography

Tim Adler, *The House of Redgrave: The Secret Lives of a Theatrical Dynasty*, Aurum Press, 2012

Lindsay Anderson, *The Diaries*, Methuen, 2004

George Baker, *The Way to Wexford: The Autobiography*, Headline, 2002

Mark Barratt, *Ian McKellen: An Unofficial Biography*, Virgin Books, 2005

Kate Bassett, *In Two Minds: A Biography of Jonathan Miller*, Oberon Books, 2012

Michael Billington (ed.), *Stage and Screen Lives: Intimate Biographies of the Famous by the Famous*, Oxford University Press, 2001

Michael Blakemore, *Stage Blood: Five Tempestuous Years in the Early Life of the National Theatre*, Faber & Faber, 2013

Melvyn Bragg, *Rich: The Life of Richard Burton*, Hodder & Stoughton, 1988

Kenneth Branagh, *Beginning*, Chatto & Windus, 1989

Peter Brook, *Threads of Time: A Memoir*, Methuen, 1999

Zoe Caldwell, *I Will Be Cleopatra: An Actress' Journey*, W.W. Norton, 2001

Simon Callow, *My Life in Pieces: An Alternative Autobiography*, Nick Hern Books, 2010

Tony Church, *A Stage for a Kingdom*, Oneiro Press, 2013

Terry Coleman, *Olivier: The Authorised Biography*, Bloomsbury, 2005

Rose Collis, *Coral Browne: 'This Effing Lady': A Biography*, Oberon Books, 2007

Jonathan Croall, *John Gielgud: Matinee Idol to Movie Star*, Methuen Drama, 2012

Alan Cumming, *Not My Father's Son: A Family Memoir*, Canongate, 2014

Elaine Dundy, *Life Itself!*, Virago Press, 2001

Richard Eyre, *National Service: Diary of a Decade at the National Theatre*, Bloomsbury, 2003

Richard Eyre, *Utopia and Other Places*, Bloomsbury, 1993

Richard Eyre, *What Do I Know? People, Politics and the Arts*, Nick Hern Books, 2014

Quentin Falk, *Albert Finney: In Character*, Robson Books, revised edition, 2002

Stephen Fay, *Power Play: The Life and Times of Peter Hall*, Hodder & Stoughton, 1995

Paul Ferris, *Richard Burton*, Weidenfeld & Nicolson, 1981

Richard Findlater, *Lilian Baylis: The Lady of the Old Vic*, Allen Lane, 1975

Richard Findlater, *Michael Redgrave: Actor*, Heinemann, 1956

Richard Findlater, *The Player Kings*, Stein & Day, 1971

Kate Fleming, *Celia Johnson: A Biography*, Weidenfeld & Nicolson, 1991

James Forsyth, *Tyrone Guthrie: The Authorised Biography*, Hamish Hamilton, 1976

Joy Leslie Gibson, *Ian McKellen: A Biography*, Weidenfeld & Nicolson, 1986

John Goodwin (ed.), *Peter Hall's Diaries: The Story of a Dramatic Battle*, Hamish Hamilton, 1983

Michael Greenwald, *Directions by Indirections: John Barton of the Royal Shakespeare Company*, University of Delaware Press, 1997

Alec Guinness, *Blessings in Disguise*, Hamish Hamilton, 1985

Tyrone Guthrie, *A Life in the Theatre*, Hamish Hamilton, 1960

Lyn Haill (ed.), *Olivier at Work: The National Years*, Nick Hern Books, 1989

Peter Hall, *Making an Exhibition of Myself: The Autobiography*, Sinclair-Stevenson, 1993

Ronald Harwood (ed.), *Dear Alec: Guinness at 75*, Hodder & Stoughton, 1989

Anthony Holden, *Olivier*, Weidenfeld & Nicolson, 1988

Michael Hordern, *A World Elsewhere: An Autobiography*, Michael O'Mara Books, 1993

Nicholas Hytner, *Balancing Acts: Behind the Scenes at the National Theatre*, Jonathan Cape, 2017

Derek Jacobi, *As Luck Would Have It: My Seven Ages*, HarperCollins, 2013

John Lahr, *Joy Ride: Lives of the Theatricals*, Bloomsbury, 2015

Anna Massey, *Telling Some Tales*, Hutchinson, 2006

Brian McFarlane, *Double-Act: The Remarkable Lives and Careers of Googie Withers and John McCallum*, Monash University Publishing, 2015

John Miller, *Judi Dench: With a Crack in Her Voice*, Weidenfeld & Nicolson, 1998

Jonathan Miller, *Subsequent Performances*, Faber & Faber, 1986

Garry O'Connor, *Alec Guinness the Unknown: A Life*, Sidgwick & Jackson, 2002

Garry O'Connor, *Paul Scofield: The Biography*, Sidgwick & Jackson, 2002

Siân Phillips, *Public Places: The Autobiography*, Hodder & Stoughton, 2001

Tim Pigott-Smith, *Do You Know Who I Am? A Memoir*, Bloomsbury, 2017

Joan Plowright, *And That's Not All: The Memoirs*, Orion, 2001

Piers Paul Read, *Alec Guinness: The Authorised Biography*, Simon & Schuster, 2003

Corin Redgrave, *Michael Redgrave My Father*, Richard Cohen Books, 1995

Michael Redgrave, *In My Mind's Eye: An Autobiography*, Weidenfeld & Nicolson, 1983

Vanessa Redgrave, *An Autobiography*, Hutchinson, 1991

Tony Richardson, *Long-Distance Runner: A Memoir*, Faber & Faber, 1993

Michael Romain, *A Profile of Jonathan Miller*, Cambridge University Press, 1992

Elizabeth Schafer, *Lilian Baylis: A Biography*, University of Hertfordshire Press, 2006

Robert Sellers, *Peter O'Toole: The Definitive Biography*, Sidgwick & Jackson, 2015

Donald Spoto, *Otherwise Engaged: The Life of Alan Bates*, Hutchinson, 2007

Robert Stephens, *Knight Errant: Memoirs of a Vagabond Actor*, Hodder & Stoughton, 1996

Alan Strachan, *Secret Dreams: A Biography of Michael Redgrave*, Weidenfeld & Nicolson, 2004

John Russell Taylor, *Alec Guinness: A Celebration*, Pavilion Books, 2000

Kathleen Tynan, *The Life of Kenneth Tynan*, Weidenfeld & Nicolson, 1987

Kenneth Tynan, *Alec Guinness: An Illustrated Study of His Work for Stage and Screen*, Macmillan, 1953

Harriet Walter, *Other People's Shoes: Thoughts on Acting*, Viking, 1999
Nicholas Wapshott, *Peter O'Toole*, Beaufort Books, 1984
Timothy West, *A Moment Towards the End of the Play … : An Autobiography*,
    Nick Hern Books, 2002.
Philip Ziegler, *Olivier*, Maclehose Press, 2013

Articles and Chapters

Frances Barber, 'Ophelia in *Hamlet*', *Players of Shakespeare 2*
Jonathan Bate and Eric Rasmussen (eds), '*Hamlet* in Performance', *Hamlet*, RSC
    edition
Richard Allan Davison, 'The Readiness Was All', Lois Potter and Arthur F. Kinney
    (eds), *Shakespeare, Text and Theatre*
Bridget Escolme, 'Mark Rylance', John Russell Brown (ed.), *The Routledge
    Companion to Directors' Shakespeare*
Philip Franks, 'Hamlet', *Players of Shakespeare 3*
Peter Holland, 'Peter Hall', John Russell Brown (ed.), *The Routledge Companion
    to Directors' Shakespeare*
Jonathan Holmes, 'Adrian Lester', John Russell Brown (ed.), *The Routledge
    Companion to Actors' Shakespeare*
Ben Kingsley, 'The Architecture of Ideas', Susannah Carson (ed.), *Shakespeare and
    Me*
Rory Kinnear, 'Character and Conundrum', Susannah Carson (ed.), *Shakespeare
    and Me*
Ben Naylor, 'Greg Hicks', John Russell Brown (ed.), *The Routledge Companion to
    Actors' Shakespeare*
Allardyce Nicoll, 'English Hamlets of the Twentieth Century', *Shakespeare Survey 9*
Benedict Nightingale, 'Shakespeare is as Shakespeare's Done', Sheridan Morley
    (ed.), *Theatre '71*
Michael Pennington, 'Hamlet', *Players of Shakespeare 1*
Paul Prescott, 'Declan Donnellan', John Russell Brown (ed.), *The Routledge
    Companion to Directors' Shakespeare*
Paul Prescott, 'Rory Kinnear', John Russell Brown (ed.), *The Routledge Companion
    to Actors' Shakespeare*
Maria Shevtsova, 'Peter Brook', John Russell Brown (ed.), *The Routledge
    Companion to Directors' Shakespeare*
Robert Smallwood, 'Shakespeare's Performances in England 1997', Stanley Wells
    (ed.), *Shakespeare Survey 51*

The Hamlet performances filmed and available on DVD include those by David
Tennant, Maxine Peake and Paapa Essiedu. Adrian Lester's is available online on
YouTube, Benedict Cumberbatch's is on NT Live.

INDEX

Numbers in bold indicate pages dealing in detail with a specific production.